PATRICK HENRY

in His Speeches and Writings
and in the Words of His Contemporaries

Compiled and Annotated by
JAMES M. ELSON
Executive Vice President Emeritus
The Patrick Henry Memorial Foundation

Patrick Henry
In His Speeches and Writings
And in the Words of His Contemporaries

Published 2007

ISBN: 0979036755
Library of Congress Control Number: 2007920033

website: jamesmelson.com

James M. Elson is the executive director emeritus of the
Patrick Henry Memorial Foundation.

Front cover:
Peter Rothermel, *Patrick Henry Before*
the Virginia House of Burgesses
Back cover:
David Silvette after a portrait
of Patrick Henry by Thomas Sully
Courtesy of the Patrick Henry Memorial Foundation,
Brookneal, Virginia.

Warwick House Publishers
720 Court Street
Lynchburg, Virginia 24504

In memory of Henry Mayer (1941-2000)

This book, I hope, will invite us to consider the claims of patriotism in its broadest sense and give us a new appreciation of the legitimacy, indeed the necessity, of political conflict in a free society.

—Henry Mayer, Preface to
*A Son of Thunder: Patrick Henry
and the American Republic*

CONTENTS

Appendices:

PREFACE

Patrick Henry, the Patriot

"Give me liberty or give me death!" cried Patrick Henry on March 23, 1775, at the Virginia Convention in St. John's Church, Richmond. For that seven-word sound bite he is remembered by Americans today. Thomas Jefferson and George Washington were also among the convention delegates. Although Jefferson was normally a reluctant public speaker, Henry's oration, according to one account, inspired him to rise and second Henry's call to arms. Washington was not unaffected: "His looks bespoke a mind absorbed in meditation on his country's fate…"

"He was certainly the man who gave the first impulse to the ball of revolution," the author of the Declaration of Independence recalled of the man towards whom he was later to have highly conflicted feelings. Jefferson, however, was not referring to Henry's "Liberty or Death" Speech, but rather to his Stamp Act Speech in Virginia's House of Burgesses at Williamsburg ten years earlier, where he was also a listener. "And in Massachusetts the effect of [Henry's] Virginia Resolves was electric," the twentieth-century historians of *The Stamp Act Crisis* have written and noted that of the original thirteen colonies, nine "eventually passed declaratory resolutions defining their rights."

The "Liberty or Death" and Stamp Act speeches are Patrick Henry's best known but certainly not his only important ones. In 1763, as a young lawyer, he first won renown in the so-called "Parson's Cause" by successfully arguing as an advocate for the people against both church and crown. In 1775, as Colonel of the Hanover Militia, Henry inspired his troops with his oratory in their march on Williamsburg, after colonial governor Lord Dunmore had removed the colony's gunpowder to British ships in the James River. Henry was a leader of the Virginia Convention of 1776, where his speaking, in the words of Edmund Randolph, "inflamed and was followed by the convention." Virginia declared itself in-dependent from English rule on May 15, 1776.

Henry served as the State of Virginia's first governor during the Revolution (1776-1779) and afterwards for two additional one-year terms (1784-1786). Until his retirement from the Virginia House of Delegates in 1790, he was undoubtedly the most power-ful politician in the Virginia legislature. "He has only to say let this be law, and it is law," wrote George Washington, the most popular man in the fledging United States of America, to James Madison in 1788.

Although Henry admired Washington more than any other American, he could not bring himself to support the new consti-tution created during the summer of 1787 at the convention in Philadelphia, which Washington had chaired (and which Henry had not attended). Henry opposed ratification, primarily because the constitution contained no bill of rights. But he was also highly suspicious of its provisions for what he called "consolidated government." Reading Henry's impassioned orations at the 1788 Virginia Convention on the Ratification of the Constitution today, we are reminded why he announced himself "a sentinel of the peo-ple." "Liberty, the greatest of all earthly blessings," he proclaimed. "Give us that precious jewel, and you may take everything else!"

Henry and his "Anti-Federalist" allies lost their fight to "Federalists" James Madison, "The Father of the Constitution," who was present at the Virginia Convention, and General Washington, not present but working diligently behind the scenes for ratification and expected by almost everyone to be the first president of the new government. Upon learning that he and his Anti-Federalists had been defeated by a vote of 89 to 79, Henry an-nounced to the convention that he would be "a peaceable citizen." "My head, my hand, and my heart shall be at liberty to retrieve the loss of liberty and remove the defects of that system—in a consti-tutional way."

Henry lost no time in putting the kind of political pressure that only he could on Madison to amend the constitution. The ora-tor and his allies made sure that Madison was denied a seat in the new United States Senate. Madison was elected to the House of Representatives only after promising to work for amendments. To his credit, he was as good as his word. Fifteen months after the conclusion of the Virginia Convention, Congress transmitted to the state legislatures twelve proposed amendments. The ten that were adopted went into effect on December 15, 1791. "I will leave to you the beguiling question of apportioning credit for the Bill of Rights," Henry Mayer, Patrick Henry's biographer, observed, "between the man who drafted the first ten amendments and the man who made him do it."

After his retirement from public service in 1790, Henry returned to the practice of law. Unlike most of the Virginia Founding Fathers, he had not inherited or married into money. Henry was determined to leave substantial bequests to those of his seventeen children who survived him. (More than one wag has suggested that he, rather than George Washington, should have been dubbed "The Father of His Country.") Henry's ability to sway a jury made him a popular and well-paid advocate for the defense in criminal cases. He surprised both friends and foes alike when he mastered the arcane precedents of international law in the British Debts Case of 1791-93, dampening the criticism of his detractors that his courtroom skills did not go beyond oratory.

Having fulfilled his financial obligations to his family, Henry withdrew to his plantations in Southside Virginia. He had no stomach for the wrangling between the new political parties (Federalists and Democratic Republicans) that originated during Washington's presidency and became endemic during the Adams administration. His health, never good after suffering a near-fatal bout of malaria in 1776, seems to have deteriorated rapidly towards the end of the 1790s.

Some close to Henry later wrote that this "debility" was mental as well as physical, citing an alleged conversion from Anti-Federalism to Federalism and a perfervid religiosity that he had not previously displayed in public. In early 1799, ex-President Washington, fearing the bitter political strife of the times might result in disunion, persuaded Henry to come out of retirement to again run for the state legislature. In March of that year, three months before his death, Henry traveled to Charlotte Court House to make his last speech. Unfortunately, there is no accurate record of what he said. It was perhaps best described by a spectator who later called it "a noble effort such as could have proceeded from none but a noble heart…" Henry was elected, but on June 6, 1799, before he could take his seat in the General Assembly, death silenced the Voice of American Liberty.

Patrick Henry, the Man

In the correspondence and documents that survive and in the memoirs of almost all who knew him, Henry, the human being, emerges as admirable as Henry, the patriot. He could be, as he was described at the First Continental Congress of 1774, "the very devil in politics—a Son of Thunder," and this remains his historical image. Yet, as Edmund Randolph, who it is said almost came to a physical confrontation with Henry during the Virginia Convention of 1788, recalled years later: "His style of oratory was vehement, without transporting him beyond the power of self command or wounding his opponents by deliberate offense. After a debate had ceased, he was surrounded by them on the first occasion with pleasantry on some of its incidents."

"I think he was the best humored man in society I almost ever knew," admitted Thomas Jefferson after Henry's death, although Jefferson's other recollections of him were not nearly so generous. In the remembrances of family, friends, and colleagues, Henry emerges as a person most of us would be pleased to have living next door. "He removed four times to places where he was personally a stranger, and always on acquaintance became a favorite neighbor," testified his cousin, Judge Edmund Winston. "He had no vice that I ever knew or ever heard of and scarcely a foible," wrote Henry's son-in-law, Judge Spencer Roane, whose relationship with him, like Judge Winston's, was both personal and professional.

Patrick Henry's Place in History

How do we rank Patrick Henry within the constellation of star patriots of his era—Washington, Jefferson, Madison, Monroe, Marshall, and Mason? This list, of course, includes only the Virginians, four of whom were among our first five presidents.

Despite the familiar seven-word sound bite, Patrick Henry remains unknown to almost all Americans. There was, for example, the visitor to Red Hill, Henry's last home and burial place, a few years ago, who asked, "Why did they hang Patrick Henry?" The list of those unfamiliar with Henry's specific accomplishments apparently includes John Ferling, a prominent historian whose *A Leap in the Dark*, published by the Oxford University Press in 2003 and acclaimed as a "first-class history of the revolutionary era," portrays Henry as uttering his immortal phrase during his Stamp Act Speech.*

Henry (1736-1799) of Virginia vies with Samuel Adams (1722-1803) of Massachusetts for the title "The Forgotten Patriot." There are similarities. Both men were the first to agitate strongly against British rule in their respective colonies (with perhaps the exception of James Otis in Massachusetts). Unfortunately, neither seems to have given much thought to his historical image. As a consequence, these pioneering patriots left extremely sparse paper trails compared to the other Founding Fathers, most of whom were greatly concerned with what posterity would think of them. Equally important for their lack of a vivid presence in today's view of the history of their time, neither held an office in the new Federal Government formed after the Constitution of the United States was ratified in 1791 (although Henry was offered quite a few).

Patrick Henry's worth as a Founder is particularly difficult to document. For what are historians to do with a man whose most

---

* The visitor was thinking of Captain Nathan Hale, a young revolutionary soldier, captured by the British in New York, who is said to have uttered the equally immortal words, "I only regret that I have one life to lose for my country," before being executed as a spy. Henry 's famous quote was heard during his "Liberty or Death" Speech in 1775, ten years after the Stamp Act Speech.

valuable contributions to American freedom vanished into thin air the moment they left his mouth, leaving only an imperfect record of what he said and—just as important—*how* he said it?

In Henry's day political speeches (unlike sermons) were not written out, and few of them survive as they were originally delivered. Henry's "Liberty or Death" and Stamp Act speeches are the two most notable examples. Fortunately, there was a stenographer present during Henry's arguments during the British Debts Case and, more importantly, during the Virginia Convention on the Ratification of the United States Constitution at Richmond in 1788. Their contents reveal much of Henry's political philosophy and are, therefore, deserving of close study. Still, the texts of Henry's orations, no matter how accurate, are not enough to convey the spell he cast over his audiences—you had to be there. Attempts by his contemporaries to describe his speaking style differ greatly and are ultimately of little help in imagining how he must have sounded. Had the technology existed to record his speeches, we would no doubt be hearing (and watching) excerpts from them today during national holidays—and political campaigns.

Many of Henry's Virginia contemporaries not only served in the United States Government but outlived him by a decade or two. After Henry's death, most of his political adversaries either had kind words for him or were silent. Thomas Jefferson, however, was not so charitable. In 1805 he described Henry to William Wirt, Henry's first biographer, as a kind of backwoods oratorical idiot savant who was "rotten hearted and avaricious." "He was a man of very little knowledge of any sort," Jefferson told Daniel Webster, visiting at Monticello in 1824. "He read nothing and had no books." As to Henry's intellectual abilities, the reader of this book has a first-hand opportunity to judge, but Jefferson's continuing enmity towards Henry cast a shadow over his image that has lasted until today.

Henry was a man who spoke with the courage of his convictions. "It has been urged against Mr. Henry by his enemies, and by the aristocrats whom he overthrew, that he always seized and advocated the popular side of the question," wrote Judge Spencer Roane to William Wirt.

> Nothing is less true. He opposed General Washington and an erring world (as he said) on the subject of the Constitution. The man who would do this cannot be suspected of want of firmness to pursue his own opinions. The man who moved the Stamp Act Resolutions and took up arms to recover the gunpowder pursued his own course. He had no certain indication of the popular opinion in either case, and both measures were esteemed by ordinary men too rash and bold to be popular. Besides, why court the popular opinion when he wanted not popularity, for he had resisted (in the latter part of his life) every distinction which was offered him?

The agrarian society of Henry's Virginia is today long gone, but does this make his setting of national priorities any less important? "You are not to inquire how your trade may be increased, nor how you are to become a great and powerful people," he reminded the Virginia Convention of 1788, "but how your liberties can be secured—for liberty ought to be the direct end of your government…"

A Note to the General Reader

A word as to how the selections in this book were chosen and arranged: Only those quotations of and stories about Patrick Henry that can be traced to him or his contemporaries have been included. Some well-known Henry anecdotes are absent or do not appear in their entirety. This is very likely because they were made up after his death or embellished upon by later authors. A few may be found in this book's Appendix F titled "Patrick Henry Apocrypha." Still, the reader may find, as Henry's first biographer William Wirt discovered, "contradictory statements" of which "*all* could not be true." Did it take six weeks or six months of study before Henry was awarded his law license? Were his eyes blue or were they gray? Did he, at his last public appearance before his death, state that the Alien and Sedition laws were "good and proper"? Did he deliver a "severe denunciation" of them? Or did he sidestep the issue by declaring they "were too deep for him"? We will never know for sure.

Most of the material in this book is arranged in chronological order to provide a sense of continuity to the reader and, where conflicting reports exist, to facilitate comparison. Occasionally I have provided *within* the text a note of explanation or correction, which always appears in brackets. Other documents and information that may be useful for reference or further study are found in the appendices, endnotes, bibliography, and indices. I want to emphasize, however, that this book is not intended to substitute for a biography (my choice is Henry Mayer's *A Son of Thunder: Patrick Henry and the American Republic*, for both its scholarship and readability).

A Note to Scholars

It has been my intention to make *Patrick Henry in His Speeches and Writings and in the Words of His Contemporaries* useful to readers who are not accustomed to eighteenth century texts. To that end, I have silently clarified spelling, punctuation, and paragraphing of those interminable sentences often beloved of the Founding Fathers. Readers of a scholarly bent will find references to original sources in this book's notes and bibliography.

Acknowledgments

I am grateful to the Patrick Henry scholars who read and commented on the draft manuscript of this book. These include Jon Kukla, Executive Vice President of the Patrick Henry Memorial Foundation at Red Hill, and author of numerous articles and seven books on Virginia and colonial history, to include *A Wilderness So Immense: The Louisiana Purchase and the Destiny of America*

(2003); Mark Couvillon, author of *Patrick Henry's Virginia* (2001) and editor of the modern edition of "The Edward Fontaine Manuscript" of 1872; Richard Schumann, who has served as the outstanding Patrick Henry interpreter at Colonial Williamsburg since 1997; and Mark Greenough of Richmond's Living History Associates, Ltd., which managed the re-enactment of the "Liberty or Death" Speech at St. John's Church from 1992 to 2003. Edith Poindexter, the Henry family genealogist at Red Hill, was also most helpful, and I offer a word of thanks to Dr. Kevin J. Hayes for permission to quote excerpts from his important manuscript, "The Library of Patrick Henry."

A special word of appreciation to Peter S. Onuf, Thomas Jefferson Memorial Foundation Professor of History at the University of Virginia and author, co-author, and editor of eleven books on Jefferson, the Revolutionary War period, and the early United States; also to Andrew Burstein, author of *The Inner Jefferson: Portrait of a Grieving Optimist* (1995) and *Jefferson's Secrets: Death and Desire at Monticello* (2005), who has also written about William Wirt, Patrick Henry's first biographer, in his *America's Jubilee* (2001). These two leading Jefferson scholars were most gracious in taking time during their summer vacations to provide objective criticism, helpful suggestions, and kind encouragement.

Last, but certainly not least, my thanks to Joyce Maddox at Warwick House Publishers, whose attention to detail combined with unfailing good humor always brighten the more routine aspects of being an author. Errors, oversights, and good advice not taken from my excellent group of advisors are, of course, no one's fault but my own.

Disclosure by the Editor

In the interests of full disclosure, the reader should know that this book is the result of my study of and reflection on Patrick Henry's life and works during eleven and one-half-years (1988-2000) as executive vice-president of the Patrick Henry Memorial

Foundation and the past seven years of my retirement. It is my hope that this book will help create a better understanding of Henry's image as it existed in his day, as well as a more accurate appraisal of the importance of his accomplishments and his character for our time.

I end this introduction by echoing the words of Judge Spencer Roane found in the closing paragraphs of his memorandum to William Wirt, which serves as the Prologue to this book:

> In giving this sketch of what I know of Mr. Henry, I have endeavored to be faithful. It will be seen whether a spirit of candor does not run through the relation and how far it is corroborated by other accounts. It was my intention "nothing to extenuate, nor set down aught in malice." If my descriptions seem extravagant, let it be remembered that he was a most remarkable man.

> James M. Elson
> Executive Vice President Emeritus
> The Patrick Henry Memorial Foundation

PROLOGUE

Spencer Roane's Memorandum of Patrick Henry to William Wirt, Henry's First Biographer (1805)[1]

Spencer Roane (1762-1822) was educated at the College of William and Mary, attended law lectures under George Wythe at Williamsburg, and continued his legal studies in Philadelphia. At the age of twenty, he successfully petitioned Governor Benjamin Harrison for a license to practice law. Shortly thereafter, in 1783, he was elected to the House of Delegates from Essex County. By 1787, he was a senator representing Essex, King and Queen, and King William counties. He was made a judge of the General Court at the age of twenty-seven. In 1794, he was appointed to the Supreme Court of Appeals and remained on the bench until his death.

As Virginia's premier jurist, Roane clashed frequently with U. S. Supreme Court Chief Justice John Marshall on matters of federal vs. state court authority. In the opinion of one scholar:

Their duel recalled the constitutional debate of the 1780s. They essentially held opposite views of America. Roane still saw a league of sovereign states, while Marshall saw a growing nation. Marshall, believing that Roane's objective was to return America to the 1780s, reminded him of the defeat of the anti-federalists and the replacement of the Articles of Confederation by the Constitution and restated the reasoning of the federalists of 1787-88—that the needs of the nation were great, that America was becoming an empire, and that it must have a government that could rule effectively and efficiently. Roane, believing that Marshall could build his new nation only upon the ruins of the states, reminded Virginians of Henry's admonition in 1788 that their mission was not to build an empire but to defend liberty.[2]

In 1786 Spencer Roane married Anne Henry, Patrick Henry's second eldest daughter. Sadly, after thirteen years as a wife and mother of seven children, Anne died in 1799, a few days before her father.

Roane was an ardent Jeffersonian Republican and states' rights advocate, but the story that President Jefferson would have appointed him Chief Justice of the United States Supreme Court in 1801 had President Adams not appointed John Marshall is surely apocryphal. Nevertheless, Roane's admiration of Jeffersonian principles adds interest to the assertion in his memorandum that "When I was last with Mr. Henry, in October '94, there was no difference between his opinions and mine that I could discover. I was extremely well pleased with all his opinions, which he communicated freely." Perhaps in this instance Roane was being a bit disingenuous, for surely at some time before 1794, in addition to his evaluations of Madison and others, Henry communicated to him his opinions on Jefferson as well—which remain conspicuous in Roane's memorandum by their absence.

Of all the memoirs sent to William Wirt by Henry's contemporaries, Roane's is the most comprehensive and successful in depicting both the statesman and the man. Wirt apparently thought so highly of Roane's judgement that he asked Roane to read and comment on manuscripts and letters from several of his other correspondents before Roane wrote his own memoir. These apparently included Jefferson's negative comments on Henry to Wirt, for, as Roane wrote in his own memorandum (at the conclusion of Section One, below), "I will enter into some particulars respecting [Henry] for the information of Mr. Wirt and animadvert by way of notes on some of the facts contained in the statements which he [Wirt] was pleased to lodge with me."

Roane seems to have genuinely admired his former father-in-law and made a conscientious effort to counter Jefferson's malicious statements about certain aspects of Henry's character. Roane's kind words for Henry and the fact that Wirt knew very well that his book's chances of success were far greater if he portrayed his subject in a heroic light were highly frustrating to Jefferson.

The result was Jefferson's disparaging comments to others about Wirt's biography after it was published.

The editor has divided the text of Roane's memorandum to Wirt into sections with a brief description of the topics covered.

[One – Roane explains his acquaintance and eventual friendship with Henry.]

My acquaintance with the late Patrick Henry did not commence till the year 1783. In the spring of that year, I met him in the general assembly as a delegate for the County of Henry and served with him in that year and the next. Although during that period I often heard him speak, I formed no very particular acquaintance with him, as I was then a very young man and was naturally averse from pushing myself into the society of so distinguished a character.

Richard Henry Lee was also a delegate during those years, and with him I was well acquainted—almost from my childhood. He had been very often at my father's house, who had long served in the assembly with him, as well as with Patrick Henry. When a young man, my father had written in the office of Colonel George Lee, the Clerk of Westmoreland and a relation of R. H. Lee's.

In the fall session of 1784, Mr. Henry was elected governor the second time, commencing in December of that year. I was elected a councilor [one of the eight members of the governor's council of state] the same session, to commence in the May following. Mr. Henry continued governor two years, and I remained in the council till the end of the year 1786, when I resigned. During that time I had an opportunity to become well acquainted with Mr. H., and especially as I had, during the time, formed connection in his family, in which I was, of course, domesticated.

After he had ceased to be governor and I had left the council, owing to the distance by which we were separated, I only saw him in the assembly, of which he was a delegate from Prince Edward and I a member of the senate, until I rode the circuit as Judge of the General Court in 1790 and the four succeeding years. I was, during those years, at least three times on his circuit, and every time left my family at his residence in Prince Edward and at Long Island and accompanied him to the courts of Prince Edward and New London, in which he then practiced, and on to Great Bridge Court, whither he went to defend a criminal. This gave me an opportunity to see him in a new character, that of a counselor in civil and criminal cases.

After I ceased to ride the circuit by being elected into the Court of Appeals and he quit the practice of law, I never again saw him, owing to the distance, though I was at his house on my last circuit in the fall of 1794. He was always in his lifetime very cordial and affectionate towards me.

I have entered into this detail to show that, although I am unable to say much of his life or character prior to 1783, except from the information of his family and others, I have had some opportunity to be well acquainted with him since that period. I will enter into some particulars respecting him for the information of Mr. Wirt and animadvert [correct] by way of notes on some of the facts contained in the statements which he [Wirt] was pleased to lodge with me. The notes will be found included in these statements.

[Two – Henry's personal and domestic character; Roane's interest in Henry's alleged debility in his last years]

With respect to the domestic character of Mr. Henry, nothing could be more amiable. In every relation, as a husband, father, master, and neighbor, he was entirely exemplary. It is no exception from this character that, I conceive, he meditated an act of injustice towards some of his first children by his last will, one of whom, too, at least, was a favorite child. That is to be ascribed to the extreme debility under which he then labored and the urgent importunity of an interested second wife, who assailed him with the claims of her nine children. (This occurrence, of course, will not be mentioned in his biography. I may be mistaken in the idea, and it had better sink into oblivion.)

The particulars of this transaction are detailed in a suit I brought in the court of chancery against his executors after his death, and in which I recovered. I have no wish to bring that transaction into this detail. I only now mention it for the purpose of declaring that even that occurrence forms no exception against his justice as a parent. It was entirely owing to the debility and to influences…[illegible].[3]

As to the disposition of Mr. Henry, it was the best imaginable. I am positive I never saw him in a passion nor apparently even out of temper. Circumstances which would have highly irritated other men had no such visible effect on him. He was always calm and collected, and the rude attacks of his adversaries in debate only whetted the poignancy of his satire. Witness his cutting reply to Francis Corbin in the Virginia Assembly about bowing, of which no doubt Mr. Wirt has been informed [see Chapter IX (3)]. It exceeded anything of the kind I ever heard. He spoke and acted this reply, and Corbin sank at least a foot in his seat.

Shortly after the Constitution was adopted, a series of the most abusive and scurrilous pieces came out against him under the signature of Decius. They were supposed to be written by Mr. John Nicholas Jr. of Albemarle County (Americanus), with the assistance of other more important men. They assailed Mr. Henry's conduct in the Virginia Convention of 1788 on the Ratification of the U. S. Constitution and slandered his character by various stories hatched up against him. These pieces were extremely hateful to all Mr. H.'s friends, and indeed to a great portion of the community. I was at his house in Prince Edward during the thickest of them, and I declare that he seemed to evince no more desire to see the newspapers containing them than the most indifferent person in the county. He evinced no feeling on the occasion and far less condescended to parry the effects thereof on the public mind. It was too puny a contest for him, and he reposed upon the consciousness of his own integrity [Roane was incorrect here; see Chapter IX, (5)].

Patrick Henry had a remarkable faculty of adapting himself to his company. Of this talent, so important to him as a public speaker, I shall presently speak—at present I have only reference to the ordinary intercourse of society. He would be pleasant and cheerful with persons of any class or condition, vicious and abandoned persons always excepted. He preferred those of character and talents, but would amuse himself with any who could contribute to his amusement. Although sufficiently tenacious of his character and dignity, he was not to be offended by rude liberties when no offense was intended. I will give one instance which struck me in a remarkable manner. He had been to Greenbrier Court to defend a criminal named Holland, of which trial I shall speak more particularly hereafter.

The trial had attracted great attention in the upper country and in Mr. Henry's own neighborhood. I was returning therefrom with Mr. H., and within fifteen miles of his house we saw a laboring man at a brake by the road, and I believe he was known to Mr. H. He accosted Mr. Henry with "How do you do, Colonel?" Mr. H. replied. He then asked Mr. H. what he had done with Holland. Mr. H. replied that he was acquitted, on which the man replied with great seeming exultation, "Hurrah for old Henry!" Mr. H., not at all offended with the coarseness of this exclamation, bid the man goodbye and jogged down the road smiling.

[Three – Henry's dress, personal habits and interests, musical accomplishments, and abilities as a businessman]

Mr. Henry was a child of nature. He preferred, I believe, being in the country and being free from the restraints of polished society, yet he could readily adapt himself to that situation. When he was governor the second time [1784-1786] (and I presume more so the first), he rarely appeared in the streets, and never without a scarlet cloak, black clothes, and a dressed wig, etc. The ideas attached to the office of governor, as handed down from the royal government, had not then got down to their present level, and I expect he considered this course a just adaptation to the public opinion. He had besides been accused by the big wigs of former times as being a coarse and common man and totally destitute of dignity, and perhaps he wished to show them that they were mistaken. With great simplicity and suavity of manner, he had as much true dignity as any man.

With respect to his family, at the time I speak of, they were furnished with an excellent coach (at a time when these vehicles were not so common as at present). They lived as genteelly and associated with as polished society as those of any governor before or since have done. He entertained as much company as others, and in as genteel a style, and when at the end of two years he resigned office, he had greatly exceeded his salary and was in debt, which was one cause that induced him to resume the practice of law [see the introduction to Chapter X]. On the other hand, when Mr. H. was in the country, he delighted to be free from these restraints. His dress was plain, as also was his house and furniture, and he was careless about his diet. He took no delight in the pleasures of the table. He was one of the most temperate men I ever knew. He rarely drank any wine or spirits, and his frequent custom was, in the country, to go to a wooden cask and drink water out of a gourd.

I believe he had been fond of hunting and fishing in his youth, but I saw nothing of it after I became acquainted with him, except that when he lived at Long Island he showed me a slope, or fish trap, which he made across a branch of the Staunton River, that furnished fish for his family, and spoke with pleasure of a buck which had recently been caught therein by having been brought down the river in the current.

I have no doubt, from report, but Mr. H. had been a good performer on the violin and was in other respects a musical man, but I never heard him play on a violin or any other instrument, or even sing or hum a tune [see Samuel Meredith's comment, Chapter I (1)]. His daughters played on musical instruments, but these seemed not much to engage his attention.

His great delight was in conversation, and in the society of his friends and family, and in the resources of his own mind. I have understood from the family that he had engaged in trade when young and had failed, but I never heard that he was ever a barkeeper, nor do I believe it. *If* his father-in-law owned a tavern, it is possible that he might have assisted gratuitously at times, but the man's nature must have changed if he could ever have been adapted to a calling of this kind. I have no conception of any man who would have been more abhorrent at mixing toddy and seeing it drunk in a tavern than Patrick Henry. The case is, however, unimportant—his rise in the world has been sufficiently remarkable without introducing into his history fiction of this kind.[4]

As to the kind of clothes in which he went dressed in his youth, according to some of the statements, we must refer (unless they be ascribed to a poverty so extreme as to have denied him better, and which I have never understood was the case) to the customs of the times in which he lived. I can myself remember when there was only one four-wheeled carriage and two pair of boots (called shoe-boots) in the wealthy and fashionable County of Essex. I myself delighted to go barefooted and in trousers until I went to college, and I have heard my father say that his father, when possessed of perhaps one hundred Negroes and when he was a colonel of militia and justice of the quorum, would in his shirt and trousers (in summer) visit two or three of his plantations and return home to breakfast.

I have said that Mr. Henry could adapt himself to all men in a remarkable manner. He was also well acquainted with the transactions of life, or, in other words, was a man of business. He could buy or sell a horse or a Negro as well as anybody and was peculiarly a judge of the value and quality of land. He made several excellent bargains for lands in the latter part of his life, owing to his foresight and judgment. When I have told him that his lands were too far from market, he once replied to me that when he lived at Leatherwood [in present-day Henry County], 180 miles from Richmond, persons passing by his house from the upper part of North Carolina envied him his contiguity to market.

[Four – Henry's modesty, his wealth, his education in the law and general education, his library]

No man ever vaunted less of his achievements than Mr. Henry. I hardly ever heard him speak of those great achievements which form the prominent part of his biography. As for *boasting*, he was an entire stranger to it; unless it be that in his latter days he seemed proud of the goodness of his lands, and, I believe, wished to be thought wealthy.

It is my opinion that he was better pleased to be flattered as to his wealth than as to his great talents. This I have accounted for by reflecting that he had long been under narrow and difficult circumstances as to property, from which he was at length happily relieved, whereas there never was a time when his talents had not shone conspicuous, though he always seemed unconscious of them.

With respect to Mr. Henry's education, he was equally silent on that subject to me. If he got a license after six weeks' reading, that was the very reason why he would not mention it, as it would look like boasting.

I never heard Mr. Henry (nor Mr. Edmund Pendleton) say that he read Mr. Pendleton's books, nor do I believe it. If he had been under any obligations to Mr. P., he would have been grateful for them. But on the contrary, I have reason to believe that he was not very fond of Mr. P., nor Mr. P. of him. I have heard Mr. Henry say that Mr. Pendleton was too much devoted to the aristocracy of former times; that he was not thorough-going enough in the Revolution; that he was in favor of an established church, when as a member of congress he was contending for civil liberty; and that Mr. P., on the bench of Caroline County Court, justified the imprisonment of several Baptist preachers, who were defended by Mr. Henry on the heinous charge of worshiping God according to the dictates of their own consciences [see Chapter III (2)]; and that Mr. Pendleton was a man of too much courtesy in his passage through life, thereby meaning that he had too little candor, etc. On the contrary, I have heard Mr. P. insinuate of Mr. H., as far as he could do so in my hearing, who was connected with him, that he was a demagogue and a popular leader, etc. He (Mr. P.) once at our table at the Swan Tavern justified himself for not offering for the office of governor in 1776 on the ground that he did not think it became those who pushed for the Revolution to get into the first offices, and on that ground he voted for Secretary Thomas Nelson Sr. [whose son, General Thomas Nelson Jr., became Virginia's third governor in 1781]. On which feeling that the remark was aimed at Mr. H., I replied that we would have cut a pretty figure if that office had been given to a man who was no Whig, as Mr. Nelson was said to have been, on which the conversation stopped. I mention these things to show that I do not believe that Mr. Henry ever read law with Mr. P. or owed him any obligations.

As to Mr. H.'s general education, I do not believe that he had a regular academical one, but I do believe that he had some knowledge of the Latin tongue and acquaintance with some of the principal branches of science. These a man of Mr. H.'s genius could not fail to acquire in a considerable degree, if not in the school room, at least at the dinner table of his father, who was a well educated man. If other men could not catch an education under these circumstances, it does not follow that Mr. H. could not, though it is said in some of the statements that he was taught by his father. His genius was as far-soaring above those of ordinary men as is the first-qualitied land of Kentucky beyond the sandy barrens of Pea Ridge (a barren ridge in King and Queen [counties]).

As to his using a translation of Livy [the Roman historian], he may have never been able to read the original with perfect ease, or have forgotten the language. I was *once* able to read Homer [the epic poet of ancient Greece] with almost as much ease as the *Spectator* [a British periodical], which I owed to our good friend John Warden [one of Roane's teachers in the law] and others, but am now obliged to read Alexander Pope's [translation of] Homer, which Dr. Samuel Johnson (I think) says, and says truly, is not Homer's Homer.

As for the general character of Mr. Henry's library, I readily believe that he had not a complete or regular one. He was not a man of regularity or system. When at his dwelling at Prince Edward County, I lodged with my family in his study (house room being scarce), and there saw his library fully. I remarked that it consisted sometimes of odd volumes, etc., but of good books. I believe that an inventory and catalogue of the books he died possessed of is filed in my former suit in the chancery court, before mentioned, and I expect it would be found to come within this description [see Appendix E "Patrick Henry's Books"]. That he was acquainted with ancient history and mythology needs no further proof than the eloquent parallel used by him in his argument on the British Debt Case between Rhadamanthus [in Greek mythology, a judge of the underworld], Nero [the Roman emperor], and George III.

I believe he was very fond of history, magazines, good poetry or plays (say Shakespeare's), and I think was a very good geographer. He was particularly well acquainted with the geography, rivers, soil, climate, etc. of America. His speeches show that he was well acquainted with mathematics and natural philosophy. After all, while I believe that although Mr. H. had not a complete education, his great merit consists in this—that he acquired it by means impervious to ordinary men.

[Five – Henry's benevolent disposition and magnanimity; stories of the effects of his oratory before the Revolution]

There was one trait in Mr. Henry, flowing from his good disposition and his magnanimity, which did him great credit and is universally admitted. He was extremely kind to young men in debate and ever ready to compliment even his adversaries where it was merited. Of the latter class, his high eulogium upon Colonel James Innes' eloquence in the Virginia Convention will be recollected. Of the former class, the instances were innumerable. I will mention one which occurred in my own case. In the spring of the year 1783, several of the most respectable of my constituents of the County of Essex tarred and feathered one James Williamson. He had been a merchant in Tappahannock, had gone to the British and endeavored to bring up tenders to burn the town during the war, and after the peace had returned to Tappahannock, where he was countenanced by some of the inhabitants. This gave such umbrage that he was pursued, caught, and tarred and feathered by the principal men of Essex. They were prosecuted for this misdemeanor in the general court. While the prosecution was still pending, these citizens sent a petition to me in the spring of 1784, praying the assembly to arrest the prosecution. I presented the petition and got a law of indemnity in some progress, taking care to state, as the fact was, that the act was committed before the definitive treaty was signed, which was some alleviation of their conduct.

Mr. Henry took me out one day and said that he admired the Whig spirit which actuated me, but that the intervention of the legislature could not be justified. I told him that the transaction was irregular, but the provocation was great and the act done, in some sense, *flagrante bello* [during hostilities]. He persisted in his opinion, and I maintained my ground, intimated that I hoped he would not oppose me, but that if he did, I must nevertheless proceed. He left me and did not oppose me, which I ascribe to the trait now in question, and the act of indemnity passed. This is one small instance, but a thousand others might be mentioned.

Although I was personally unacquainted with Mr. Henry until 1783, I was no stranger to his character before that time. A volunteer at the age of thirteen, armed with a short carbine and tomahawk, and clothed in a hunting shirt with the words "Liberty or Death" engraved in capitals over my left breast, I could not be indifferent to the character of that man who electrified the American public by his eloquence in council and roused them to resistance at a critical time by taking the field.

I had even before this formed a high opinion of this man's eloquence, talents, and patriotism. My father, a burgess for Essex from 1768 to the Revolution, and once or twice during the war, always came home in raptures with the man. That a plain man of ordinary though respected family should beard the aristocracy, by whom we were then cursed and ruled, and overthrow them in the cause of independence was grateful to a man of my father's Whig principles. He considered Henry as the organ of the great body of the people—as the instrument by whom the big wigs were to be thrown down and liberty and independence established.

It is among the first things I can remember that my father paid the expenses of a Scotch tutor residing in his family named Bradfute, a man of learning, to go with him to Williamsburg to hear Patrick Henry speak; and that he laughed at Bradfute, on his return, for having been so much enchanted with his eloquence as to have unconsciously spurt tobacco juice from the gallery on the heads of the members and to have nearly fallen from the gallery into the house. At a subsequent time, too, my father carried another tutor and myself, when not ten years old, to Williamsburg on purpose to hear Patrick Henry speak, but no occasion brought him out before the vacation had expired and we returned home. It was about this time, I presume, that the circumstance took place which often I have heard Major Joseph Scott relate. Mr. H. was declaiming against the British king and ministry, and such was the effect of his eloquence that all at once the spectators in the gallery rushed out. It was at first supposed that the house was on fire. Not so; but some of the most prominent of these spectators ran up into the cupola and dowsed the royal flag which was there suspended! Notwithstanding these and such like "effects," it was still said by some that Patrick Henry was only a declaimer. Because he spoke with force of feeling, it was inferred that he wanted arguments. On the same principle, Andrew Roland was reputed to be a great lawyer because he was a miserable speaker.

[Six– Henry as an orator compared to Richard Henry Lee. Madison could not compete with Henry in oratory. Henry's letters prove he could write well.]

With these impressions, I met Patrick Henry in the general assembly in May 1783. I also then met with Richard Henry Lee. I lodged with Lee one or two sessions, and was perfectly acquainted with him while I was as yet a stranger to Mr. Henry. These two gentlemen were the great leaders in the House of Delegates and were almost constantly opposed. Not withstanding my habits of intimacy with Mr. Lee, I found myself obliged to vote with Patrick Henry against him in 1783 and against Madison in 1784 (in which year, I think, R. H. Lee was sent to congress), but with several important exceptions. I voted against him (P.H.), I recollect, on the subject of the refugees—he was for permitting their return, on the subject of a general assessment, and the act of incorporating the Episcopal Church [see Chapter VII]. I voted with him in general because he was, I thought, a more practical statesman than Madison (time has made Madison more practical) and less selfish than Lee.

As an orator, Mr. Henry demolished Madison with as much ease as Sampson did the cords that bound him before he was shorn. Mr. Lee held a greater competition. There were many other great men in the house, but as orators they cannot be named with Henry or Lee. Mr. Lee was a polished gentleman. His person was not very good, and he had lost the use of one of his hands, but his manner was perfectly graceful. His language was always chaste, and although somewhat too monotonous, his speeches were always pleasing. Yet he did not ravish your senses nor carry away your judgment by storm. His was of the mediate class of eloquence described by Rollin in his *Belles Lettres*. He was like a beautiful river meandering through a flowery meadow, but which never overflowed its banks. It was Henry who was the mountain torrent that swept away everything before it. It was he alone who thundered and lightened. He alone attained that sublime species of eloquence also mentioned by Rollin.[5]

It has been one of the greatest pleasures of my life to hear these two great masters, almost constantly opposed to each other, for several sessions. I had no relish for any other speaker. Henry was almost always victorious. He was as much superior to Lee in temper as in eloquence. For while the former would often apologize to the house for being so often obliged to differ from the latter, which he assured them was from no want of respect for him, I once heard Mr. Lee say in a pet, after sustaining a great defeat, that if the votes were weighed instead of being counted, he would not have lost it.

Mr. Henry was inferior to Mr. Lee in the gracefulness of his action, and perhaps also the chasteness of his language. Yet his language was seldom incorrect and his address always striking. He had a fine blue eye and an earnest manner which made it impossible not to attend him. His speaking was unequal and always rose with the subject and the exigency. In this respect he entirely differed from Mr. Lee, who was always equal. At some times Mr. Henry would seem to hobble (especially in the beginning of his speeches) and at others his tones would be almost disagreeable. Yet it was by means of his tones and the happy modulation of his voice that his speaking had, perhaps, its greatest effect. He had a happy articulation and a clear, distinct, strong voice, and every syllable was uttered. He was very unassuming as to himself, amounting almost to humility and very respectful towards his competitor. The consequence was that no feeling of disgust or animosity was arrayed against him. His exordiums [introductions], in particular, were often hobbling, and always unassuming. He knew mankind too well to promise much. They were of the *menin aeide* ["I sing of the wrath"] cast (of Homer) rather than of the *fortunam Priami* ["I sing of the fortune (luck) of Priam"] of some author whose name is forgotten [Horace, *Ars Poetica*].

He was great at a reply, and greater in proportion to the pressure which was bearing upon him. The resources of his mind and of his eloquence were equal to any drafts which could be made upon them. He took but short notes of what fell from his adversaries and disliked the drudgery of composition, yet it is a mistake to say he could not write well. Many of his public letters prove the contrary. I do not know that he ever wrote anything for the press.

[Seven – Henry as an independent politician, a man of the people, and leader of the Revolution]

It has been urged against Mr. Henry by his enemies, and by the aristocrats whom he overthrew, that he always seized and advocated the popular side of the question. Nothing is less true. He opposed General Washington and an erring world (as he said) on the subject of the Constitution [see Chapter VIII]. The man who would do this cannot be suspected of want of firmness to pursue his own opinions. The man who moved the Stamp Act Resolutions and took up arms to recover the gunpowder pursued his own course. He had no certain indication of the popular opinion in either case, and both measures were esteemed by ordinary men too rash and bold to be popular. Besides, why court the popular opinion when he wanted not popularity, for he had resisted (in the latter part of his life) every distinction which was offered him? [For a list of these, see the introduction to Chapter XI.]

On this subject, I take the fact to be that he generally thought like the most of people because he was a plain, practical man, because he was emphatically one of the people, and because he detested, as a statesman, the projects of theorists and bookworms. His prejudices against statesmen of this character were very strong. He emphatically led the people in promoting and effecting the Revolution.

[Eight – Henry's skill as a lawyer and as an orator in court; examples of his abilities in both the tragic and the comic line]

At the bar, Mr. Henry was equally successful. When I saw him there, he must necessarily have been very rusty; yet I considered him a good lawyer. He was acquainted with the rules and canons of property. He would not, indeed, undergo the drudgery necessary for complicated business, yet I am told that in the British Debt Case he astonished the public not less by the matter than manner of his speech. It was as a criminal lawyer that his eloquence had the fairest scope, and in that character I have seen him. He was perfect master of the passions of his auditory, whether in the tragic or the comic line. The tones of his voice, to say nothing of his matter and gestures, were insinuated into the feelings of his hearers in a manner that baffled all description. It seemed to operate by mere sympathy, and by his tones alone, it seemed to me that he could make you cry or laugh at pleasure. Yet his gesture came powerfully in aid, and if necessary would approach almost to the ridiculous. This was the case in the "roasting case" to be presently mentioned. Also in Francis Corbin's case. Corbin had accused him of inconsistency in not acquiescing under the new constitution after having declared somewhere emphatically that he would deem it his duty to bow down to the majesty of the people. Henry yielded the palm of bowing to Corbin, who, he said, had been at the Court of St. James, but said he would in his plain way stand up for the rights of the people. At this he straightened himself in a remarkable manner [see Chapter IX].

I will endeavor to give some account of his tragic and comic effect in two instances that came before me: About the year 1792, one Holland killed a young man in Botetourt County. The young man was popular and lived, I think, with King, a merchant of Fincastle, who employed John Breckenridge to assist in the prosecution of Holland. Holland had gone up from Louisa County as a schoolmaster, but had turned out badly and was very unpopular. The killing was in the night and was generally believed to be murder. He was the son of one Dr. Holland, who was yet living in Louisa and had been one of Mr. Henry's juvenile friends and acquaintances. At the insistence of the father, and for a reasonable fee, Mr. Henry undertook to go to Greenbrier Court to defend Holland. Mr. Edmund Winston and myself were the judges. Such were the prejudices there, as I was afterward informed by Thomas Madison, that the people declared that even Patrick Henry need not come to defend Holland unless he brought a jury with him.

The day of the trial the courthouse was crowded, and I did not move from my seat for fourteen hours, and had no wish to do so. The examination took up a great part of the time, and the lawyers were probably exhausted. Breckenridge was eloquent, but Henry left no dry eye in the courthouse. The case, I believe, was murder, though possibly manslaughter only. Henry laid hold of this possibility with such effect as to make all forget that Holland had killed the storekeeper, and presented the deplorable case of the jury killing Holland, an innocent man. He also presented, as it were at the clerk's table, old Holland and his wife, who were then in Louisa, asked what must be the feelings of this venerable pair at this awful moment, and what the consequences to them of a mistaken verdict affecting the life of their son. He caused the jury to lose sight of the murder they were trying and weep with old Holland and his wife, whom he painted, and perhaps proved to be, very respectable. All this was done in a manner so solemn and touching, and a tone so irresistible, that it was impossible for the stoutest heart not to take sides with the criminal. During the examination the bloody clothes were brought in. Mr. Henry objected to this exhibition and applied most forcibly and pathetically Antony's remarks on Caesar's wounds—on those dumb mouths which would raise the stones of Rome to mutiny [Shakespeare, *Julius Caesar*, III, ii, 227-234]. He urged that this sight would totally deprive the jury of their judgment, which would be merged in their feelings. The motion fell, Mr. Winston being of opinion to reject them. I was of opinion to receive them as explanatory of the nature of the crime, by showing in what direction the strokes were given.

The result of the trial was that, after a retirement of a half or a quarter of an hour, the jury brought in a verdict of *not guilty!* But on being reminded by the court that they might find an inferior degree of homicide, they then brought in a verdict of manslaughter.

Mr. Henry was equally successful in the comic line. Mr. Wirt has heard, no doubt, how he choused [tricked] John Hook out of his cause by raising the cry of "Beef" against him [see Chapter X (2)]. I will give a similar instance. About the year 1792, there were many suits on the south of the James River for inflicting Lynch Law [summary punishment, but which did *not* include hanging]. A verdict of $500 had been given in Prince Edward County District Court in a case of this kind. This alarmed the defendant in the next case, who employed Mr. Henry to defend him. The case was that a wagoner and the plaintiff were traveling to Richmond, and the wagoner knocked down a turkey and put it into his wagon. Complaint was made to the defendant, a justice. Both the parties were taken up, and the wagoner agreed to take a whipping rather than be sent to jail, but the plaintiff refused. The justice, however, gave him a small whipping, and for this the suit was brought. The plaintiff's plea was that he was wholly innocent of the act committed. Mr. Henry on the contrary, contended that he was a party in aiding and assisting. In the course of his remarks, he thus expressed himself: "But, gentlemen of the jury, this plaintiff tells you that he had nothing to do with the turkey—I dare say, gentlemen, not until it was *roasted*," etc. He pronounced the word *roasted* with such rotundity of voice and comicalness of manner and gesture that it threw everyone into a fit of laughter at the plaintiff, who stood up in the place usually allotted to criminals, and the defendant was let off with little or no damage.

I have likened this faculty of Mr. Henry of operating upon the feelings, whether tragic or comic, by the mere tone of his voice to the experiment of ringing a series of glasses by rubbing one of them with the finger. It operated by sympathy. Yet he ranted not, nor did he distress himself or his audience by an unnatural stretching of his throat. He had a perfect command of a strong and musical voice, which he raised or lowered at pleasure and modulated so as to fall in with any given chord of the human heart.

It is to be also observed that although his language was plain and free from unusual or high-flown words, his ideas were remarkably bold, strong, and striking. By the joint effect of these two faculties—I mean of the power of his tone or voice and the grandness of his conceptions—he had a wonderful effect upon the feelings of his audience. Both of these concurred in the famous speech in the Convention of 1788, which was interrupted by a storm [see Chapter VIII (11)], and of which I see Mr. Wirt has a note. The question of adoption was approaching, and from that cause everyone had an awful and anxious feeling. This was, as it were, the parting speech of Mr. Henry, and he was depicting the awful immensity of the question and its consequences as it respected the present and future generations. He stated that the ethereal beings were awaiting with anxiety the decision of a question which involved the happiness or misery of more than half the human race. He had presented such an awful picture, and in such feeling colors, as to interest the feelings of the audience to the highest pitch. When lo! a storm at that moment arose, which shook the building in which the convention were sitting, and broke it up in confusion. So remarkable a coincidence was never before witnessed, and it seemed as if he had indeed the faculty of calling up spirits from the vasty deep.

[Nine – Henry's understanding of human nature as a major factor in his accomplishments; his preference for "men of genius"]

Mr. Henry was remarkably well acquainted with mankind. He knew well all the springs and motives of human action. This arose from mingling freely with mankind and from a keen and constant observation. From this faculty and his great command of temper, he would have made a great negotiator. In fact, he was a great negotiator, for in managing a jury or a popular assembly he measured and gauged them by a discriminating judgment. He knew how much they would bear and what was the proper string to touch them upon. The same faculty and discernment which enabled him to buy a tract of land or a Negro on good terms and to govern a jury or a popular assembly at pleasure by measuring the depth of those with whom he was dealing would have enabled him to fathom the views and feelings of courts and cabinets.

The advantage of Mr. Henry's education consisted in this, that it arose from some reading which he never forgot and much observation and reflection. It was remarked of Montesquieu's *Spirit of the Laws* that it was a good book for one travelling in a stagecoach, for that you might read as much of it in half an hour as would serve you to reflect upon a whole day. Such was somewhat the proportion between Mr. Henry's education as drawn from reading and from observation and reflection. He read good books as it were for a text and filled up the picture by an acute and penetrating observation and reflection and by mingling in the society of men. He had practiced law in the county courts, a school remarkably well adapted to acquaint a person with mankind in general.

Mr. Henry was very fond of men of genius, and on this ground he was much attached to Dr. James McClurg [1746-1823] and had a great agency in getting him into the council in May 1784. Dr. McClurg, I believe, would not have been then elected but for a speech of his just before the ballot. As he spoke, many members were seen to tear up their ballots prepared for other candidates. Henry took the ground for Dr. McClurg that he was a man of great genius and eminence in his profession. At this time party had not thrown our citizens so far asunder [Dr. McClurg eventually ended up in the Federalist camp].

Mr. Henry did not permit political prejudices to tear asunder his friendships. I have heard that he interfered with the Committee of Hanover in favor of Mr. Peter Lyons, an old friend and fellow-practitioner at the bar, and got him excused when suspected of some disaffection. He acted a very friendly and liberal part towards Mr. Jaqueline Ambler when Treasurer, who by some means sustained a considerable loss of public money, and for which Mr. Ambler was grateful.

Mr. Henry's talent for humor showed itself sometimes in a remarkable manner. About the year 1790, as I think I have heard him or some of the family say, General Edward Lawson applied to him for his friendly advice touching the state of his affairs, which were deplorably bad. Lawson had been a revolutionary patriot and soldier and a colleague of Mr. Henry in the assembly and Convention of 1788. Mr. Henry secured a full and frank disclosure. After he was done, Mr. H. paused, and Lawson requested his opinion; on which Henry, looking at him significantly, said, "Why, faith, General, you had better run away." This, which was perhaps a jest in Henry, was literally followed by Lawson, who ran to Kentucky, spent his estate, and came to a wretched end.

[Ten – Difficulties Henry surmounted to achieve success; his courage—personal and political—and his military career; Henry's opinions of George Mason and James Madison]

In estimating Mr. Henry's standing and endowments, the difficulties under which he labored ought to be taken into consideration. He was without a regular academical education. He was poor, married young, and had a numerous family. For a great part of his life (though he died rich) he was struggling in debt and difficulties. Where were his means and leisure for improvement? Contrast him in these respects with Madison, for example. Madison was born to affluence. His father early gave him a competent fortune, which also, I believe, he managed for him. And Madison lived with his father, I believe, till past the age of forty, unencumbered with the cares of a family or with keeping house. He had, besides, received a finished education at Princeton. He had every opportunity for improvement, and his life was that of a recluse and student. Had Mr. Henry had these advantages and been as studious as Madison, he would have excelled him if possible, as much in the knowledge of books as he actually did in that of men, the great source of his superiority over Madison in public assemblies.

It has been said of Patrick Henry that he was not a military man and *surmised* that he was deficient in personal courage [this very likely in response to a comment by Thomas Jefferson to William Wirt]. As to the last, he was so good-tempered a man that I never heard of his having a quarrel. He did call on Edmund Randolph in 1788 on account of some personalities [offensive personal remarks] used toward him in the Convention of 1788 [see Chapter VIII (6)] with old Will Cabell [Colonel William Cabell Sr. of Union Hill (c. 1729-1798)] as his friend. I heard the latter say that Mr. Henry acted with great firmness and propriety. He let Mr. Randolph down, however, pretty easily, owing to the extreme benignity of his disposition. He had, however, what suited us much better, an astonishing portion of political courage. Perhaps it is not too much to affirm that it is owing to this one quality of this single man that our revolution took place at the time it did. As to his being a military man, he was certainly not a man of system and regularity, nor do I believe that he was a good tactician. He may nevertheless have had a genius which would have made him adequate (with the aid of subalterns) to great military operations. As to his resigning the command of the First Virginia Regiment, it is probable that he may have thought himself slighted by the Committee of Safety, though I never heard him complain of it [see Chapter V (2)]. Indeed, he seldom complained (as to himself) of anybody. That committee, however, had a spice of the old aristocracy in it, by whom Henry was much hated, and it might have been agreeable to some of them to mortify him. Pendleton, the eclipsed rival of Henry, presided in the committee and had his party with him.

The principal reason, I believe, why he resigned was that he was called by the public voice as governor, and was perhaps indispensably necessary in that station. His competitor for that office was Secretary Thomas Nelson Sr., who was beaten easily by Patrick Henry, although supported by all the aristocracy, and by Pendleton and perhaps a few others of plebian standing.

Henry had strong prejudices for and against many of his political associates, though he only expressed them to his particular friends. He had the highest opinion of George Mason's talents, patriotism, and republican principles. He considered him as a man well acquainted with the interests of the people and warmly attached to the liberty of his country. A cordial friendship existed between them. Of Richard Henry Lee, he did not think quite so well, and they were very often opposed to each other. Yet they coalesced on great questions, as that of independence and opposition to the federal constitution. In 1788, Mr. Henry nominated Lee and William Grayson as senators (taking the unusual liberty of nominating *two*) against Madison, and they were elected. He was very fond of John Tyler as a warm-hearted patriot and an honest, sensible man, and many others not necessary to be now mentioned. As to Mr. Madison, he considered him in 1783 and 84 as a man of great acquirements but too theoretical as a politician, and that he was not well versed in the affairs of men. This opinion increased in the Convention of 1788. He was astonished that Madison would take the Constitution, admitting its defects, and in a season of perfect peace, and believed him too friendly to a strong government and too hostile to the governments of the states. On these grounds, he was rejected as a senator in 1788, and probably this rejection was useful to Madison, for, to regain the confidence of his native state, he brought forward the amendments introduced in 1789 into the Constitution [see Chapter IX].

[Eleven - Henry's political opinions during his last years and Roane's explanation of the reasons for them— again, his alleged debility; Henry's Christian religion and his tolerance; Roane's belief that Henry remained "a true Republican" until his death]

Henry's prejudice against Madison always remained in some degree, and to this cause may in some measure be ascribed his alleged secession from the Republican Party, now headed by Madison, toward the close of his life. With respect to this alleged change of his political principles, I shall say what I know about it. When I was last with him, in October of 1794, there was no difference between his opinions and mine that I could discover. I was extremely well pleased with all his opinions, which he communicated freely. He had, after the adoption of the Constitution, taken the anti-federal side in the assembly on all occasions. After this, matters seeming to come to extremities in relation to our foreign affairs, I understood—for I never saw him again—that he disapproved the policy of embarking in the cause of France and running the risk of a war with Britain. Possibly his sagacious mind foresaw the issue of the French Revolution and dreaded the effect of a war with England upon our free government and upon the finances of the United States.

After it began to be rumored that he had changed his opinions, he wrote me several letters alluding to the report, and averring that his opinions were not changed, and that he was too old to change them, but admitting that he differed from the Republican leaders as to some of their measures, which he considered unwise and impolitic. I saw another long letter to one of his daughters, who had apprised him that he was charged with a change of his opinions, entirely to the same effect [probably the August 20, 1796, letter to Betsey Henry Aylett, see Chapter XI (4)]. According to the best of my recollection, this letter had some cant of religious professions and complaint of the decay of virtue, etc., which I rather think indicated a change in him and some debility or gloom in his understanding. The particular date of it is not recollected, but I rather think it was within the two years in which Judge Edmund Winston says he gradually declined before his death. The alleged change must, I presume, have been subsequent to the fall of 1796, for in that session he was elected governor for the third time, with a view to keep out General James Wood, who was deemed a Federalist. Mr. Henry was voted for zealously by all the Republicans. He declined, however, and Wood was then elected.

It must have been about the same time that he was chosen a senator of the United States, which I see is asserted in one of the statements furnished, though I have at present no distinct recollections of that fact (*quere de hoc*) ["it is necessary to investigate the matter." Henry was chosen a senator but declined.]. I have understood that for two or three years before he died he became much debilitated (see [Judge Edmund] Winston's narrative [Appendix A, Section Six]). He was very retired and much out of the way of correct information. I have also understood that he became then more religious and that it became a frequent topic of his conversation. This I must ascribe to the debility just mentioned, for though I believe him to have been always a Christian, he was remarkably tolerant to others and never obtruded that as the subject of conversation. In this state of seclusion and debility, he was a fit subject to be worked upon by artful politicians to widen a breach which would not otherwise have been so great. That debility which, in the instance of the will before mentioned, made him an easy prey to intrigues of a domestic character, laid him equally open to the arts of crafty politicians.

Before this time, General Washington, no doubt informed of some difference in opinion between him and the Republican leaders, wrote him flattering letters. He had appointed him Secretary of State, and he and President Adams appointed him one of a trio of ambassadors to go to France or England, and also a minister to the Court of Spain—all of which appointments Mr. Henry declined [see Chapter XI]. I do not think that at the time these appointments were offered Mr. Henry was in this state of debility. Nor do I assert anything about this debility but from information and belief. I have no personal knowledge of it. They were, however, offered after Patrick Henry began to diverge from the Republican Party, and measures were afterward taken to widen the breach and to inflame him against the Republican leaders.

As to these measures, General Henry ["Light-Horse Harry"] Lee was the principal agent. He misrepresented the views and conduct of the Republicans, and flattered Mr. Henry, and assailed him on his weak side in the trading for valuable lands, which Mr. H. wished to acquire for the sons of his second marriage. By means like this, I believe, it was that Lee got from him a political letter, which he used to the injury of the Republican cause in a contested election in the Northern Neck.

I well remember that when I visited Mrs. Henry, on her invitation, after Mr. Henry's death, I mentioned this fact to her and stated the injury it had done to Mr. Henry with the Republicans. She seemed to agree with me on the subject, but concluded, with a laugh, that Henry Lee had been a great friend to their family, for that Mr. Henry had got two fine tracts of land from him! This was the instrument by which the influence of this infirm and declining old man was to be drawn from the Republican cause. This was the panacea for every injury. It must have been by similar means that a letter was got from Mr. Henry favoring John Marshall in his election contest with John Clopton [see Chapter XII (1)]. It was written to a man (Archibald Blair) who, I well know, was hardly in the habit of conversing with Mr. Henry in his more prosperous days. On the whole, it is my decided opinion and belief (but I only give it *as* my opinion and belief) that Mr. Henry was operated upon by the artfulness and misrepresentation of artful and designing men under circumstances of seclusion and debility, arising from the infirmity of age and disease peculiarly fitting him for the operation, and that by this means, he was carried to greater lengths against the measures of the Republicans than he would otherwise have gone.

The effect now supposed can only be ascribed to debility. Formerly no man was more armed against seductions of every kind than Patrick Henry. Offices had now no charm for him, for he declined them all before the time in question, and he was hackneyed through life to flattery and compliments. As a proof how impenetrable he had been to attempts of this kind, when Leven Rowell and Charles Simons and others professed a willingness to vote for him as president, but not for Jefferson, he declined the thing by a short notification in the *Virginia Gazette*. If, therefore, he was operated upon, as I have supposed, it must be ascribed to debility, and to it only. Under other circumstances, he could have got Lee's land without any sacrifice of opinion, for he was a match for Lee in bargaining.

Mr. Winston says Mr. Henry died in June 1799, after "a gradual decline of about two years." I suspect it will be found that his most violent complaints against the Republicans took place within those two years. This decline was not, perhaps, attended with effects palpably visible, for he was elected from Charlotte County in April 1799, but it made him gloomy on the subject of religion and querulous on that of politics. In short, I believe it made him a different man from what he had before been. At the same time, I readily admit that he had before differed from the Republicans in some degree as to measures of policy, in some instances—in some of which, perhaps, time has shown that he was not mistaken. As to fundamentals, however, I must always believe he remained a true Republican.

[Twelve - Roane's profession of candor in his memorandum of Henry; the impossibility of preserving his eloquence in writing; Henry's many virtues and one fault; a physical description of Henry]

In giving this sketch of what I knew of Mr. Henry, I have endeavored to be faithful. It will be seen whether a spirit of candor does not run through the relation and how far it is corroborated by other accounts. It was my intention "nothing to extenuate, nor set down aught in malice." If my descriptions seem extravagant, let it be remembered that he was a most remarkable man. As for his public conduct and opinions, they are already before the world, who will judge of them. It is only his eloquence, character, and virtue to which my details have related. In forming an estimate of his eloquence, no reliance can be placed on the printed speeches. No reporter whatever could take down what he actually said—and if he could, it would fall far short of the original. Much of the effect of his eloquence arose from his voice, gesture, etc., which in print is entirely lost.

As to the character of Mr. Henry: With many sublime virtues, he had no vice that I knew or ever heard of and scarcely a foible. I have thought, indeed, that he was too much attached to property; a defect, however, which might be excused on the largeness of a beloved family and the straitened circumstances in which he had been confined during a great part of his life.

Mr. Henry was a man of middling stature. He was rather stoop-shouldered (after I knew him), probably the effect of age. He had no superfluous flesh. His features were distinctly marked and his complexion rather dark. He was somewhat bald and always wore a wig in public. He was, according to my recollection, very attentive to his teeth, his beard, and his linen. He was not a handsome man, but his countenance was agreeable and full of intelligence and interest. He had a fine blue eye and an excellent set of teeth, which, with the aid of a mouth sufficiently wide, enabled him to articulate very distinctly. His voice was strong, harmonious, and clear, and he could modulate it at pleasure.

The miniature shown by Mr. Wirt has some resemblance of Mr. Henry, but is not a good likeness. It makes him too thin and wrinkled and to appear older than he appeared when I last saw him. I saw that miniature about the time it was taken and gave this opinion then. The portrait I mentioned to Mr. Wirt, if in existence, affords a better likeness.[6]

CHAPTER I

HENRY'S EARLY LIFE TO THE PARSON'S CAUSE CASE, 1763

"Until he arrived to eminence at the bar, there was nothing very remarkable in the person, mind, or manners of Mr. Henry."
—Samuel Meredith, who grew up with Patrick Henry in Hanover County, Virginia, 1805

(1) Henry's early life: excerpts from Samuel Meredith's memorandum to William Wirt (1805)

Samuel Meredith (1732-1808), four years older than Henry, grew up with him in Hanover County. He married Jane Henry, the one of Patrick's seven sisters closest to him in age. His entire memorandum appears in this book as Appendix B. [1]

Patrick Henry was born in Hanover County on May 29, 1736. His father was a Scotchman from Aberdeen of a very liberal and extensive education. He was sent to a common English school until about the age of ten years, where he learned to read and write and acquired some little knowledge of arithmetic. He never went to any other school, public or private, but remained with his father, who was his only tutor. With him he acquired a knowledge of the Latin language and a smattering of Greek. He became well acquainted with mathematics, of which he was very fond. At the age of fifteen he was well versed in both ancient and modern history. His uncle had nothing to do with his education. [The uncle, the Reverend Patrick Henry, was an Anglican minister and held a master's degree from the King's College of Aberdeen University in Scotland. For years the younger Patrick Henry signed his name

"Patrick Henry Junior." John Henry, young Patrick's father, attended Aberdeen University for four years but did not graduate.]

Until he arrived to eminence at the bar, there was nothing very remarkable in the person, mind, or manners of Mr. Henry. His disposition was very mild, benevolent, and humane. He was quiet and inclined to be thoughtful, but fond of society. From his earliest days he was an attentive observer of everything of consequence that passed before him. Nothing escaped his attention. He was fond of reading, but indulged in innocent amusements. He was remarkably fond of his gun. He interested himself much in the happiness of others, particularly of his sisters, of whom he had eight, and whose advocate he always was when any favor or indulgence was to be procured from their mother.

In his youth he seemed regardless of the appearance of his outside dress, but was unusually attentive in having clean linen and stockings. He was not remarkable for an uncouth or genteel appearance (the preceding remarks are particularly applicable to Mr. Henry's youth), and in fact there was nothing in early life for which he was remarkable except his invariable habit of close and attentive observation. He had a nice ear for music, and when he was about the age of twelve, he had his collar bone broken, and during the confinement learned to play very well on the flute. He was also an excellent performer on the violin...

About the age of fifteen he became clerk for some merchant in Hanover. He continued in that employment for one year, when his father purchased a parcel of goods for him and his brother William, and they commenced business on their own account. They were jointly interested, but Patrick was the principal manager. They, however, did not continue business longer than one year, when it was found necessary to abandon it, as they had injured themselves by granting too extensive credit.

P. H. was then engaged in winding up the business of the concern until he was married, the fall after he was eighteen, to a daughter of Mr. John Shelton, who lived in the forks of Hanover. She was a woman of some fortune and much respectability, by whom he had six children. She died about the year 1770 or 1771 [correct date, 1775]. In April 1776 [correct date, 1777] he was married to a daughter of Mr. Nathaniel Dandridge, now the wife of Judge Edmund Winston, by whom he had nine children—living at, or some short time before, his death...[2]

(2) Patrick Henry receives his law license, according to Thomas Jefferson and John Tyler.

On July 23, 1805, William Wirt (1772-1834) wrote from Williamsburg to then-President Thomas Jefferson (1743-1826) at Monticello "begging your aid of your memory towards a little literary project which I have on foot. I am collecting memoirs of the late Patrick Henry. His life and example appear to me to afford some fine lessons. His faults as well as his virtues will be instructive, and propose to myself to be his biographer, not his panegyrist..."

Jefferson responded quickly (August 4, 1805) to Wirt, stating at the beginning of his letter, "I feel every disposition to comply with your request respecting Mr. Henry, but I fear to promise from a doubt whether my occupations would permit me the time requisite to recollect and commit to paper the facts respecting him which were within my own knowledge..."

After finishing his brief letter with "Accept my friendly salutations and assurances of sincere esteem and respect," Jefferson signed it, then appended a postscript of his recollections of Henry approximately eight times the letter's length, which began: [3]

My acquaintance with Mr. Henry commenced in the winter of 1759-60 on my way to the college [The College of William and Mary]. I passed the Christmas holidays at Colonel Nathaniel West Dandridge's in Hanover, to whom Mr. Henry was a near neighbor. During the festivity of the season I met him in society every day, and we became well acquainted, although I was much his junior, being then in my seventeenth year and he a married man. The spring following, he came to Williamsburg to obtain a license as a lawyer, and he called on me at the college. He told me he had been reading law only six weeks. Two of the examiners, however,

Peyton and John Randolph, men of great facility of temper, signed his license with as much reluctance as their dispositions would permit them to show. Mr. Wythe absolutely refused [Jefferson was mistaken about this].[4] Robert C. Nicholas refused also at first, but, on repeated importunities and promises of future reading, he signed. The two Randolphs acknowledged he was very ignorant of law, but they perceived him to be a young man of genius and did not doubt he would soon qualify himself.

John Tyler (1747-1813), governor of Virginia (1808-11) and father of President John Tyler, in a memorandum to William Wirt (1805), who noted, "This account of Mr. Henry's examination is given by Judge Tyler, who states it as having come from Mr. Henry himself:" [5]

On this preparation, however, he obtained a license to practice the law. How he passed with two of the examiners, I have no idea, but he himself used to relate his interview with the third. This was no other than Mr. John Randolph [father of Edmund Randolph], who was afterward the king's attorney-general for the colony; a gentleman of the most courtly elegance of person and manners, a polished wit, and a profound lawyer. At first he was so much shocked by Mr. Henry's very ungainly figure and address that he refused to examine him. Understanding, however, that he had already obtained two signatures, he entered, with manifest reluctance, on the business. A very short time was sufficient to satisfy him of the erroneous conclusion which he had drawn from the exterior of the candidate. With evident marks of increasing surprise (produced no doubt by the peculiar texture and strength of Mr. Henry's style and the boldness and originality of his combinations), he continued the examination for several hours, interrogating the candidate not on the principles of municipal law, in which he no doubt soon discovered his deficiency, but on the laws of nature and of nations, on the policy of the feudal system, and on general history, which last he found to be his stronghold.

During the very short portion of the examination which was devoted to the common law, Mr. Randolph dissented, or affected to dissent, from one of Mr. Henry's answers and called upon him to assign the reasons for his opinion. This produced an argument, and Mr. Randolph now played off on him the same arts which he had so often practiced on his country customers—drawing him out by questions, endeavoring to puzzle him by subtleties, assailing him with declamation, and watching continually the defensive operations of his mind. After a considerable discussion, he said: "You defend your opinions well, sir, but now to the law and to the testimony." Hereupon, he carried him to his office, and, opening the authorities, said to him: "Behold the face of natural reason. You have never seen these books, nor this principle of the law, yet you are right and I am wrong. And from the lesson which you have given me (you must excuse me for saying it), I will never trust to appearances again. Mr. Henry, if your industry be only half equal to your genius, I augur that you will do well and become an ornament and honor to your profession.

(3) Edmund Winston traces Henry's rise in his profession in his memorandum to William Wirt (1805).

Edmund Winston (1745-1818) was not only Patrick Henry's first cousin but a longtime friend, with many professional, as well as personal, associations. In 1788 he was elected a judge of the General Court and served until 1813. He was appointed an executor of Patrick Henry's estate and married his widow, Dorothea, in 1801, two years after Henry's death. His entire memorandum appears as Appendix A. [6]

In May 1754, at the age of eighteen, [Patrick Henry] married the daughter [Sarah Shelton] of Mr. John Shelton, a planter living in the neighborhood [Hanover County], and soon after removed to a small farm and other properties given him by his father and father-in-law. Here he was obliged to labor with his own hands to obtain a scanty support for his family...

In the winter of 1760, he obtained a license to practice law, after six weeks reading such books as he could borrow, without other assistance. He may be considered to have been at the time a virtuous young man, unconscious of the power of his own mind— in very narrow circumstances, making a last effort to supply the wants of his family…

I believe in [the Parson's Cause Case of 1763] he gave the first indication of superior talents. I was not present, but a few days after, Colonel Henry [John Henry, Patrick's father] mentioned it to me in nearly the following words: "Patrick spoke in this cause for near an hour without hesitation or embarrassment, and in a manner that surprised me, and showed himself well informed on a subject of which I did not think he had any knowledge…"

In 1764 [Henry] attended the Committee of Privileges, as counsel in a contested election in the House of Burgesses. Some time after, a member of the House, speaking to me of this occurrence, observed he had for a day or two observed an ill-dressed young man sauntering in the lobby. He seemed to be a stranger to everybody, and he had not the curiosity to inquire his name. But attending when the case of the contested election came on before the committee, he was surprised to find this same person was counsel for one of the parties, and still more so when he delivered an argument superior to anything he had ever heard…

In 1769 [Henry] went to the bar of the General Court. The profits of his practice must have been very moderate, for about this time he thought his property was [illegible] worth not more than 1,400 pounds, adding [illegible]. He entered here into a competition [in the practice of law] with Mr. Pendleton, the Attorney General John Randolph, Mr. Wythe, Mr. Nicholas, Mr. Mercer, and Mr. Jefferson, all of them men of eminence in their profession. It will perhaps be admitted that in reasoning on general principles he did not lose in comparison with any man, and I never heard that he betrayed a want of legal knowledge. It will naturally be asked, how is that possible? To which I can only answer that without much labor, he acquired that information which, in the case of other men, is the result of painful research.

(4) Jefferson praises Henry and also condemns him— particularly in matters of law.

Excerpts from Thomas Jefferson's reply to William Wirt's first letter concerning Wirt's proposed Henry biography (August 4, 1805): [7]

[W]e had a very familiar intercourse for upwards of twenty years, and ran our course nearly together. During this our political principles being the same, we acted in perfect concert until the year 1781. I witnessed the part he bore in nearly all the great questions of that period and perhaps could recollect some anecdotes not uninteresting. He was certainly the man who gave the first impulse to the ball of revolution. Were I to give his character in general terms, it would be of mixed aspect. I think he was the best humored man in society I almost ever knew, and the greatest orator that ever lived. He had a consummate knowledge of the human heart, which directing the efforts of his eloquence enabled him to attain a degree of popularity with the people at large never perhaps equaled. His judgment in other matters was inaccurate; in matters of law it was not worth a copper. He was avaricious and rotten hearted. His two great passions were the love of money and of fame, but when these came into competition, the former predominated...

Mr. Henry began his career with very little property. He acted, as I have understood, as a bar keeper in the tavern at Hanover Court House for some time [Jefferson seems to be correct about this; see note 4 of the Prologue, Section Three]. He married very young, settled, I believe, at a place called Roundabout in Louisa [County], got credit for some little store of merchandize, but very soon failed [Jefferson's chronology is a bit off here]. From this he turned his views to the law, for the acquisition or practice of which, however, he was too lazy. Whenever the courts were closed for the winter season, he would make up a party of poor deer hunters of his neighborhood, would go off with them to the piney woods of Fluvanna, and pass weeks in hunting deer, of which he was passionately fond, sleeping under a tent before a fire, wearing the same shirt the whole time, and covering all the dirt of his dress with a hunting shirt.

He never undertook to draw pleadings if he could avoid it or to manage that part of a cause, and very unwillingly engaged but as an assistant to speak in the cause. And the fee was an indispensable preliminary, observing to the applicant that he kept no accounts, never putting pen to paper, which was true [not true; see note following]. His powers over a jury were so irresistible that he received great fees for his services and had the reputation of being insatiable about money.

After about ten years practice in the county courts, he came to the general court, where, however, being totally unqualified for anything but mere jury cases, he devoted himself to these, and chiefly to the criminal business. From these poor devils, it was always understood that he squeezed exorbitant fees of fifty, one hundred, and two hundred pounds. From this source he made great profits, and they were said to be great. His other business, exclusive of the criminal, would never, I am sure, pay the expenses of his attendance at court... [8]

(5) Edmund Randolph's observation on the different approaches of Jefferson and Henry to the law: [9]

On two signal arguments before the General Court in which Mr. Henry and [Mr. Jefferson] were coadjutors, each characterized himself. Mr. Jefferson drew copiously from the law, Mr. Henry from the recesses of the human heart.

(6) The Parson's Cause Case, Hanover Court House, 1 December 1763

Henry first won renown as an orator by arguing successfully to a jury that clergy (parsons) of the state-supported Anglican Church should receive only a token amount of back pay, which had been awarded them by a royal decree overruling a law passed by the colonial legislature. Thus, Henry stood in opposition to

*both church and crown, while gaining notoriety and popularity as
an advocate for the people.*

*According to the Reverend James Maury, the clergyman on
whose behalf the suit was brought:*[10]

Mr. Henry rose and harangued the jury for near an hour. This
harangue turned upon points as much out of his own depth, and
that of the jury, as they were foreign from the purpose, which
it would be impertinent to mention here. However, after he had
discussed those points, he labored to prove "that the act of 1758
had every characteristic of a good law, that it was a law of general
utility, and could not, consistently with what he called the original
compact between king and people, stipulating protection on one
hand and obedience on the other, be annulled." Hence, he inferred,
"that a king, by disallowing acts of this salutary nature, from being
the father of his people degenerated into a tyrant and forfeits all
right to his subjects' obedience."

He further urged "that the only use of an established church
and clergy in society is to enforce obedience to civil sanctions
and the observance of those which are called duties of imperfect
obligation; that when a clergy ceases to answer these ends, the
community has no further need of their ministry and may justly
strip them of their appointments; that the clergy of Virginia, in
this particular instance of their refusing to acquiesce in the law
in question, had been so far from answering that they had most
notoriously counteracted those great ends of their institution; that,
therefore, instead of useful members of the state, they ought to
be considered as enemies of the community; and that, in the case
now before them, Mr. Maury, instead of countenance and protection and damages, very justly deserved to be punished with signal
severity..."

You'll observe I do not pretend to remember his words, but
take this to have been the sum and substance of this part of his
labored oration. When he came to that part of it where he undertook to assert "that a king, by annulling or disallowing acts of so
salutary a nature, from being the father of his people degenerated

into a tyrant and forfeits all right to his subjects' obedience," the more sober part of his audience were struck with horror. Mr. Lyons [Peter Lyons, the opposing attorney] called out aloud, and with an honest warmth, to the bench "that the gentleman had spoken treason" and expressed his astonishment "that their worships could hear it without emotion or any mark of dissatisfaction." At the same instant, too, amongst some gentlemen in the crowd behind me, was a confused murmur of "Treason, Treason!" Yet Mr. Henry went on in the same treasonable and licentious strain without interruption from the bench, even without receiving the least exterior notice of their disapprobation.

One of the jury, too, was so highly pleased with these doctrines, that, as I was afterwards told, he every now and then gave the traitorous declaimer a nod of appreciation. After the court was adjourned, [Henry] apologized to me for what he had said, alleging that his sole view in engaging in the cause and in saying what he had was to make himself popular…

A fragment of Henry's argument to the jury according to a spectator at the trial:[11]

We have heard a great deal about the benevolence and holy zeal of our reverend clergy, but how is this manifested? Do they manifest their zeal in the cause of religion and humanity by practicing the mild and benevolent precepts of the Gospel of Jesus? Do they feed the hungry and clothe the naked? Oh, no, gentlemen! Instead of feeding the hungry and clothing the naked, these rapacious harpies would, were their powers equal to their will, snatch from the hearth of their honest parishioner his last hoe cake, from the widow and her orphan children their last milk cow!—the last bed, nay, the last blanket from the lying-in woman!

Samuel Meredith to William Wirt, 1805, on the Parsons' Cause Case[12]

On the day of the trial in Hanover, [Patrick Henry Jr.] appeared as a volunteer on the side of the people in opposition to the clergy, of whom at least twenty attended. Among them was the uncle of P.H. [Patrick Henry Sr., one of the "parsons" who might eventually gain if the suit was successful], an old respectable and venerable clergyman [of the Anglican Church], who rode to the courthouse in his carriage. As soon as he alighted, he was met by P.H., who accosted him most respectfully and requested him not to appear in the courthouse on that day.

"Why?" said the gentleman. "Because I am engaged in opposition to the clergy, and your appearance there might strike me with such awe as to prevent me from doing justice to my cause." "Rather than that effect should be produced, Patrick," said his uncle, "I will not only absent myself from the courthouse but return home," and accordingly got into his carriage and drove off. P. H. delighted and astonished the audience and the court. His father was then sitting as the judge of the court and shed tears [of pride at the demonstration of his son's forensic abilities] most profusely. The issue of the trial is well known. The people were so delighted that they carried him about the yard on their shoulders. Here began his fame and his popularity. From this time his rise was rapid...

CHAPTER II

HENRY IN THE VIRGINIA HOUSE OF BURGESSES
THE STAMP ACT SPEECH, 1765

"I attended the debate, however, at the door of the lobby
of the House of Burgesses and heard the splendid display
of Mr. Henry's talents as a popular orator. They were great
indeed; such as I have never heard from any other man.
He appeared to me to speak as Homer wrote."
—Thomas Jefferson on Henry's Stamp Act Speech,
in his *Autobiography*, 1821

**(1) Henry, newly elected to the Virginia House of Burgesses,
took his seat on May 20, 1765.**

*Four days later, as Thomas Jefferson related in his August 4,
1805, letter to William Wirt, Henry made his second major public
stand:* [1]

He was elected a representative of the county of [Louisa] and
brought himself into public notice on the following occasion...
The gentlemen of this country [Virginia] had at that time become
deeply involved in that state of indebtedness which has since
ended in so general a crush of their fortunes. [John] Robinson,
the Speaker [of the House of Burgesses], was also Treasurer, an
officer always chosen by the assembly. He was an excellent man,
liberal, friendly, and rich. He had been drawn in to lend, on his
own account, great sums of money to persons of this description,
and especially those who were of the assembly. He used freely
for this purpose the public money, confiding, for its replacement
in his own means and the securities he had taken on those loans.
About this time, however, he became sensible that his deficit to the

public [had] become so enormous as that a discovery must soon take place, for as yet the public had no suspicion of it. He devised therefore, with his friends in the assembly, a plan for a public loan office to a certain amount, from which monies might be lent on public account, and on good landed security, to individuals. This was accordingly brought forward in the House of Burgesses, and had it succeeded, the debts due to Robinson on these loans would have been transferred to the public and his deficit thus completely covered.

This state of things, however, was not yet known; but Mr. Henry attacked the scheme, on other general grounds, in that style of bold, grand, and overwhelming eloquence for which he became so justly celebrated afterwards. He carried with him all the members of the upper counties and left a minority composed merely of the aristocracy of the [colony]. From this time his popularity swelled apace, and Robinson, dying [the following year], his deficit was brought to light and discovered the true object of the proposition.

In a letter to Wirt nine years later (August 14, 1814), Jefferson further recalled of the same incident: [2]

I can never forget a particular exclamation of [Henry] in the debate, which electrified his hearers. It had been urged that from certain unhappy circumstances of the colony, men of substantial property had contracted debts, which, if exacted suddenly, must ruin them and their families, but with a little indulgence of time might be paid with ease. "What sir?" exclaimed Mr. Henry, in animadverting on this, "Is it proposed then to reclaim the spendthrift from his dissipation and extravagance by filling his pockets with money?" Those expressions are indelibly impressed on my memory. He laid open with so much energy the spirit of favoritism on which the proposition was founded and the abuses to which it would lead that it was crushed in its birth.

(2) The Stamp Act Speech and Stamp Act Resolves, May 29, 1765

Henry, a member of the House of Burgesses for only nine days, introduced his Stamp Act Resolutions on his twenty-ninth birthday. "What Henry said and what the Burgesses did are clear in legend but cloudy in history," wrote historians Edmund S. and Helen M. Morgan in their definitive work on the Stamp Act.[3]

Thomas Jefferson, who heard Henry's Stamp Act Speech, called it "the dawn of the Revolution," although he at first indicated to William Wirt that Henry did not write the Stamp Act resolutions himself. This was part of Jefferson's portrayal of Henry to Wirt as an orator capable of "torrents of sublime eloquence" who could not write.

Thomas Jefferson in his letter to William Wirt of August 4, 1805:[4]

The next great occasion on which he signalized himself was that which may be considered the dawn of the Revolution in May 1765. The British Parliament had passed resolutions preparatory to levying a revenue on the colonies by a stamp tax. The Virginia Assembly at their next session prepared and sent to England very elaborate representations addressed in separate forms to the King, Lords, and Commons against the right to impose such taxes. The famous Stamp Act was, however, passed in January 1765, and in the session of the Virginia Assembly the May following, Mr. Henry introduced the celebrated resolutions of that date. These were drawn by George Johnston, a lawyer of the Northern Neck, a very able and correct speaker. Mr. Henry moved and Johnston seconded these resolutions successively. They were opposed by Randolph, Bland, Pendleton, Nicholas, Wythe, and all the old members whose influence in the house had, till then, been unbroken. They did it, not from any question of our rights, but on the ground that the same sentiments had been at the preceding session expressed in a more conciliatory form, to which the answers were not yet received.

But torrents of sublime eloquence from Mr. Henry, backed by the solid reasoning of Johnston, prevailed. The last, however, and strongest resolution was carried out by a single vote. The debate on it was most bloody. I was then but a student and was listening at the door of the lobby (for as yet there was no gallery) when Peyton Randolph, after the vote, came out of the house and said, as he entered the lobby, "By God, I would have given 500 guineas for a single vote." For as this would have divided the house, the vote of Robinson, the Speaker, would have rejected the resolution.

Mr. Henry left town that evening, and the next morning before the meeting of the House, I saw Peter Randolph, then of the Council, but who had formerly been clerk to the house, for an hour or two at the clerk's table, searching the old journals for a precedent of a resolution of the house, *erased*, while he was clerk for the journals, by a subsequent order of the house. Whether he found it or not, I do not remember, but when the house met, a motion was made and carried to erase that resolution, and he entirely under the control of the governor, I do not know that this resolution ever appeared in print. I write this from memory, but the impression made on me at the time was as such as to fix the facts indelibly in my mind.

A decade later in a letter to William Wirt (August 5, 1815), Jefferson modified his opinion as to the author of the Stamp Act Resolves.[5]

I can readily enough believe these resolutions were written by Mr. Henry himself. They bear the stamp of his mind, strong without precision. That they were written by Johnston, who seconded them, was only the rumor of the day and very possibly unfounded.

(3) The ending of the Stamp Act Speech

Generally, historians have been more convinced of Henry's authorship of the Stamp Act Resolves and less sure of exactly how his speech concluded. William Wirt's ending was generally accepted for more than a century.

An excerpt from Wirt's biography of 1817 containing John Tyler Sr.'s version of the ending: [6]

It was in the midst of this magnificent debate, while he was descanting on the tyranny of the obnoxious act, that he exclaimed in a voice of thunder, and with the look of a god: "Caesar had his Brutus—Charles the First, his Cromwell—and George the Third—('Treason!' cried the speaker—'Treason, treason!' echoed from every part of the house. It was one of those trying moments which is decisive of character. Henry faltered not for an instant; but rising to a loftier attitude, and fixing on the speaker an eye of the most determined fire, he finished his sentence with the firmest emphasis)—*May profit by their example. If this* be treason, make the most of it."*

According to the footnote (*) added by Wirt after the ending of his account, Jefferson was in agreement with Tyler. [7]

* I had frequently heard the above anecdote of the cry of treason, but with such variations of the concluding words, that I began to doubt whether the whole might not be fiction. With a view to ascertain the truth, therefore, I submitted it to Mr. Jefferson, as it had been given to me by Judge Tyler, and this is his answer: "I well remember the cry of treason, the pause of Mr. Henry at the name of George III, and the presence of mind with which he closed his sentence, and baffled the charge vociferated." The incident, therefore, becomes authentic history.

Edmund Randolph, who did not hear the speech, reported its conclusion in his History of Virginia *like this:* [8]

In [Henry's] harangue, he certainly indulged a strain never before heard in the royal capitol. This circumstance passed while he was speaking: "Caesar," cried he, "had his Brutus; Charles the first his Cromwell; and George the third—" "Treason, sir," exclaimed the speaker, to which Henry instantly replied, "And George the third may never have either." This dexterous escape or retreat, if it did not savor of lively eloquence, was itself a victory...

An excerpt from a letter dated October 3, 1815, by Paul Carrington (1733-1818) to William Wirt, who heard the speech as a newly elected member of the House of Delegates. [9]

But when the fifth and last [resolution] came to be considered, meaning that which Mr. Jefferson called the strongest and most bloody, Mr. Henry's manly eloquence surpassed everything of the kind I had ever heard before. It was that which brought forward Speaker Robinson crying out, "Treason, treason!" and Mr. Henry's presence of mind in reply, of which you must have read or heard...

A "French Traveler in the Colonies" who heard the Stamp Act Speech reported an entirely different ending. [10] *The journal, written in English, was discovered during the second decade of the twentieth century in the archives of the* Service Hydrographique de la Marine *at Paris. The anonymous Frenchman (or possibly an Irish agent working for the French) related that he*

went immediately to the assembly which was sitting, where [he] was entertained with very strong debates concerning duties that the parliament wants to lay on the American colonies, which they call or style stamp duties. Shortly after I came in, one of the members stood up and said he had read that in former times Tarquin and Julius [Caesar] had their Brutus, Charles [I] had his Cromwell, and he did not doubt but some good American would stand up in favor of his country, but (says he) in a more moderate manner. [He] was going to continue, when the Speaker of the House rose and said, he, the last that stood up, had spoke treason, and [he, the Speaker,] was very sorry to see that not one of the members of the house was loyal enough to stop him before he had gone so far.

Upon which, the same member stood up again (his name is Henry) and said that if he had affronted the Speaker or the House, he was ready to ask pardon, and he would show his loyalty to His Majesty, King George III, at the expense of the last drop of his blood. But what he had said must be attributed to the interest of his country's dying liberty, which he had at heart, and the heat of passion might have led him to have said something more than he intended. But, again, if he said anything wrong, he begged the Speaker and the House's pardon. Some other members stood up and backed him, on which that affair was dropped.

(4) Which of Henry's resolves were passed by the House of Burgesses?

As Jefferson noted in his August 4, 1805, letter to William Wirt (above), it was "the last... and strongest resolution" that set off the "bloody debate," which was "carried out by a single vote." But Henry left town that evening, and when the House of Burgesses met the following day, "a motion was made and carried to erase that resolution." Jefferson was correct in stating that because the only printer in Williamsburg was under the control of the governor, none of the resolutions were published in Virginia.

However, by the middle of June as many as seven resolutions began to circulate in colonies north of Virginia. The Newport (Rhode Island) Mercury *was the first newspaper to print them and was eventually followed by several others. Subsequent entries in the French traveler's journal make it clear that news of Henry's speech and resolutions had made an impact in the towns he visited after leaving Williamsburg. "And in Massachusetts the effect of the Virginia Resolves was electric," wrote Edmund S. and Helen M. Morgan, authors of* The Stamp Act Crisis: Prologue to

Revolution. *The Morgans noted that "every colony which later participated in the Revolution, with the exception of Georgia, North Carolina, Delaware, and New Hampshire, eventually passed declaratory resolutions defining their rights, and in all of these the limits set on Parliament's authority excluded the right to tax the colonies."* [11]

In the printed Journals of the House the Stamp Act Resolutions stand as follows: [12]

Resolved: That the first adventurers and settlers of this, His Majesty's colony and dominion, brought with them and transmitted to their posterity and all other His Majesty's subjects since inhabiting in this, His Majesty's said colony, all the privileges, franchises, and immunities that have at any time been held, enjoyed and possessed by the people of Great Britain.

Resolved: That by two royal charters granted by King James I the colonists aforesaid are declared entitled to all the privileges, liberties, and immunities of denizens and natural-born subjects to all intents and purposes as if they had been abiding and born within the realm of England.

Resolved: That the taxation of the people by themselves, or by persons chosen by themselves to represent them, who can only know what taxes the people are able to bear and the easiest mode of raising them and are equally affected by such taxes themselves, is the distinguishing characteristic of British freedom, and without which the ancient constitution cannot subsist.

Resolved: That His Majesty's liege people of this most ancient colony have uninterruptedly enjoyed the right of being thus governed by their own assembly in the article of their taxes and internal policy, and that the same has never been forfeited or any other way given up, but has been constantly recognized by the kings and people of Great Britain.

After Patrick Henry's death in 1799, a sealed letter was found with his will, on which was written, "Enclosed are the resolutions of the Virginia Assembly, in 1765, concerning the Stamp Act. Let my executors open this paper." Henry's fifth resolution was: [13]

Resolved: Therefore that the General Assembly of this colony have the only and sole exclusive right and power to lay taxes and impositions upon the inhabitants of this colony, and that every attempt to vest such power in any person or persons whatsoever other than the General Assembly aforesaid has a manifest tendency to destroy British as well as American freedom.

(5) John Tyler Sr., in his memorandum to William Wirt (1805), recalled Henry making this declaration in regard to his initial challenges to Church and Crown. [14]

Why Henry gave the Stamp Act & Speech & the Resolves

In a conversation with him once at his own house, upon his first essay into the political world, I asked him how he ventured to lift his voice against so terrible a junto as that he had to oppose, when he first stirred the country to assert its political rights…

His reply was that he was convinced of the rectitude of the cause and his own views, and that although he well knew that many a just cause had been lost and, for wise purposes, Providence might not interfere for its safety, yet he was well acquainted with the great extent of our back country, which would always afford him a safe retreat from tyranny. But he was always satisfied that a united sentiment and sound patriotism would carry us safely to the wished-for port. And if the people would not die or be free, it was of no consequence what sort of government they lived under.

CHAPTER III

Towards the First
Continental Congress, 1774

"I am not a Virginian but an American,"
—Patrick Henry at the First Continental Congress

(1) Excerpts from a "fragment of a manuscript found with his papers," late 1760s: [1]

This somewhat rambling meditation by Patrick Henry in his early thirties is noteworthy for its musings on the baneful effects of slavery, religious intolerance, and the lack of artisans and manufacturing capabilities in colonial Virginia. According to William Wirt Henry, Henry's grandson and biographer, the manuscript was in Patrick Henry's handwriting and "the earliest production of his pen remaining."

Reprehension seldom is the duty of a minister. A good life is the best lecture. But if it happens that a life is so wicked as to become notoriously offensive (in which case only a minister is supposed to make personal application), such a man ceases to be popular. For I dare affirm that vice never in any country was held in reverence for its own sake, and so far as a man is openly wicked, he is unpopular. If it should be that a dependent minister, having incurred the displeasure of a powerful person and for doing his duty, should raise such an opposition as he could not be able to resist, the unprejudiced everywhere would revere him as a victim to wicked intrigues and heap their deserved benefactions upon him. But I have proved above that the toleration proposed is the surest method to give us a virtuous clergy. It is the business of a virtuous clergyman to censure vice in every appearance of it.

Therefore under a general toleration this duty will be commonly attended to.

Will anyone censure me as an innovator? I care not. 'Tis prudent to adopt the policy of other countries when experience shows it to be wiser than our own in anything. Most nations have learned from abroad those sciences and arts that embellish and sweeten human life. This is the greatest advantage arising from a social intercourse among nations and keeps the civilized world cemented together like one great family. The example of the northern colonies is striking. England received the manufactures of wool, glasses, paper, hats, etc., from the Flemish and French workmen, invited there under the direction of the wisest sovereigns. The English shipbuilders are allured to the neighboring states by the greatest rewards. The best-policied countries borrow improvements in the art of war from their neighbors, and under foreign generals have been led to victory and conquest. The period in which the present settlement of religion was made here [in Virginia] does no great honor to the English nation. [Other] Colonies on this continent have experienced a more enlarged [i.e., tolerant] system, and their growth and real prosperity are the just encomiums of that policy from which those colonies received their happy constitutions.

I cannot do justice to a subject so copious and important in a few pages. I abridge everything. Much learning has been displayed to show the necessity of establishing one church in England in the present form. But these reasonings do not reach the case of this colony, and, granting they did, perhaps I could not answer them, as I have neither the leisure nor abilities to write a volume on the subject.

It is out of my province to attempt a reformation in the church, nor should I have meddled with it, but I see clearly the evils we feel can only be redressed by the proposed alteration. The disadvantage from the great number of slaves may perhaps wear off when the present stock and their descendants are scattered through the immense deserts in the West. To re-export them is now impracticable, and sorry I am for it.

If anyone doubts the truths asserted here, I beseech him to reflect wherefore is it that a country I say the happiest for situation on this continent, blest with a soil producing not only the necessaries but the luxuries of life; full of rivers, havens, and inlets that invite the visits of commerce for the products of industry; and bordered with extended plains—that instead of lonely scattered huts, might be covered with magnificent cities. Wherefore is it that a country producing the choicest grain, stock, wool, fish, hemp, flax, metals of the North, together with the corn, pulp, rice, wine, fruits, and most of those delicacies found in southern climes, should want the common conveniences, the necessaries of life? I will not enumerate the good things our country may produce. Let me ask what it will not produce? The truth is anything but inhabitants sensible of its value.

How comes it that the lands in Pennsylvania are five times the value of ours? Pennsylvania is the country of the most extensive privileges with few slaves. A Dutch, Irish, or Scotch emigrant finds there his religion, his priest, his language, his manners, and everything but that poverty and oppression he left at home. Take an instance nearer to us. The country beyond the mountains is settled on a plan of economy very different from ours. Europeans, instead of Africans, till the lands and manufacture. The tax to the established church is scarcely felt. The people brought their priests with them. The lands in some parts there are almost as dear as at Williamsburg, and not withstanding the many disadvantages arising from situation, they are the most flourishing parts of Virginia, and this in a few years. Manufacturers have [obliterated in MS] them. By this means, they have [ditto] the money [ditto] produced.

I agree entirely with those who insist on the necessity of home manufactures. We differ in the means of procuring them. To what purpose do we offer premiums, when experience tells us no one will obtain them? Common sense informs us that the first thing to be thought of is manufacturers. The present inhabitants of the colony must manufacture under great disadvantage, for the countries with whom we are connected send continual supplies to our doors, offering to take in barter those commodities, the culture of which we understand. If attempts are made, we find the many difficulties attending them too great to be conquered. It must ever be so till we have procured numbers of skillful artisans. A planter willing to go upon the new plan can't have spinners of wool and flax, a tanner, a shoemaker, a weaver, a fuller, etc. in his own family. He must travel continually great distances to find these several people, and when he has found them, they are bunglers and extravagant in their charges. He is rid of this trouble and perplexity by going to a store.

But I need not say anything to prove the great utility of importing good artisans. A general toleration of religion appears to me the best means of peopling our country and enabling our people to procure those necessaries among themselves, the purchase of which from abroad has so nearly ruined a colony enjoying from nature and time the means of becoming the most prosperous on the continent. Our country will be peopled. The question is, shall it be with Europeans or Africans? To do it with the latter will take many years; with the former 'tis quickly done. Is there a man so degenerate as to wish to see his country the gloomy retreat of slaves? No; while we may, let us people our lands with men who secure our internal peace and make us respectable abroad; who will contribute [obliterated in MS] influence and establish in posterity the benefit of the British Constitution.

Tell me no more of ideal wealth. Away with the schemes of paper money and loan offices, calculated to feed extravagance and revive expiring luxury. To many the observations above will seem of small weight. When I say that the article of religion is deemed a trifle by our people in the general, I assert a known truth. But when we suppose that the poorer sort of European emigrants set as light by it, we are greatly mistaken. The free exercise of religion has stocked the northern part of the continent with inhabitants, and although Europe has in great measure adopted a more moderate policy, yet the profession of Protestantism is extremely inconvenient in many places there. A Calvinist, a Lutheran, or Quaker who has felt these inconveniences in Europe sails not to Virginia, where they are felt perhaps in a greater degree.

(2) Patrick Henry defends the persecuted Baptists, late 1760s-early 1770s.

In the late 1760s, a systematic persecution of the rapidly increasing number of Baptists in Virginia began, led by, among others, Henry's political nemesis, Edmund Pendleton [see the Prologue, Section Four]. Preachers were dragged from the pulpit, beaten, imprisoned, and threatened with death. During this period, Henry frequently, and on occasion at his own expense, defended these unfortunate evangelists.

On November 15, 1770, Patrick Henry qualified to practice law in Spotsylvania County. A colorful account of his successful defense of the Spotsylvania Baptists, first published in 1850, was "made up in after years on doubtful traditions," according to William Wirt Henry, Patrick Henry's grandson and biographer (see Appendix F, "Patrick Henry Apocrypha"). However, there can be no doubt concerning the tribute of Baptist historian Robert Semple, published in 1810. [2]

It was in making these attempts [to obtain a license to preach] that [ministers] were so fortunate as to interest in their behalf the celebrated Patrick Henry. Being always the friend of liberty, he only needed to be informed of their oppression, when, without hesitation, he stepped forward to their relief. From that day until the day of their complete emancipation from the shackles of tyranny, the Baptists found in Patrick Henry an unwavering friend. May his name descend to posterity with unsullied honor!

(3) Henry's appearance and manner in court, circa 1772, as described by St. George Tucker in his memorandum to William Wirt (1805):

Judge Tucker (1752-1827) recalled his observations of Henry in action while he was a student at the College of William and Mary. [3]

The General Court met in April. Mr. Henry practiced as a lawyer in it. I attended very frequently and generally sat near the clerk's table, directly opposite to the bar. I had now for the first time a near view of Mr. Henry's face. He wore a black suit of clothes and (as was the custom of the bar then) a tie wig, such as Mr. Edmund Pendleton wore till his death. His appearance was greatly improved by these adventitious circumstances.

His visage was long, thin, but not sharp—dark, without any appearance of blood in his cheeks, somewhat inclining to sallowness. His profile was of the Roman cast, though his nose was rather long than high; his forehead high and straight, but forming a considerable angle with the nose; his eyes a dark gray [others described them as blue], not large, penetrating, deep-set in his head; his eyelashes long and black, which, with the color of his eyebrows, made his eyes appear almost black—a superficial view would indeed make it be supposed they were perfectly black. His nose was of the Roman stamp, as I have already said; his cheekbones rather high, but not like a Scotsman's—they were neither as large, as near the eyes, nor as far apart as is the natives' of Scotland; his cheeks hollow; his chin long but well formed and rounded at the end, so as to form a proper counterpart to the upper part of his face. I find it difficult to describe his mouth, in which there was nothing remarkable—except when about to express a modest dissent from some opinion upon which he was commenting. He then had a half sort of smile, in which the want of conviction was, perhaps, more strongly expressed than that cynical or satirical emotion which probably prompted it.

His manner and address to the court and jury might be deemed the excess of humility, diffidence, and modesty. If, as rarely happened, he had occasion to answer any remark from the bench, it was impossible for meekness herself to assume a manner less presumptuous. But in the smile, of which I have been speaking, you might anticipate the want of conviction expressed in his answers, at the moment that he submitted to the "superior wisdom" of the court with a grace that would have done honor to the most polished courtier in Westminster Hall. In his reply to counsel, his remarks on the evidence, and on the conduct of the parties, he preserved the same distinguished deference and politeness, still accompanied by the never-failing index of this skeptical smile when the occasion prompted.

His manner was solemn and impressive, his voice neither remarkable for its pleasing tones, or the variety of its cadence, or for harshness. If it was never melodious (as I rather think), it was never, however, raised, harsh. It was clear, distinct, and capable of that emphasis which I incline to believe constituted one of the greatest charms in Mr. Henry's manner. His countenance was grave (even when clothed with the half smile I have mentioned), penetrating, and marked with the strong lineaments of deep reflection. When speaking in public he never (even on occasions when he excited it in others) had anything like pleasantry in his countenance, his manner, or the tone of his voice. You would swear he had never uttered or laughed at a joke.

In short, in debate either at the bar or elsewhere, his manner was so earnest and impressive, united with a contraction or knitting of his brows, which appeared habitual, as to give his countenance a severity sometimes bordering upon the appearance of anger or contempt suppressed, while his language and gesture exhibited nothing but what was perfectly decorous. He was emphatic, without vehemence or declamation; animated but never boisterous; nervous, without recourse to intemperate language; and clear, though not always methodical.

(4) The earliest of Patrick Henry's letters known to exist and his most extensive meditation on slavery [4]

Henry wrote to Robert Pleasants, a Quaker leader who had educated his slaves, then freed them.

Hanover, January 18th, 1773

Dear Sir,

I take this opportunity to acknowledge the receipt of Anthony Benezet's book against the slave trade. I thank you for it. It is not a little surprising that the professors of Christianity, whose chief excellence consists in softening the human heart and in cherishing and improving its finer feelings, should encourage a practice so totally repugnant to the first impressions of right and wrong. What adds to the wonder is that this abominable practice has been introduced in the most enlightened ages. Times that seem to have pretensions to boast of high improvements in the arts and sciences and refined morality have brought into general use, and guarded by many laws, a species of violence and tyranny which our rude and barbarous, but more honest, ancestors detested.

Is it not amazing that at a time when the rights of humanity are defined and understood with precision, in a country above all others fond of liberty; that in such an age and in such a country we find men professing a religion the most humane, mild, gentle, and generous, adopting a principle as repugnant to humanity as it is inconsistent with the Bible and destructive to liberty? Every thinking, honest man rejects it in speculation; how few in practice from conscientious motives?

The world in general has denied your people a share of its honors, but the wise will ascribe to you a just tribute of virtuous praise for the practice of a train of virtues among which your disagreement to slavery will be principally ranked. I cannot but wish well to a people whose system imitates the example of Him whose life was perfect. And, believe me, I shall honor the Quakers for their noble effort to abolish slavery. It is equally calculated to promote moral and political good.

Would anyone believe I am the master of slaves of my own purchase! I am drawn along by the general inconvenience of living here without them. I will not, I cannot justify it. However culpable my conduct, I will so far pay my devoir to virtue, as to own the excellence and rectitude of her precepts and lament my want of conformity to them.

I believe a time will come when an opportunity will be offered to abolish this lamentable evil. Everything we can do is to improve it, if it happens in our day. If not, let us transmit to our descendants, together with our slaves, a pity for their unhappy lot and an abhorrence of slavery. If we cannot reduce this wished-for reformation to practice, let us treat the unhappy victims with lenity. It is the furthest advance we can make toward justice. It is a debt we owe to the purity of our religion—to show that it is at variance with that law which warrants slavery.

Here is an instance that silent meetings (scoffed at by reverend doctors) have done, yet which learned and elaborate preaching could not effect. So much preferable are the genuine dictates of conscience and a steady attention to its feelings about the teachings of those men who pretend to have a better guide. I exhort you to persevere in so worthy a resolution. Some of your people disagree or at least are lukewarm in the abolition of slavery. Many treat the resolution of your meeting with ridicule. And among those who throw contempt on it are clergymen, whose surest guard against both ridicule and contempt is a certain act of assembly.

I know not when to stop. I could say many things on the subject, a serious view of which gives a gloomy perspective to future times. Excuse this scrawl and believe me with esteem,

Your humble servant,
Patrick Henry, Junior

(5) Excerpt from a letter by revolutionary statesman George Mason (1725-1792) of Gunston Hall in Virginia's Northern Neck to his friend Martin Cockburn, May 26, 1774 [5]

At the request of the gentlemen concerned, I have spent an evening with them upon the subject [the expected dissolution of the House of Burgesses by Lord Dunmore, the Royal Governor], when I had an opportunity of conversing with Mr. Henry, and knowing his sentiments, as well as hearing him in the house since on different occasions. He is by far the most powerful speaker I ever heard. Every word he says not only engages, but commands the attention, and your passions are no longer your own when he addresses them. But his eloquence is the smallest part of his merit. He is in my opinion the first man upon this continent in abilities as well as in public virtues. And had he lived in Rome about the time of the first Punic war, when the Roman people had arrived at their meridian glory and their virtues not yet tarnished, Mr. Henry's talents would have put him at the head of that glorious Commonwealth.

(6) Patrick Henry at the First Continental Congress, Philadelphia, September-October 1774

Henry was one of the seven delegates from Virginia. The others were Peyton Randolph, Richard Henry Lee, George Washington, Richard Bland, Benjamin Harrison Sr., and Edmund Pendleton.

Excerpt from the diary of John Adams (1735-1826) for September 5, 1774: [6]

Charles Francis Adams, John Adams' grandson and the mid-nineteenth century editor of his Works, *noted, "This is probably all that has been saved of the celebrated speech of Patrick Henry at the opening of the Congress, which has earned for him the national reputation he has ever since enjoyed."*

Government is dissolved. Fleets and armies and the present state of things show that government is dissolved. Where are your landmarks, your boundaries of colonies? We are in a state of nature, sir... The distinctions between Virginians, Pennsylvanians, New Yorkers, and New Englanders are no more. I am not a Virginian but an American.

On September 10, 1774, Silas Deane (1737-1789), a delegate from Connecticut wrote to his wife concerning Henry: [7]

[He is] the most complete speaker I ever heard, but in a letter I can give you no idea of the music of his voice, or the high-wrought, yet natural, elegance of his style and manner.

Roger Atkinson of Mansfield, near Petersburg, Virginia, wrote to his brother-in-law Samuel Pleasants, a resident of Philadelphia on October 1, 1774, describing the Virginia delegates to the First Continental Congress. [8]

A real half-Quaker, Patrick Henry, your brother's man—moderate and mild, in religious matters a saint but the very devil in politics—a Son of Thunder... He will shake the senate and some years ago had liked to have talked treason to the house. In these times a very useful man, a notable American, very stern and steady in his country's cause, and at the same time such a fool that I verily believe it would puzzle a king to buy him off.

In a letter to ex-president Jefferson, dated November 12, 1813, ex-president Adams wrote: [9]

In the Congress of 1774, there was not one member, except Patrick Henry, who appeared to me sensible of the precipice, or rather, the pinnacle on which he stood and had the candor and courage to acknowledge it.

An excerpt from a letter from John Adams to Henry biographer William Wirt, dated January 23, 1818: [10]

When [the First Continental] Congress finished their business, as they thought, in the autumn of 1774, I had with Mr. Henry, before we took leave of each other, some familiar conversation in which I expressed a full conviction that our resolves, declarations of rights, enumeration of wrongs, petitions, remonstrances, and addresses, associations, and non-importation agreements—however they might be expected by the people in America and however necessary to cement the union of the colonies—would be but waste paper in England. Mr. Henry said they might make some impression among the people of England, but agreed with me that they would be totally lost upon the government.

I had but just received a short and hasty letter, written to me by Major Joseph Hawley of Northampton, containing "a few broken hints," as he called them, of what he thought was proper to be done and concluding with these words: "After all we must fight." This letter I read to Mr. Henry, who listened with great attention; and as soon as I had pronounced the words, "After all, we must fight," he raised his head, and with an energy and vehemence that I can never forget, broke out with, "By G—D, I am of that man's mind." I put the letter into his hand, and when he read it, he returned it to me with an equally solemn asseveration that he agreed entirely in opinion with the writer. I considered this as a sacred oath upon a very great occasion and could have sworn it as religiously as he did, and by no means inconsistent with what you say in some part of your book, that he never took the sacred name in vain…

The other delegates from Virginia returned to their state, in full confidence that all our grievances would be redressed. The last words that Richard Henry Lee said to me when we parted were, *"We shall infallibly carry all our points; you will be completely relieved. All the offensive acts will be repealed; the army and fleet will be recalled; and Britain will give up her foolish project."*

Washington only was in doubt. He never spoke in public. In private he joined with those who advocated a non-exportation, as well as a non-importation, agreement. With both he thought we should prevail; without either he thought it doubtful. Henry was clear in one opinion, Richard Henry Lee in an opposite opinion, and Washington doubted between the two. Henry, however, appeared in the end to be exactly in the right.

An appraisal of Patrick Henry's performance at the First Continental Congress of 1774 by Thomas Jefferson (who was not there) from his August 4, 1805, letter to William Wirt:[11]

In ordinary business he was a very inefficient member. He could not draw a bill on the most simple subject which would bear legal criticism or even the ordinary criticism which looks to correctness of style and idea. For indeed there was no accuracy of idea in his head. His imagination was copious, poetical, sublime; but vague also. He said the strongest things in the finest language, but without logic, without arrangement, desultorily. This appeared eminently and in a mortifying degree in the first sessions of the First Congress, which met in September 1774.

CHAPTER IV

THE "LIBERTY OR DEATH" SPEECH AND THE CLASH WITH DUNMORE, 1775

"We must fight!"
—Patrick Henry, St. John's Church,
Richmond, March 23,1775

(1) Henry's "Liberty or Death" Speech

Patrick Henry's most famous oration was given slightly less than a month before "the shot heard 'round the world" in Massachusetts, that marked the beginning of the American Revolution. Among his listeners were George Washington, Thomas Jefferson, Richard Henry Lee, Thomas Nelson Jr., Edmund Pendleton, and other Virginians who would make significant contributions to the Revolution. With his speech, Henry offered the Second Virginia Convention, meeting in Richmond away from the colony's capital and the Royal Governor Dunmore, a set of resolutions for the establishment of a provincial militia. Despite his spellbinding oratory, they passed by only a narrow margin.

Henry's resolutions for arming Virginia: [1]

Resolved that a well regulated militia composed of gentlemen and yeomen is the natural strength and only security of a free government: that such a militia in this colony would forever render it unnecessary for the mother country to keep among us for the purpose of our defense any standing army of mercenary forces, always subversive of the quiet and dangerous to the liberties of the people; and would obviate the pretext of taxing us for their support:

That the establishment of such a militia is at this time peculiarly necessary by the state of our laws for the protection and defense of the country, some of which are already expired and others will shortly do so, and that the known remissness of government in calling us together in a legislative capacity renders it too insecure in this time of danger and distress to rely; that opportunity will be given of renewing them in general assembly or making any provision to secure our inestimable rights and liberties from those further violations with which they threatened.

Resolved therefore that this colony be immediately put into a posture of defense; and that Mr. [Patrick] Henry, Mr. [Richard Henry] Lee, Mr. Treasurer [Robert Carter Nicholas], Mr. [Benjamin] Harrison, Mr. Lemuel Riddick, Mr. [George] Washington, Mr. Steven [Adam Stephen], Mr. Andrew Lewis, Mr. [William] Christian, Mr. [Edmund] Pendleton, Mr. [Thomas] Jefferson and Mr. [Isaac] Zane to be a committee to prepare a plan for embodying, arming and disciplining such a number of men as may be sufficient for that purpose.

The "Liberty or Death" Speech as it appears in Wirt's biography:[2]

He rose at this time with a majesty unusual to him in an exordium [Henry was known for beginning his speeches haltingly—probably to make his perorations more dramatic.], and with all that self-possession by which he was so invariably distinguished. "No man," he said, "thought more highly than he did of the patriotism, as well as abilities, of the very worthy gentlemen who had just addressed the house. But different men often saw the same subject in different lights; and, therefore, he hoped it would not be thought disrespectful to those gentlemen, if, entertaining as he did, opinions of a character very opposite to theirs, he should speak forth *his* sentiments freely, and without reserve.

"This," he said, "was no time for ceremony. The question before this house was one of awful moment to the country. For his own part, he considered it as nothing less than a question of freedom or slavery. And in proportion to the magnitude of the subject ought to be the freedom of debate. It was only in this way that they could hope to arrive at truth and fulfill the great responsibility which they held to God and country. Should he keep back his opinions at such a time, through fear of giving offence, he should consider himself as guilty of treason toward his country and of an act of disloyalty toward the majesty of heaven, which he revered above all earthly kings.

"Mr. President," said he, "it is natural to man to indulge in the illusions of hope. We are apt to shut our eyes against a painful truth—and listen to the song of that siren, till she transforms us into beasts. Is this," he asked, "the part of wise men, engaged in a great and arduous struggle for liberty? Were we disposed to be of the number of those, who having eyes, see not, and, having ears, hear not the things which so nearly concern their temporal salvation? For his part, whatever anguish of spirit it might cost, *he* was willing to know the whole truth—to know the worst and provide for it.

"He had," he said, "but one lamp by which his feet were guided, and that was the lamp of experience. He knew of no way of judging of the future but by the past. And judging by the past, he wished to know what there had been in the conduct of the British ministry for the last ten years to justify those hopes with which gentlemen had been pleased to solace themselves and the house? Is it that insidious smile with which our petition has been lately received? Trust it not, sir; it will prove a snare to your feet. Suffer not yourselves to be betrayed with a kiss.

"Ask yourselves how this gracious reception of our petition comports with those warlike preparations which cover our waters and darken our land. Are fleets and armies necessary to a work of love and reconciliation? Have we shown ourselves so unwilling to be reconciled that force must be called in to win back our love? Let us not deceive ourselves, sir. These are the implements of war and subjugation—the last arguments to which kings resort.

"I ask gentlemen, sir, what means this martial array, if its purpose be not to force us into submission? Can gentlemen assign any other possible motive for it? Has Great Britain any enemy in this quarter of the world to call for all this accumulation of navies and armies? No sir, she has none. They are meant for us; they can be meant for no other. They are sent over to bind and rivet upon us those chains which the British ministry has been so long forging. And what have we to oppose them? Shall we try argument? Sir, we have been trying that for the last ten years. Have we anything new to offer upon the subject? Nothing. We have held the subject up in every light of which it is capable, but it is all in vain. Shall we resort to entreaty and humble supplication? What terms shall we find which have not been already exhausted?

"Let us not, I beseech you, sir, deceive ourselves longer. Sir, we have done everything that could be done to avert the storm which is now coming on. We have petitioned; we have remonstrated; we have supplicated; we have prostrated ourselves before the throne and have implored its interposition to arrest the tyrannical hands of the Ministry and Parliament. Our petitions have been slighted; our remonstrances have produced additional violence and insult; our supplications have been disregarded; and we have been spurned with contempt from the foot of the throne.

"In vain, after these things, may we indulge the fond hope of peace and reconciliation? *There is no longer any room for hope.* If we wish to be free; if we mean to preserve inviolate those inestimable privileges for which we have been so long contending; if we mean not basely to abandon the noble struggle in which we have been so long engaged and which we have pledged ourselves never to abandon until the glorious object of our contest shall be obtained; we must fight! I repeat it, sir, we must fight! An appeal to arms and to the God of Hosts is all that is left to us!

"They tell us," continued Mr. Henry, "that we are weak—unable to cope with so formidable an adversary. But when shall we be stronger? Will it be the next week or the next year? Will it be when we are totally disarmed and when a British guard shall be stationed in every house? Shall we gather strength by irresolution and inaction? Shall we acquire the means of effectual resistance by lying supinely on our backs and hugging the delusive phantom of hope until our enemies shall have bound us hand and foot? Sir, we are not weak, if we make a proper use of those means which the God of nature has placed in our power.

"Three millions of people armed in the holy cause of liberty and in such a country as that which we possess are invincible by any force which our enemy can send against us. Besides, sir, we shall not fight our battles alone. There is a just God who presides over the destinies of nations and who will raise up friends to fight our battles for us. The battle, sir, is not to the strong alone. It is to the vigilant, the active, the brave. Besides, sir, we have no election. If we were base enough to desire it, it is now too late to retire from the contest. There is no retreat but in submission and slavery! Our chains are forged. Their clanking may be heard on the plains of Boston! The war is inevitable—and let it come!! I repeat it, sir, let it come!!!

"It is vain, sir, to extenuate the matter. Gentlemen may cry, peace, peace—but there is no peace. The war is actually begun! The next gale that sweeps from the North will bring to our ears the clash of resounding arms. Our brethren are already in the field. Why stand we here idle? What is it that gentlemen wish? What would they have? Is life so dear or peace so sweet, as to be purchased at the price of chains and slavery? Forbid it, Almighty God! I know not what course others may take; but as for me," cried he, with both his arms extended aloft, his brow knit, every feature marked with the resolute purpose of his soul, and his voice swelled to its boldest note of exclamation, "Give me liberty or give me death!"

The "Liberty or Death" Speech was reconstructed by Henry's biographer, William Wirt, more than thirty years after it was given, principally from a memorandum sent him by St. George Tucker, and possibly with some assistance from John Tyler Sr.[3-4] *These were fortunate circumstances, for the two men primarily responsible for the early nineteenth-century report of Henry's speech, Tucker and Wirt, were both gifted writers.*[5] *Tucker, in addition to his accomplishments as a jurist and legal scholar, was also a poet of some distinction,[6] while Wirt, in addition to his success as an author and attorney, was considered one of the premier orators of his day. Tucker's memorandum to William Wirt was destroyed circa 1900.[7]*

The historian Moses Coit Tyler, however, had access to the Tucker memorandum during the 1880s while writing his biography of Henry and quoted the following two excerpts of Tucker's description of the speech:[8]

It was on that occasion that I first felt a full impression of Mr. Henry's powers. In vain should I attempt to give you any idea of his speech. He was calm and collected—touched upon the origin and progress of the dispute between Great Britain and the colonies—the various conciliatory measures adapted by the latter, and the uniformly increasing tone of violence and arrogance on the part of the former.

After Henry's "An appeal to arms and to the God of Hosts is all that is left to us!" Wirt inserted this note:[9]

"Imagine to yourself," says my correspondent, (Judge Tucker), "this sentence delivered with all the calm dignity of Cato of Utica [who, having been defeated in battle by Caesar in 46 BC, took his own life by the sword]—imagine to yourself the Roman senate, assembled in the capitol, when it was entered by the profane Gauls, who, at first, were awed by their presence, as if they had entered an assembly of the gods!—imagine that you heard that Cato addressing such a senate—imagine that you saw the handwriting on the wall of Belshazzar's palace [as described in the Old Testament, Daniel, Chapter Five]—imagine you heard a voice as from heaven uttering the words: '*We must fight,*' as the doom of fate, and you may have some idea of the speaker, the assembly to whom he addressed himself, and the auditory, of which I was one."

An excerpt from Edmund Randolph's description of the "Liberty or Death" Speech in his History of Virginia: [10]

There is no record that Randolph, himself, was present at St. John's Church, but he undoubtedly heard many accounts of the speech—particularly from his uncle, Peyton Randolph, who presided at the convention. Although Jefferson characteristically avoided public speaking whenever he could, Edmund Randolph portrays him "arguing closely, profoundly, and warmly on the same side." George Washington, whose "looks bespoke a mind absorbed in meditation on his country's fate" during the speech, left to posterity this account of the day: "Dined at Mr. Patrick Coote's and lodged where I had done the night before."

Accordingly, a resolution was passed for immediately putting the colony into a posture of defense and for preparing a plan of embodying and disciplining such a number of men as might be sufficient for that purpose. Henry moved and Richard Henry Lee seconded it. The fangs of European criticism might be challenged to spread themselves against feeling and acting with his country. Demosthenes [Henry] invigorated the timid, and Cicero [Lee] charmed the backward. The multitude, many of whom had traveled to the convention from a distance, could not suppress their emotion.

Henry was his pure self. Those who had toiled in the artifices of scholastic rhetoric were involuntarily driven into an inquiry within themselves, whether rules and forms and niceties of elocution would not have choked his native fire. It blazed so as to warm the coldest heart. In the sacred place of meeting, the church, the imagination had no difficulty to conceive, when he launched forth in solemn tones various causes of scruple against oppressors, that the British king was lying prostrate from the thunder of heaven. Henry was thought in his attitudes to resemble Saint Paul while preaching at Athens and to speak as man was never known to speak before.

After every illusion had vanished, a prodigy yet remained. It was Patrick Henry, born in obscurity, poor, and without the advantages of literature, rousing the genius of his country and binding a band of patriots together to hurl defiance at the tyranny of so formidable a nation as Great Britain. This enchantment was spontaneous obedience to the workings of the soul. When he uttered what commanded respect for himself, he solicited no admiring looks from those who surrounded him. If he had, he must have been abased by meeting every eye fixed upon him. He paused, but he paused full of some rising eruption of eloquence. When he sat down, his sounds vibrated so loudly, if not in the ears, at least in the memory of his audience, that no other member, not even his friend who was to second him, was yet adventurous enough to interfere with that voice which had so recently subdued and captivated.

After a few minutes Richard Henry Lee fanned and refreshed with a gale of pleasure, but the vessel of the Revolution was still under the impulse of the tempest which Henry had created. Artificial oratory fell in copious streams from the mouth of Lee, and rules of persuasion accomplished everything which rules could effect. If elegance had been personified, the person of Lee would have been chosen. But Henry trampled upon rules and yet triumphed, at this time perhaps beyond his own expectation.

Jefferson was not silent. He argued closely, profoundly, and warmly on the same side. The post in this revolutionary debate belonging to him was that at which the theories of republicanism were deposited. Washington was prominent, though silent. His looks bespoke a mind absorbed in meditation on his country's fate, but a positive concert between him and Henry could not more effectually have exhibited him to view than when Henry with indignation ridiculed the ideas of peace "when there was no peace" and enlarged on the duty of preparing for war.

Excerpt from a letter dated April 6, 1775, by James Parker, a Tory merchant of Norfolk, Virginia, writing to his superior, Charles Steuart of Glasgow, Scotland, not long after Henry's speech: [11]

You never heard anything more infamously insolent than P. Henry's speech. He called the K[ing] a tyrant, a fool, a puppet, and a tool to the ministry and said there were now no Englishmen, no Scots, no Britons, but a set of wretches sunk in luxury. They had lost their natural courage and were unable to look the brave Americans in the face. He could not have been more completely scurrilous if he had been possessed of John Wilkes' [a radical British political reformer] vocabulary. This creature is so infatuated that he goes about praying and preaching amongst the common people.

(2) Colonel Henry, commander of the Hanover Militia, reacts to Colonial Governor Lord Dunmore's removal of the gunpowder from the arsenal at Williamsburg

On April 19, 1775, British attempts to destroy American military stores at Concord, Massachusetts, led to the beginning of the Revolution. Late in the night of April twentieth, John Murray, Earl of Dunmore, colonial governor of Virginia, successfully accomplished a similar mission when he seized the small supply of arms and gunpowder at Williamsburg and transferred them to a British ship in the James River.

An excerpt from Edmund Randolph's account in his History of Virginia: [12] *Although Randolph was not a participant in the Gunpowder Expedition, his description of it is a good overview of the activities of the Hanover Militia and possesses the virtues of being both brief and generally accurate.*

In April 1775, Dunmore, eager to acquit himself with some noise toward his royal master and misconceiving action, whether well or ill directed, to be synonymous with duty, adopted a measure which in any aspect could not promote his interest, as a scheme to deprive the city of Williamsburg of ammunition and arms must inevitably precipitate a general tumult. There was a paltry magazine in that city, the then-metropolis, which had served as a receptacle for a few military stores of government and for the gunpowder of the merchants there, who from caution retained but small quantities for the course of retail. Those were, by Dunmore's order, secretly, in the night, conveyed on board a vessel of war; thus adopting a policy in one sense groveling, and in another not far removed from assassination, as it was believed at the time, and more strongly suspected from what happened afterwards, that he designed, by disarming the people, to weaken the means of opposing an insurrection of the slaves, whom he purposed to invite to his standard, and for a protection against whom in part the magazine was at first built.

The citizens ran to arms as soon as the rapine was detected and would have assaulted the governor in his residence had they not been dissuaded by the calmer counsels of Peyton Randolph and Robert Carter Nicholas. The violence projected was, however, rather suspended than extinguished. It was suspended to afford to the governor an opportunity of promising to replace the gunpowder, in conformity with an address from the corporation. But instead of the candor and frankness incumbent on official stations, he replied with evasion and falsehood. Public office, if it cannot gratify with pleasant things, ought at least not to sap confidence by the desertion of truth. Dunmore says that "hearing of an insurrection in a neighboring county, he had removed the gunpowder from the magazine, where he did not think it secure, to a place of perfect security, and that upon his word and honor, whenever it was wanted in any insurrection, it should be delivered in half an hour; that he was surprised to hear that the people were under arms on this occasion, and that he should not think it prudent to put powder into their hands in such a situation." The impetuosity of a multitude, once arrested, does not instantly return to its former extravagance, although their demands may not be completely satisfied; and now, after some further effervescence, it gradually subsided into perfect tranquility.

In other parts of Virginia, Dunmore's excuse for the removal of the powder was spurned at with indignation for its departure from the fact, and his equivocation about an insurrection, the interpretation of which when it might happen he reserved to himself. In the county of Hanover, in which Patrick Henry lived, the standing committee created by the Convention and the armed volunteer company refused to acquiesce; and Henry at the head of the latter marched to extort from the king's receiver general, Richard Corbin, out of the royal coffer, the value of the powder. That officer drew a bill of exchange on London for the amount, being upward of 300 pounds sterling, which sum was paid into the treasury. It was Henry's ulterior intention to visit Williamsburg with his company of men, and in some manner or other, to hold Dunmore responsible for the restitution of the powder. But when he had advanced within fifteen miles of that city, he was met by Robert Carter Nicholas and Thomas Nelson, who represented to him that as his object had been accomplished in the bill of exchange, he and his party would best consult the peace of Virginia by returning in peace, and they prevailed upon him to return. Of itself the money was of no account, but the occurrence disrobed the regal government of superstitious reverence and thereby forwarded a most essential branch of the impending Revolution. Henry was proclaimed a traitor by Dunmore, and his personal safety was thereby incorporated with the American cause. It conferred upon him a degree of military prominence, which might be a basis for future elevation in any line.

Excerpt from George Dabney's memo to William Wirt, May 14, 1805: [13]
William Wirt seems to have been puzzled as to how to construct his account of the Gunpowder Expedition from the different versions he received from the various participants. He used quotation marks for Henry only in a short passage from Captain George Dabney's account (Appendix C) and seems to have made up the speech he ascribes Henry delivering to the Hanover Militia (see Appendix F, "Patrick Henry Apocrypha"). According to Dabney, a militia member:

[Patrick Henry] on his way to meet a committee which were to confer on the occasion... observed to Colonel Richard Morris and myself that it was a fortunate circumstance which would arouse the people from North to South:

> You may in vain mention the duties to them upon tea, and etc. These things will not affect them. They depend on principles too abstracted for their apprehension and feeling. But tell them of the robbery of the magazine, and that the next step will be to disarm them, you bring the subject home to their bosoms, and they will be ready to fly to arms to defend themselves.

(3) Lord Dunmore reacts to the Gunpowder Expedition by issuing a proclamation against Henry and the Hanover Militia, May 6, 1775. [14]

By his excellency, the Right Hon. John, Earl of Dunmore, His Majesty's Lieutenant and Governor General of the Colony and Dominion of Virginia, and Vice Admiral of the same:

A PROCLAMATION
Virginia, to wit:

Whereas, I have been informed, from undoubted authority, that a certain Patrick Henry of the County of Hanover and a number of deluded followers have taken up arms, chosen their officers, and styling themselves an independent company, have marched out of their county, encamped, and put themselves in a posture of war. They have written and dispatched letters to diverse parts of the country, exciting the people to join in these outrageous and rebellious practices, to the great terror of all his majesty's faithful subjects and in open defiance of law and government. They have committed other acts of violence—particularly in extorting from His Majesty's Receiver General the sum of 330 pounds under pretense of replacing the powder I thought proper to order from the magazine.

Whence it undeniably appears that there is no longer the least security for the life or property of any man. Wherefore I have thought proper, with the advice of His Majesty's Council and in His Majesty's name, to issue this, my proclamation, strictly charging all persons upon their allegiance not to aid, abet, or give countenance to the said Patrick Henry or any other persons concerned in such unwarrantable combinations. But, on the contrary, to oppose them and their designs by every means. These designs must otherwise inevitably involve the whole country in the most direful calamity, as they will call for the vengeance of offended majesty and the insulted laws to be exerted here to vindicate the constitutional authority of government.

Given under my hand and the seal of the colony at Williamsburg, this 6th day of May 1775, and in the 15th year of His Majesty's reign.

DUNMORE

God save the King.

CHAPTER V

HENRY LEADS VIRGINIA
INTO THE REVOLUTION, 1776

"He entered into no subtlety of reasoning but was roused
by the now apparent spirit of the people as a pillar of fire,
which notwithstanding the darkness of the prospect,
[he] would conduct to the promised land."
—Edmund Randolph, *History of Virginia*, ca. 1810

(1) Patrick Henry at the Second Continental Congress

*Henry took his seat in the Second Continental Congress at
Philadelphia on May 18, 1775, twelve days after Dunmore's proclamation against him. Jefferson was a first-time member of the
Virginia delegation. Although historians agree that Henry made
no notable contribution to the body's deliberations, contrary to
Jefferson's assertion, he did remain until it adjourned on August
first.*

*Excerpt from Thomas Jefferson's August 4, 1805, letter to
William Wirt:* [1]

I found Mr. Henry to be a silent and almost unmedling member
in Congress. On the original opening of that body, while general
grievances were the topic, he was in his element and captivated all
with his bold and splendid eloquence. But as soon as they came
to specific matters, to sober reasoning and solid argumentation,
he had the good sense to perceive that his declamation, however
excellent in its proper place, had no weight at all in such an assembly as that, of coolheaded, reflecting, judicious men. He ceased
therefore in a great measure to take any part in the business. He

seemed indeed very tired of the place and wonderfully relieved when, by appointment of the Virginia Convention to be colonel of their First Regiment, he was permitted to leave Congress about the last of July.

(2) Henry as colonel of the Virginia Militia

On August 5, 1775, the Virginia Convention elected Patrick Henry colonel of the first of two Virginia regiments and the commander in chief of all regular forces in Virginia. During the next five months Colonel Henry did not always receive the support of the Convention's Committee of Safety, whose chairman was Edmund Pendleton, his sometime adversary in political matters. Although a popular commander, there were doubts as to whether Henry had enough military experience for success in the field. On February 13, 1776, the Continental Congress merged the two Virginia regiments into six continental regiments representing all thirteen colonies. Henry, finding former subordinates promoted above him to general officer rank, declined a colonel's commission in the Continental Army, thus ending his military career.

On March 1, 1776, Purdie's Virginia Gazette *of Williamsburg published this account:* [2]

Yesterday morning the troops in this city, being informed that Patrick Henry, Esquire, Commander in Chief of the Virginia Forces resigned his commission the day preceding and was about to leave them, the whole went into mourning, and, under arms, waited on him at his lodgings, when they addressed him...

After the officers had received Colonel Henry's kind answer to their address, they insisted on his dining with them, at the Raleigh Tavern before his departure. After dinner a number of them proposed escorting him out of town, but were prevented by some uneasiness getting among the soldiery, who assembled in a tumultuous manner and demanded their discharge, and declaring their unwillingness to serve under any other commander. Upon which Colonel Henry found it necessary to stay a night longer in town, which he spent in visiting the several barracks, and used every argument in his power with the soldiery to lay aside their imprudent resolution and to continue in the service which he had quitted from motives in which his honor alone was concerned. And that, although he was prevented from serving his country in a military capacity, yet his utmost abilities should ever be exerted for the real interest of the United Colonies in support of the glorious cause in which they had engaged... And we have now the pleasure to assure the public that those brave fellows are now pretty well reconciled and will spend the last drop of their blood in their country's defense.

Edmund Randolph later wrote in his History of Virginia: [3]

The Convention had organized a large corps of militia, styled minutemen, who were to be trained at convenient seasons and ready for service at all times. Two regiments of regular infantry had been also raised, the command of which was given to Patrick Henry, then a member of Congress sitting in Philadelphia. Officers with military experience were rare: Virginia was compelled to rely principally on those elements of character which were indispensable in a soldier. Henry was seconded by men who had been active in the French and Indian War of 1755, and their imperfect lessons promised to render him with his ambition and attention an able defender of liberty in the field, as he had been in the forum.

Washington had obviously not yet heard of Henry's declining a Continental Army commission when he wrote the following, but his view that Henry would be of far greater value to the Revolution in government rather than in the military was undoubtedly correct.

Excerpt from a letter by General Washington to Joseph Reed, his adjutant general, March 7, 1776: [4]

I think my countrymen made a capital mistake when they took Henry out of the senate to place him in the field, and pity it is that he does not see this and remove every difficulty by a voluntary resignation.

(3) Edmund Randolph on Patrick Henry at the Virginia Convention of 1776

When the Virginia Convention again met on May 6, 1776, Patrick Henry was one of its members, as were the young James Madison (1751-1836) and Edmund Randolph (1753-1813), both of whom were destined to become Henry's future political adversaries. Years later, Randolph wrote these remembrances of Henry at the Convention of 1776.

Henry waits to call for a Virginia Declaration of Independence until he believes the Convention is ready for it. [5]

When the disposition of the people as exhibited by their representatives could not be mistaken, Henry had full indulgence of his own private judgment, and he concerted with [Thomas] Nelson [Jr.] that he, Nelson, should introduce the question of independence and that Henry should enforce it. Nelson affected nothing of oratory except what ardent feelings might inspire… It was expected that a declaration of independence would certainly be pressed, and for obvious reasons Mr. Henry seemed allotted to crown his political conduct with this supreme stroke. And yet for a considerable time he talked of the subject as being critical, but without committing himself by a pointed avowal in its favor or a pointed repudiation of it.

He thought that a cause which put at stake the lives and fortunes of the people should appear to be their own act, and that he ought not to place upon the responsibility of his eloquence a revolution of which the people might be wearied after the present stimulus should cease to operate. But after some time he appeared in an element for which he was born. To cut the knot, which calm prudence was puzzled to untie, was worthy of the magnificence of his genius. He entered into no subtlety of reasoning but was roused by the now apparent spirit of the people as a pillar of fire,

which notwithstanding the darkness of the prospect would conduct to the promised land. He inflamed, and was followed by, the
convention…

The principles of Paine's pamphlet [Thomas Paine, *Common
Sense* (1776)] now stalked in triumph under the sanction of the
most extensive, richest, and most commanding colony in America.
The event had been vehemently desired by a majority of [the
Continental] Congress, who would not venture to originate it with
themselves. They were aware of its favorable influence on the affairs of America with respect to foreign nations.

*Virginia declared itself independent from English rule on
May 15, 1776, and instructed its delegation in the Continental
Congress to do likewise. On June 12, Virginia's Declaration of
Rights was unanimously accepted by the Convention. George
Mason, Patrick Henry, James Madison, and Edmund Randolph,
were members of the declaration's drafting committee. Most
scholars attribute authorship of the declaration's sixteen articles
to Mason. However, according to Randolph's* History of Virginia,
*it was Henry who proposed the fifteenth and sixteenth articles.
Randolph remembered, "The latter [Article Sixteen], coming
from a gentleman who was supposed to be a dissenter, caused an
appeal to him whether it was designed as a prelude to an attack
on the established [Anglican] church, and he disclaimed such an
object."* [6]

Article Fifteen. That no free government, or the blessing of
liberty, can be preserved to any people but by a firm adherence
to justice, moderation, temperance, frugality, and virtue, and by
frequent recurrence to fundamental principles.

Article Sixteen. That religion, or the duty which we owe to
our Creator, and the manner of discharging it can be directed only
by reason and conviction, not by force or violence, and therefore
all men are equally entitled to the free exercise of religion according to the dictates of conscience; and that it is the mutual duty of
all to practice Christian forbearance, love, and charity.

On June 29, 1776, the Virginia Convention adopted a constitution for the new commonwealth. It established a republican form of government for Virginia. The governor, who was elected annually by the bicameral legislature, was advised by an executive council, and there was a separate judiciary. Henry, realizing that Virginia's first governor would, in wartime, need strong executive powers and that he would very likely himself be chosen, argued vigorously for them. His efforts, according to Randolph, seem to have been only partially successful, as Governors Henry (1776-1779) and Jefferson (1779-1881) were to learn through bitter experience. [7]

After creating the office of governor, the convention gave way to their horror of a *powerful* chief magistrate without waiting to reflect how much stronger a governor might be made for the benefit of the people, and yet be held with a republican bridle. These were not times of terror indeed, but every hint of a power which might be stigmatized as being of royal origin obscured, for a time, a part of that patriotic splendor with which the mover had before shone.

No member but Henry could with impunity to his popularity have contended as strenuously as he did for an executive veto on the acts of the two houses of legislation. Those who knew him to be indolent in literary investigations were astonished at the manner in which he exhausted this topic, unaided as he was believed to be by any of the treatises on government except Montesquieu [the early eighteenth-century French political philosopher, admired by many of the Founding Fathers]. Amongst other arguments, he averred that a governor would be a mere phantom, unable to defend his office from the impulse or ferment in that body, and that he would otherwise be ultimately a dependent instead of a coordinate branch of power. His eloquence, however, had an effect only personal to himself: it only stopped the wheel of popular favor, while as to him in this respect it was inclining to roll backwards.

(4) Henry accepts election as Governor of Virginia.

On July 1, 1776, Henry sent this letter to the Virginia Convention: [8]

To the Honorable President and House of Convention:

Gentlemen: The vote of this day appointing me Governor of the Commonwealth has been notified to me in the most polite and obliging manner by George Mason, Henry Lee, Dudley Digges, John Blair, and Bartholomew Dandridge, Esquires.

A sense of the high and unmerited honor conferred upon me by the convention fills my heart with gratitude, which I trust my whole life will manifest. I take this earliest opportunity to express my thanks, which I wish to convey to you, gentlemen, in the strongest terms of acknowledgment.

When I reflect that the tyranny of the British king and parliament has kindled a formidable war, now raging throughout this wide-extended continent, and in the operations of which this commonwealth must bear so great a part; and that from the events of this war the lasting happiness or misery of a great proportion of the human species will finally result; that in order to preserve this commonwealth from anarchy and its attendant ruin, and to give vigor to our councils and effect to all our measures, government has been necessarily assumed and new modeled; that it is exposed to numberless hazards and perils in its infantine state; that it can never attain to maturity or ripen into firmness unless it is guarded by an affectionate assiduity and managed by great abilities; I feel my mind filled with anxiety and uneasiness to find myself so unequal to the duties of that important office to which I am called by the favor of my fellow citizens at this truly critical conjuncture. The errors of my conduct shall be atoned for, so far as I am able, by unwearied endeavors to secure the freedom and happiness of our common country.

I shall enter upon the duties of my office when you, gentlemen, shall be pleased to direct, relying upon the known wisdom and virtue of your honorable house to supply my defects and to permanency and success to that system of government, which you have formed and which is so wisely calculated to secure equal liberty and advance human happiness.

I have the honor to be, gentlemen,

Your most obedient and very humble servant,

P. Henry, Junior

At approximately the time he became Virginia's first elected governor, Patrick Henry was stricken with malaria. His illness was so serious that it was rumored he had died of it. Henry spent July and August 1776 in his sick bed at his home, Scotchtown, in Hanover County, and did not take up his duties as governor full time until the middle of September. The malaria would recur at intervals for the remainder of his life.

Excerpt from the diary of Landon Carter (1710-1778) dated July 13, 1776. Carter was a wealthy Tidewater planter and a political enemy of Henry: [9]

Came here after dinner Mr. John Selden, who told us Captain Burgess Bull wrote from Hampton that Patrick Henry, the late elected governor, died last Tuesday evening. So that being the day our [artillery] batteries began to play on Dunmore's gang and they being routed, we ought to look on those two joined as two glorious events, particularly favorable by the hand of Providence.

Members of an association of Baptists meeting in Louisa County, whose religious freedom Henry had frequently defended in court—sometimes at his own expense (see Chapter III, 2)—wrote to Henry, congratulating him on his election and his "constant attachment to the cause of liberty and the rights of conscience." Henry replied on August 13, 1776: [10]

To the Ministers and Delegates of the Baptist Churches and to the Members of Communion:

Gentlemen: I am exceedingly obliged to you for your very kind address, and the favorable sentiments you are pleased to entertain respecting my conduct, and the principles which have directed it. My constant endeavor shall be to guard the rights of all my fellow citizens from every encroachment.

I am happy to find a catholic spirit prevailing in our country, and that those religious distinctions which formerly produced some heats are now forgotten. Happy must every friend to virtue and America feel himself to perceive that the only contest among us, at this critical and important period, is who shall be foremost to preserve our religious and civil liberties.

My earnest wish is that Christian charity, forbearance, and love may unite all different persuasions as brethren who must perish or triumph together. And I trust that the time is not far distant when we shall greet each other as peaceable possessors of that just and equal system of liberty adopted by the last convention, and in support of which may God crown our arms with success.

I am gentlemen,

   Your most obedient and very humble servant,
   P. Henry, Junior

CHAPTER VI

Henry as Revolutionary War Governor, 1776-1779

"I have the honor to transmit to you an account of necessaries sent off in nine wagons for the Virginia regiments in Continental service…"
—Governor Henry to General Washington,
September 20, 1776

(1) Governor Henry does his best to keep General Washington supplied.

One of Governor Henry's first official acts upon recuperating from his illness was to write to General Washington on September 20, 1776. Washington responded in a letter from "Heights of Harlem"(NY) dated October 5, congratulating Henry "most cordially upon your appointment to the government, and, with no less sincerity, on your late recovery. Your correspondence will confer honor and satisfaction, and, whenever it is in my power, I shall write to you with pleasure." Thus began a correspondence that continued through Henry's three terms as Virginia's wartime governor (1776-1779). [1]

The following exchange of letters took place when Washington's struggling army was encamped near Valley Forge, Pennsylvania, during the winter of 1777-1778. Henry to Washington, Williamsburg, December 6, 1777: [2]

Sir: Enclosed I have the honor to transmit you an account of necessaries sent off in nine wagons for the Virginia Regiments in Continental service… It is my wish that the troops of Virginia shall have them. I also send a list of some other articles, chiefly linens that will shortly set out from our public store, for the same uses.

Added to this supply, fifteen thousand pounds worth of woolens, etc., proper for the soldiers, will set out from Petersburg in a few days. These last are procured under an act of assembly, empowering me to seize necessaries for our troops wherever they may be found. I have given orders, in consequence, to proper persons in different parts of the state, which I expect will produce many necessaries, if not enough for the Virginia troops. Orders are sent to both Carolinas for blankets, particularly, and soldiers' clothes; and nothing possible for me to effect will be left undone in getting whatever the troops are in want of...

The lenity of your publications respecting deserters is very apparent. But nevertheless, a great many of them are yet skulking on the Eastern Shore, and really I think their case peculiar. Their officers took up the general opinion that their service would be confined to that shore and promised them to remain there. Their desertion followed upon orders to march away. I beg leave to observe that if your Excellency would offer them a pardon upon their enlistment to serve this state, it would forward the general service by enabling us to spare so many more troops for the Grand Army. I beg leave to assure you of the highest esteem and regard, with which I have the honor to be, Sir, your Excellency's

Most obedient and humble servant,

Patrick Henry

His Excellency George Washington

George Washington to Patrick Henry, from "Camp 14 miles from Philadelphia, 19th Dec. 1777:" [3]

Sir: On Saturday evening I was honored with your favor of the 6th instant and am much obliged by your exertions for clothing for the Virginia Troops. The articles you send shall be applied to their use, agreeable to your wishes—It will be difficult for me to determine when the troops are supplied, owing to their fluctuating and deficient state. However, I believe there will be little reason to suspect that the quantities that may be procured will much exceed the necessary demands. It will be a happy circumstance and of great saving if we should be able in future to clothe our army comfortably. Their sufferings hitherto have been great, and from our deficiencies in this instance we have lost many men and have generally been deprived of a large proportion of our force…

I am persuaded that many desertions have proceeded from the cause you mention. The officers were highly culpable in making such assurances—The expedient you propose might, and I believe would, bring in several, but I cannot consider myself authorized to adopt it…

I have nothing material to inform you of, except that we are told by the Boston paper that a ship has arrived from France at one of the eastern ports with fifty pieces of brass artillery, 5,000 stands of arms and other stores. There are letters also which mention her arrival, but not the particular amount of the stores.

I have the honor to be, with great respect and regard, sir, your most obedient servant,

George Washington

His Excellency, Gov. Patrick Henry

(2) Governor Henry authorizes George Rogers Clark to head a military expedition north of the Ohio River, January 2, 1778.

In addition to the fighting going on in states both to the north and south and potential problems of civil defense within Virginia, Governor Henry had to contend with enemies, foreign and native, on the western frontier. Perhaps the state's most notable military achievement during Patrick Henry's three terms as Virginia's Revolutionary War governor was George Rogers Clark's conquest of the Northwest. After Henry authorized Clark to attack British forces north of the Ohio River, Clark captured their out-

post at Kaskaskia on July 4, 1778. In December of the same year,
the Virginia General Assembly created the vast new territory of
Illinois. [4]

Lieutenant Colonel George Rogers Clark:

You are to proceed with all convenient speed to raise seven companies of soldiers to consist of fifty men each, officered in the usual manner and armed most properly for the enterprise, and with this force attack the British post at Kaskaskia.

It is conjectured that there are many pieces of cannon and military stores to considerable amount at that place, the taking and preservation of which would be a valuable acquisition to the state. If you are fortunate, therefore, as to succeed in your expectation, you will take every possible measure to secure the artillery and stores and whatever may advantage the state.

For the transportation of the troops, provisions, etc., down the Ohio, you are to apply to the commanding officer at Fort Pitt for boats, and during the whole transaction you are to take especial care to keep the destination of your force secret. Its success depends upon this...

It is earnestly desired that you show humanity to such British subjects and other persons as fall into your hands. If the white inhabitants at that post and the neighborhood will give undoubted evidence of their attachment to this state (for it is certain they live within its limits) by taking the test prescribed by law and by every other way and means in their power, let them be treated as fellow citizens and their persons and property duly secured. Assistance and protection against all enemies, whatever shall be afforded them, and the Commonwealth of Virginia is pledged to accomplish it. But if these people will not accede to these reasonable demands, they must feel the miseries of war, under the direction of that humanity that has hither distinguished Americans and which it is expected you will ever consider as the rule of your conduct, from which you are in no instance to depart.

The corps you are to command are to receive the pay and allowances of militia and to act under the laws and regulations of this state now in force as militia. The inhabitants at this post will be informed by you that in case they accede to the offers of becoming citizens of this commonwealth, a proper garrison will be maintained among them and every attention bestowed to render their commerce beneficial—the fairest prospects being opened to the dominions of both France and Spain.

It is in contemplation to establish a post near the mouth of the Ohio. Cannon will be wanted to fortify it. Part of those at Kaskaskia will be easily brought thither or otherwise secured as circumstances will make necessary.

You are to apply to General Hand for powder and lead necessary for this expedition. If he can't supply it, the person who has that which Captain Lynn brought from Orleans can. Lead was sent to Hampshire by my orders and that may be delivered to you. Wishing you success, I am, Sir,

Your humble servant,
P. Henry

(3) Henry stands by General Washington, and Washington shows his appreciation. George Washington to Patrick Henry, from Valley Forge, March 27, 1778.

With the American defeats at Brandywine and Germantown, and the British occupation of Philadelphia, there was, in some quarters, much dissatisfaction with General Washington's leadership. In mid-February 1778, Governor Henry received an unsigned letter designed to secure his cooperation in replacing Washington. This intrigue, sometimes called "The Conway Cabal" after one of the dissident generals involved, seems, however, not to have been a formal conspiracy. Henry immediately forwarded the correspondence to Washington with a note of his own which began, "You will no doubt be surprised at seeing the enclosed letter, in which the encomiums bestowed on me are as undeserved as the censures aimed at you are unjust. I am sorry there should be one man who counts himself my friend who is not yours." Washington replied: [5]

Dear Sir:

About eight days past I was honored with your favor of the twentieth of last month. Your friendship, sir, in transmitting to me the anonymous letter you had received lays me under the most grateful obligations, and if my acknowledgments can be due for anything more, it is for the polite and delicate terms in which you have been pleased to communicate the matter.

I have ever been happy in supposing that I had a place in your esteem, and the proof of it you have afforded on this occasion makes me peculiarly so. The favorable light in which you hold me is truly flattering, but I should feel much regret if I thought the happiness of America so intimately connected with my personal welfare, as you so obligingly seem to consider it. All I can say is that she has ever had, and I trust she ever will have, my honest exertions to promote her interest. I cannot hope that my services have been the best, but my heart tells me they have been the best that I could render.

That I may have erred in using the means in my power for accomplishing the object of the arduous exalted station with which I am honored, I cannot doubt. Nor do I wish my conduct be exempted from reprehension farther than it may deserve. Error is the portion of humanity, and to censure it, whether committed by this or that public character, is the prerogative of free men. However, being intimately acquainted with the man I conceive to be the author of the letter transmitted, and having always received from him the strongest professions of attachment and regard, I am constrained to consider him as not possessing, at least, a great degree of candor and sincerity, though his views in addressing you should have been the result of conviction and founded in motives of public good.

This is not the only secret, insidious attempt that has been made to wound my reputation. There have been others equally base, cruel, and ungenerous, because conducted with as little frankness and proceeding from views, perhaps, as personally interested. I am, dear sir, with great esteem and regard, your much obliged friend and servant,

George Washington

To His Excellency P. Henry, Esquire, Governor of Virginia.

(4) Henry, in poor health and spirits, writes to Governor Thomas Jefferson from "Leatherwood," his new home in Henry County, February 15, 1780.

Henry served the three one-year terms as governor permitted by Virginia's constitution (1776-1779) and retired with "the unanimous approbation" of both the state's Senate and House of Delegates. Exhausted from his recurring malaria and overwork, he moved with his family to Southside Virginia. The pessimistic tone of this letter reflects both his poor health and his estimate of Virginia at this point in the Revolution. [6]

Dear Sir:

I return many thanks for your favor by Mr. Sanders. The kind notice you were pleased to take of me was particularly obliging, as I have scarcely heard a word of public matters since I moved up in the retirement where I live. I have had many anxieties for our commonwealth, principally occasioned by the depreciation of our money. To judge by this, which somebody has called the pulse of the state, I have feared that our body politic was dangerously sick. God forbid it may not be unto death. But I cannot forbear thinking the present increase in prices is in great part owing to a kind of habit which is now of four or five years growth, which is fostered by a mistaken avarice and, like other habits, hard to part with, for there is really very little money hereabouts.

What you say of the practices of our disguised Tories perfectly agrees with my own observation, and the attempts to raise prejudices against the French, I know, were begun when I lived below. What gave me the utmost pain was to see some men, indeed very many, who were thought good Whigs keep company with the miscreants, wretches, who, I am satisfied, were laboring for our destruction. This countenance shown them is of fatal tendency. They should be shunned and execrated, and this is the only way to supply the place of legal conviction and punishment. But this is an effort of virtue, small as it seems, of which our countrymen are not capable.

Indeed, I will own to you, my dear sir, that observing this impunity, and even respect, which some wicked individuals have met with, while their guilt was clear as the sun, has sickened me, and made me sometimes wish to be in retirement for the rest of my life. I will, however, be down on the next assembly, if I am chosen. My health, I am satisfied, will never again permit a close application to sedentary business, and I even doubt whether I can remain below long enough to serve in the assembly. I will, however, make the trial.

But tell me, do you remember any instance where tyranny was destroyed and freedom established on its ruins among a people possessing so small a share of virtue and public spirit? I recollect none, and this more than the British arms makes me fearful of final success without a reform. But when or how this is to be effected, I have not the means of judging. I most sincerely wish you health and prosperity. If you can spare time to drop me a line now and then, it will be highly obliging to, dear sir, your affectionate friend and obedient servant,

P. Henry

To His Excellency, Thomas Jefferson, at Richmond

(5) Henry incurs Jefferson's enmity.

Henry's retirement from government lasted less than a year. In May 1780, he traveled from his home in Henry County to the new capital in Richmond where he became leader of Virginia's House of Delegates. During May of the following year, the General Assembly was forced to meet in Charlottesville because British troops were threatening the entire eastern part of the state. As it turned out, even Charlottesville was not safe from the British cavalry, and the Virginia legislature had to beat a quick retreat over the Blue Ridge Mountains to the frontier town of Staunton. Governor Jefferson, whose second term expired at the end of May 1781, retired to his Poplar Forest plantation near present-day Lynchburg and did not return to Monticello until early August.

There was some controversy concerning Jefferson's per-
formance as governor and about his disappearance afterwards,
although he held no public office following the expiration of his
second term. By October, however, the British had surrendered
at Yorktown, and the matter no longer seemed as important as
it had previously. On December 12, 1781, the Virginia House of
Delegates passed a resolution declaring "that the sincere thanks
of the General Assembly be given to our former Governor,"
praising Jefferson for the conduct of his administration and pro-
claiming "the high opinion which they entertain of Mr. Jefferson's
ability, rectitude and integrity as chief magistrate, and mean by
thus publicly avowing their opinion to obviate all future and re-
move all former unmerited censure." [7]

Edmund Randolph described the proceedings in his History
of Virginia *with considerable tact:* [8]

At [the June 1781] session of the assembly [after its flight
from Charlottesville at the end of May], the usual antidote for
public distress was resorted to. Two persons were named with ac-
rimony as delinquent, Baron Steuben, for not having succeeded in
protecting the stores in the vicinity of Point of Fork, and Thomas
Jefferson, the governor at the time of [Benedict] Arnold's invasion, as not having made some exertions which he might have
made for the defense of the country... Colonel George Nicholas
and Mr. Patrick Henry were those who charged Mr. Jefferson.
They aimed to express themselves with delicacy toward him,
without weakening the ground on which they supposed that their
suspicions would be found ultimately to stand. But probably without design, they wounded by their measured endeavor to avoid the
infliction of a wound.

Colonel Nicholas moved, however, for an inquiry into the
conduct of the governor at the succeeding session. The motion
was carried with the concurrence of [Jefferson's] friends and his
foes; of the former to afford him an opportunity for exculpation; of
the latter who conceived him to be ruined. He appeared at that session as a delegate from Albemarle and at the appointed day called

for some accusation. Neither of those gentlemen having pledged themselves to become prosecutors, they did not feel it to be a personal duty of either to appear as such.

But Mr. Jefferson did not affect to be ignorant of the general imputation which had been circulated, but was destitute of any precise shape; and in an address to the house, which amounted to a challenge of impeachment, he reviewed his administration so as to draw forth votes of eulogium, which by some men unambitious of true fame would have been deemed cheaply purchased by past calumnies. He ought to have been satisfied, because they were the undivided voice of his country [state], which had been prejudiced against him.

Despite the commendation by the General Assembly, Jefferson never forgave Henry for what he perceived as Henry's leadership in introducing the motion to censure him.

Excerpt from a letter by Thomas Jefferson to Isaac Zane, December 24, 1781: [9]

The trifling body [George Nicholas] who moved the matter [the motion to censure] was below contempt; he was more an object of pity. His natural ill temper was the tool worked by another hand. He was like the minnows which go in and out of the fundament of the whale. But the whale himself [Henry] was discoverable enough by the turbulence of the water under which he moved.

CHAPTER VII

PEACE: HENRY IN THE LEGISLATURE, GOVERNOR FOR A SECOND TIME (1784-1786), AND A FAMILY MATTER

"It is in your power, my dear sir, to do more good and prevent
more mischief than any man in this state."
—George Mason to Patrick Henry, May 6, 1783

(1) George Mason reaffirms Henry's preeminence in Virginia politics.

After the surrender of Cornwallis at Yorktown in October 1781, active hostilities in the war ceased. With the prospect of the peace treaty with Great Britain in mind, which was concluded in September 1783, Mason wrote to Henry on May 6 from his home, Gunston Hall:[1]

I congratulate you most sincerely on the accomplishment of what I know was the warmest wish of your heart, the establishment of American independence and the liberty of our country. We are now to rank among the nations of the world, but whether our independence shall prove a blessing or a curse must depend upon our own wisdom or folly, virtue or wickedness. Judging of the future from the past, the prospect is not promising. Justice and virtue are the vital principles of republican government, but among us a depravity of manners and morals prevails to the destruction of all confidence between man and man.

It greatly behooves the assembly to revise several of our laws and to abolish all such as are contrary to the fundamental principles of justice. And, by a strict adherence to the distinctions between right and wrong for the future, to restore that confidence and reverence in the people for the legislature, which has been so greatly impaired by a contrary conduct and without which our laws can never be much more than a dead letter.

It is in your power, my dear sir, to do more good and prevent more mischief than any man in this state, and I doubt not that you will exert the great talents with which God has blessed you in promoting the public happiness and prosperity.

(2) Upon cessation of hostilities, Henry advocated free trade with England in the May 1783 session of the Virginia Legislature.

According to Judge John Tyler, on the first day of the session Henry moved the repeal of the act prohibiting the importation of British goods.[2]

Mr. Henry espoused the measure which took off the restraints on British commerce before any treaty was entered into. I opposed him on this ground—that that measure would expel from this country the trade of every other nation on account of our habits, language, and the manner of conducting business between us and them. Also on this ground, in addition to the above, I argued that if we changed the then-current of commerce, we should drive away all competition and never perhaps regain it (which has literally happened).

In reply to these observations, he was beyond all expression eloquent and sublime. After painting the distress of the people struggling through a perilous war, cut off from commerce so long that they were naked and unclothed, he concluded with a figure, or rather with a series of figures which I shall never forget, because, beautiful as they were in themselves, their effect was heightened beyond all description by the manner in which he acted what he spoke:

"Why," said he, "should we fetter commerce? If a man is in chains, he droops and bows to the earth, for his spirits are broken (looking sorrowfully at his feet). But let him twist the fetters from his legs, and he will stand erect (straightening himself and assuming a look of proud defiance). Fetter not commerce, sir—let her be as free as the air. She will range the whole creation and return on the wings of the four winds of heaven to bless the land with plenty."

(3) According to Judge Tyler, Henry, in the same session of the legislature, advocated open immigration and prophesied a great nation.[3]

The personal feeling of a politician ought not to be permitted to enter those walls. The question (he said) was a national one, and in deciding it, if they acted wisely, nothing would be regarded but the interest of the nation. On the altar of his country's good he was willing to sacrifice all personal resentments, all private wrongs, and he flattered himself that he was not the only man in the house who was capable of making such a sacrifice.

"We have, sir," said he, "an extensive country without population. What can be more obvious policy than that this country ought to be populated? People, sir, form the strength and constitute the wealth of a nation. I want to see our vast forests filled up by some process a little more speedy than the ordinary course of nature. I wish to see these states rapidly ascending to the rank which their natural advantages authorize them to hold among the nations of the earth. Cast your eye, sir, over this extensive country. Observe the salubrity of your climate, the variety and fertility of your soil, and see that soil intersected in every quarter by bold navigable streams, flowing to the east and to the west as if the finger of heaven were marking out the course of your settlements, inviting you to enterprise and pointing the way to wealth.

"Sir, you are destined at some time or other to become a great agricultural and commercial people. The only question is whether you choose to reach this point by slow gradations and at some distant period—lingering on through a long and sickly minority, subjected meanwhile to machinations, insults, and oppressions of enemies, foreign and domestic, without sufficient strength to resist and chastise them—or whether you choose rather to rush at once, as it were, to the full enjoyment of those high destinies and be able to cope single-handed with the proudest oppressors of the old world.

"If you prefer the latter course, as I trust you do, encourage emigration, encourage the husbandmen, the mechanics, the merchants of the old world to come and settle in this land of promise. Make it the home of the skillful, the industrious, the fortunate, the happy, as well as the asylum of the distressed. Fill up the measure of your population as speedily as you can by the means which heaven has placed in your hands. And I venture to prophesy there are those now living who will see this favored land among the most powerful on earth—able, sir, to take care of herself without resorting to that policy which is always so dangerous, although sometimes unavoidable, of calling in foreign aid. Yes, sir, they will see her great in arts and in arms, her golden harvests waving over fields of immeasurable extent, her commerce penetrating the most distant seas, and her cannon silencing the vain boasts of those who now proudly affect to rule the waves.

"But, sir, you must have men. You cannot get along without them. Those heavy forests of valuable timber under which your lands are groaning must be cleared away. Those vast riches which cover the face of your soil, as well as those which lie hid in its bosom, are to be developed and gathered only by the skill and enterprise of men. Your timber, sir, must be worked up into ships to transport the production of the soil from which it has been cleared. Then you must have commercial men and commercial capital to take off your productions and find the best markets for them abroad. Your great want, sir, is the want of men; and these you must have and will have speedily, if you are wise.

"Do you ask how you are to get them? Open your doors, sir, and they will come in. The population of the old world is full to overflowing. That population is ground, too, by the oppressions of the governments under which they live. Sir, they are already standing on tiptoe upon their native shores and looking to your coasts with a wistful and longing eye. They see here a land blessed with natural and political advantages which are not equaled by those of any other country upon earth—a land on which Providence has emptied the horn of abundance, a land over which peace has now stretched forth her white wings, and where contentment and plenty lie down at every door!

"Sir, they see something more attractive than all this. They see a land in which Liberty has taken up her abode—that Liberty whom they had considered as a fabled goddess existing only in the fancies of poets. They see her here a real divinity—her altars rising on every hand throughout these happy states, her glories chanted by three millions of tongues, and the whole region smiling under her blessed influence. Sir, let but this, our celestial golden goddess Liberty, stretch forth her fair hand toward the people of the old world. Tell them to come and bid them welcome, and you will see them pouring in from the north, from the south, from the east, and from the west. Your wildernesses will be cleared and settled, your deserts will smile, your ranks will be filled, and you will soon be in a condition to defy the powers of any adversary.

"But gentlemen object to any accession from Great Britain, and particularly to the return of British refugees. Sir, I feel no objection to the return of those deluded people. They have, to be sure, mistaken their own interests most woefully, and most woefully have they suffered the punishment due to their offenses. But the relations which we bear to them and to their native country are now changed. Their king has acknowledged our independence. The quarrel is over. Peace has returned and found us a free people.

"Let us have the magnanimity, sir, to lay aside our antipathies and prejudices, and consider the subject in a political light. Those are an enterprising, moneyed people. They will be serviceable in taking off the surplus produce of our lands and supplying us with necessaries during the infant state of our manufactures. Even if they be inimical to us in point of feeling and principle, I can see no objection in a political view in making them tributary to our advantage. And as I have no prejudices to prevent my making this use of them, so, sir, I have no fear of any mischief that they can do us.

"Afraid of them! What, sir," said he, rising to one of his loftiest attitudes and assuming a look of the most indignant and sovereign contempt, "shall we, who have laid the proud British lion at our feet, now be afraid of his whelps?"

(4) Archibald Stuart tells of Henry making his case through humor in the Virginia Legislature, ca. 1784.[4]

At your request, I attempt a narrative of the extraordinary effects of Mr. Henry's eloquence in the Virginia Legislature, about the year 1784, when I was present as a member of that body:

The finances of the country had been much deranged during the war, and public credit was at a low ebb. A party in the legislature thought it then high time to place the character and credit of the state on a more respectable footing by laying taxes commensurate with all the public demand. With this view, a bill had been brought into the house and referred to a committee of the whole, in support of which the then-speaker (Mr. Tyler), Henry Tazewell, Mann Page, William Ronald, and many other members of great respectability (including, to the best of my recollection, Richard H. Lee, and perhaps Mr. Madison), took an active part. Mr. Henry, on the other hand, was of the opinion that this was a premature attempt, and that policy required that the people should have some repose after the fatigues and privations to which they had been subject during a long and arduous struggle for independence.

The advocates of the bill, in committee of the whole house, used their utmost efforts and were successful in conforming it to their views by such a majority (say thirty) as seemed to ensure its passage. When the committee rose, the bill was instantly reported to the house, when Mr. Henry, who had been excited and roused by his recent defeat, came forward again in all the majesty of his power. For some time after he commenced speaking, the countenance of his opponents indicated no apprehension of danger to their cause.

The feelings of Mr. Tyler, which were sometimes warm, could not on that occasion be concealed, even in the chair. His countenance was forbidding, even repulsive, and his face turned from the speaker. Mr. Tazewell was reading a pamphlet, and Mr. Page was more than usually grave. After some time, however, it was discovered that Mr. Tyler's countenance gradually began to relax. He would occasionally look at Mr. Henry and sometimes smile. His attention by degrees became more fixed. At length it became completely so. He next appeared to be in good humor. He leaned towards Mr. Henry, appeared charmed and delighted, and finally lost in wonder and amazement. The progress of these feelings was legible in his countenance.

Mr. Henry drew a most affecting picture of the state of poverty and suffering in which the people of the upper counties had been left by the war. His delineation of their wants and wretchedness was so minute, so full of feeling, and withal so true, that he could scarcely fail to enlist on his side every sympathetic mind. He contrasted the severe toil by which they had to gain their daily subsistence with the facilities enjoyed by the people of the lower counties. The latter, he said, residing on the salt rivers and creeks, could draw their supplies at pleasure from the waters that flowed by their doors. And then he presented such a ludicrous image of the members who had advocated the bill (the most of whom were from the lower counties), peeping and peering along the shores of the creeks to pick up their mess of crabs or paddling off to the oyster rocks to rake for their daily bread, as filled the house with merriment.

Mr. Tazewell laid down his pamphlet and shook his sides with laughter. Even the gravity of Mr. Page was affected. A corresponding change of countenance prevailed through the ranks of the advocates of the bill, and you might discover that they had surrendered their cause. In this they were not disappointed, for on a division, Mr. Henry had a majority of upwards of thirty against the bill.

(5) Jefferson's enmity towards Henry seems to have increased exponentially between 1781 and 1784.

Excerpt from a letter by Thomas Jefferson to George Rogers Clark, November 26, 1782. This was in response to a letter from Clark to Jefferson in which he expressed anger that his services during the war had not received appropriate recognition. "That you have made enemies you must not doubt, when you reflect that you have made yourself eminent," Jefferson informed Clark. [5]

I was not a little surprised, however, to find a person hostile to you, as far as he [Henry] has the courage to show hostility to any man. Who he is you will probably have heard, or may know him by his description as being all tongue and without head or heart.

Excerpt from a letter by Thomas Jefferson to James Madison, December 8, 1784 (The words in italics, note the editors of The Papers of Thomas Jefferson, *were written to Madison in a code known only to the two men.) :*[6]

While Mr. Henry lives, another bad constitution would be formed and saddled forever on us. What we have to do, I think, *is devoutly to pray* for *his death.*

(6) Henry is "kicked upstairs," and as a result, his legislation fails to pass.

James Madison, unlike Thomas Jefferson who was in France, was a member of Virginia's House of Delegates during 1783-84 and found himself pitted against Henry on nearly every major issue of the time, although he never resorted to personal attacks.

On November 17, 1784, Henry was elected Governor of Virginia for a fourth term—"without competition or opposition," as Madison informed Jefferson, apparently with some satisfaction. Madison was one of three members of the House committee appointed to notify Henry of his election.

On November 14, 1784, Madison wrote to James Monroe that the House of Delegates was "still occupied" with a bill for a general assessment for Christian denominations, which Madison opposed. The bill, based on a resolution introduced and strongly advocated by Henry, called for a "moderate tax contribution" for such a purpose. It had been passed by a vote of 47 to 32 in the House Committee of the Whole, and, so it appeared, would be easily carried when it came to the floor for final action.

Two weeks later, Madison informed Monroe that the bill had still not been considered for final passage and noted, "Mr. Henry, the father of this scheme... will no more sit in the House of Delegates, a circumstance very inauspicious to his offspring." Madison was right; the bill was never brought up again. Thomas Jefferson's bill for establishing religious freedom in Virginia became law in January 1786. The preamble to the General Assessment Bill follows: [7]

Whereas the general diffusion of Christian knowledge hath a natural tendency to correct the morals of men, restrain their vices, and preserve the peace of society, which cannot be effected without a competent provision for learned teachers, who may be thereby enabled to devote their time and attention to the duty of instructing such citizens as, from their circumstances and want of education, cannot otherwise attain such knowledge; and it is judged such provision may be made by the legislature, without counteracting the liberal principle heretofore adopted and intended to be preserved, by abolishing all distinctions of pre-eminence amongst the different societies of Christians.

In November 1784 Henry proposed two pieces of legislation favoring amicable relations with the Indians.

The first bill directed the Governor of Virginia to adopt such measures as he found necessary "to avert the dangers of hostilities with the Indians and to incline them to treat with the commissioners of congress." Henry's second bill for achieving peace with the Indians was much more specific—and much more controversial. It

called for cash payments, tax incentives, and educational incen-
tives for whites who married Indians. Moreover, offspring of these
mixed marriages were to have the same legal rights and privileges
as offspring of free white people. The "Bill for the encouragement
of intermarriage of whites with Indians," whose preamble follows,
was passed through two readings and was engrossed for final pas-
sage.[8] *But soon after Henry became governor, and, in his absence*
from the House, it was defeated on the third reading.

Whereas, intermarriages between the citizens of this commonwealth and the Indians living in its neighborhood may have
great effect in conciliating the friendship and confidence of the
latter, whereby not only their civilization may in some degree be
finally brought about, but, in the meantime, their hostile inroads
be prevented.

Excerpt from a letter by John Marshall to James Monroe,
December 1784 on Henry's bill: [9]

We have rejected some bills which, in my conception, would
have been advantageous to this country. Among these I rank the
bill for encouraging intermarriages with the Indians. Our prejudices, however, oppose themselves to our interests and operate too
powerfully on them.

(7) Henry writing to his sister, Anne Henry Christian, upon learning of the death of her husband, Colonel William Christian, seeks consolation in his Christian faith.

Colonel Christian had moved his family to Kentucky in August
1785 and was killed while pursuing an Indian raiding party across
the Ohio River. Henry assumed the responsibility of serving as
executor of his estate. After his sister's death a few years later, he
took her young son, Johnny, into his household and provided for
his education. [10]

Richmond, May 15th, 1786

I am at a loss how to address you, my dear sister. Would to God I could say something to give relief to the dearest of women and sisters. My heart has felt in a manner new and strange to me, insomuch that while I am endeavoring to comfort you, I want a comforter myself. I forbear to tell you how great was my love for my friend and brother. I turn my eyes to heaven where he is gone. I trust and adore with humility the unsearchable ways of that Providence which calls us off the stage of action at such time and in such a manner as its wisdom and goodness directs. We cannot see the reason of these dispensations now, but we may be assured they are directed by wisdom and mercy.

This is one of the occasions that calls your and my attention back to the many precious lessons of piety given us by our honored parents, whose lives were indeed a constant lesson and worthy of imitation. This is one of the trying scenes, in which the Christian is eminently superior to all others and finds a refuge that no misfortunes can take away. To this refuge let my dearest sister fly with humble resignation. I think I can see some traces of a kind Providence to you and the children in giving you a good son-in-law, so necessary at this time to take charge of your affairs. It gives me comfort to reflect on this. Pray tell Mr. Bullitt [Alexander Scott Bullitt (1761-1816), Anne Henry Christian's son-in-law] I wish to hear from him and to cultivate an intimacy with him, and that he may command any services from me.

I could wish anything remained in my power to do for you and yours. And if at any time you think there is, pray let me know it and depend on me to do it to the utmost. I need not tell you how much I shall value your letters, particularly now, for I am anxious to hear from you and how everything goes on in your affairs. As so few of the family are left, I hope we shall not fail to correspond frequently. It is natural to me to increase in affection to the survivors as the number decreases.

I am pained on reflecting that my letters always are penned as dictated by the strongest love and affection to you, but that my actions have not kept pace. Opportunities being wanting must be the excuse. For indeed, my dearest sister, you never knew how much I loved you or your husband. My heart is full—perhaps I may never see you in this world. Oh, may we meet in that heaven to which the merits of Jesus will carry those who love and serve him. Heaven will, I trust, give you its choicest comforts and preserve your family. Such is the prayer of him who thinks it his honor and pride to be your affectionate brother.

P. Henry

To Mrs. Anne Christian, Kentucky.

CHAPTER VIII

PATRICK HENRY AT THE VIRGINIA CONVENTION ON THE RATIFICATION OF THE CONSTITUTION OF THE UNITED STATES, RICHMOND, JUNE 1788

"Liberty, the greatest of all earthly blessings. Give us that precious jewel, and you make take everything else."
—Patrick Henry at the Virginia Convention,
June 15, 1788

Patrick Henry did not attend the convention that met in Philadelphia in the summer of 1787 "to render the constitution of the Federal Government adequate to the exigencies of the Union," even though his name had appeared just after Washington's on the Virginia Assembly's list of delegates. "I smelt a rat," has been attributed to Henry by a nineteenth-century Virginia historian to explain his absence. The quote is catchy but cannot be ascribed to Henry by any contemporary source. His principal reason for not attending the gathering in Philadelphia was very likely his tenuous financial situation. During his fourth and fifth terms as governor (1784-1786), according to Spencer Roane [Prologue, Section Three], "he had greatly exceeded his salary and was in debt." Henry settled his family in rural Prince Edward County with hopes of educating his sons at nearby Hampden-Sydney College and improving his financial status by returning to the practice of law (see the introduction to Chapter X).

The Philadelphia Convention, meeting in secret, jettisoned the Articles of Confederation and devised an entirely new constitution. When Virginia's ratification convention met in June 1788 in Richmond, eight of the required nine states had already assented to adoption. "The example of Virginia is a powerful thing," Henry admonished the delegates. Indeed it was. The Old Dominion was, at the time, the largest, most populous, and arguably the richest state in the new nation.

Even with the absence of George Washington (ostensibly remaining aloof but exercising considerable influence for ratification) and Thomas Jefferson (serving as ambassador to France), the Virginia Ratification Convention boasted an impressive collection of statesmen. The participants included Patrick Henry, George Mason, James Madison, Edmund Randolph, John Marshall, James Monroe, John Tyler, Edmund Pendleton, Benjamin Harrison, and Henry ("Light Horse Harry") Lee. James Madison, the "father" of the document being considered, and Edmund Randolph (who initially refused to sign at Philadelphia but later changed his mind) led the forces for ratification, known as the "Federalists." Patrick Henry and George Mason (who had also refused to sign and had not changed his mind) led the opposition, known as the "Anti-federalists."

Henry's oratory at the Virginia Convention deserves extensive study. Only on this occasion and during the British Debts Case (see Chapter X) were Henry's speeches transcribed. The stenographer, a Petersburg lawyer named David Robertson, admitted that he had missed a great deal of their content—and undoubtedly much of their eloquence. But even as imperfectly recorded, Henry's oratory is remarkable reading.

The fifty-two-year-old Henry was at the top of his form. In his attacks against what he regarded as the proposed constitution's too centralized and overbearing system of government, he was by turns cynical, skeptical, and suspicious. But Henry was not the great dissenter only. He spoke for a Bill of Rights, which the framers of the proposed constitution had not considered necessary, and he spoke, as he always had, for liberty: "The necessity of a Bill of Rights appears to me to be greater in this government than ever it was in any government before!" he asserted. "Liberty, the greatest of all earthly blessings," he declared. "Give us that precious jewel, and you may take everything else!"

Henry and his forces lost the ratification vote. Or did they? A Bill of Rights was added to the Constitution in 1791, and, as we *shall see in the following chapter, due in no small part to Henry's efforts. Moreover, Patrick Henry, in his final speech to the Virginia Convention on June 25th, was the first of the Founding Fathers to teach us an important lesson of constitutionalism the hard way—through losing. You make your case, you take a vote, and, if the vote is not in your favor, you seek to make changes in a lawful manner.*

(1) Henry politely warns Washington of his opposition, October 19, 1787. [1]

Henry was undoubtedly sincere in expressing his regrets for having to oppose his former commander in chief, whom he admired more than any other living American. He was perhaps less candid in suggesting the possibility of changing his "present sentiments into a conformity with the opinions of those personages for whom I have the highest reverence."

Dear Sir:

I was honored by the receipt of your favor, together with a copy of the proposed federal constitution, a few days ago, for which I beg you to accept my thanks. They are also due to you from me as a citizen, on account of the great fatigue necessarily attending the arduous business of the late convention.

I have to lament that I cannot bring my mind to accord with the proposed constitution. The concern I feel on this account is really greater than I am able to express. Perhaps mature reflection may furnish me reasons to change my present sentiments into a conformity with the opinions of those personages for whom I have the highest reverence. Be that as it may, I beg you will be persuaded of the unalterable regard and attachment with which I ever shall be, dear sir,

Your obliged and very humble servant,

P. Henry

Excerpt from a letter by Patrick Henry in Richmond to Thomas Madison, his brother-in-law, in Washington County, Southwest Virginia, October 21, 1787:[2]

For such is the warmth of all the members of assembly concerning the new constitution, that no kind of business can be done until that is considered, so far at least as to recommend a convention of the people. Great divisions are likely to happen, and I am afraid for the consequences. I can never agree to the proposed plan without amendments, though many are willing to swallow it in its present form. Pray how are politics your way? The Friends of Liberty will expect support from the back [country] people…

(1) Judge Edmund Winston (who was a delegate) recalls Henry's oratory at the Virginia Convention of 1788 to William Wirt, 1805. [3]

In 1788 the opposition to the new frame of government before the convention devolved on him, almost alone. While he was speaking, there was a perfect stillness throughout the house and in the galleries. There was no inattention or appearance of weariness. When any other member spoke, the members and the audience would in half an hour be going out or moving from their seats…

(3) Wednesday, June 4, 1788.
Patrick Henry's Opening Speech: [4]

Mr. Chairman:

The public mind, as well as my own, is extremely uneasy at the proposed change of government. Give me leave to form one of the number of those who wish to be thoroughly acquainted with the reasons of this perilous and uneasy situation—and why we are brought hither to decide on this great national question. I consider myself as the servant of the people of this commonwealth, as a sentinel over their rights, liberty, and happiness. I represent their feelings when I say that they are exceedingly uneasy, being brought from that state of full security which they enjoyed to the present delusive appearance of things.

A year ago, the minds of our citizens were at perfect repose. Before the meeting of the late federal convention at Philadelphia a general peace and a universal tranquility prevailed in this country. But since that period they are exceedingly uneasy and disquieted. When I wished for an appointment to this convention, my mind was extremely agitated for the situation of public affairs. I conceive the republic to be in extreme danger. If our situation be thus uneasy, whence has arisen this fearful jeopardy? It arises from this fatal system. It arises from a proposal to change our government...

This proposal of altering our federal government is of a most alarming nature. Make the best of this new government. Say it is composed by anything but inspiration. You ought to be extremely cautious, watchful, jealous of your liberty—for instead of securing your rights, you may lose them forever. If a wrong step be now made, the republic may be lost forever. If this new government will not come up to the expectation of the people and they should be disappointed, their liberty will be lost, and tyranny will arise. I repeat it again, and I beg gentlemen to consider—that a wrong step made now will plunge us into misery, and our republic will be lost...

And here I would make this inquiry of those worthy characters who composed a part of the late federal convention. I am sure they were fully impressed with the necessity of forming a great consolidated government instead of a confederation. That this is a consolidated government is demonstrably clear, and the danger of such a government is, to my mind, very striking. I have the highest veneration for those gentlemen. But sir, give me leave to demand what right had they to say *We, the people*? My political curiosity, exclusive of my anxious solicitude for the public welfare, leads me to ask who authorized them to speak the language of *We, the people,* instead of *We, the states*? States are the characteristics and the soul of a confederation. If the states be not the agents of this compact, it must be one great consolidated national government of the people of all the states.

I have the highest respect for those gentlemen who formed the convention, and were some of them not here, I would express some testimonial of my esteem for them—a confidence which was well placed. And I am sure, sir, I would give up anything to them. I would cheerfully confide in them as my representatives. But, sir, on this great occasion I would demand the cause of their conduct—even from that illustrious man [George Washington] who saved us by his valor I would have a reason for his conduct. That liberty which he has given us by his valor tells me to ask this reason, and I am sure, were he here, he would give us that reason. But there are other gentlemen here who can give us this information...

The federal convention ought to have amended the old system. For this purpose they were solely delegated. The object of their mission extended to no other consideration. You must, therefore, forgive the solicitation of one unworthy member to know what danger could have arisen under the present confederation, and what are the causes of this proposal to change our government.

(4) Thursday, June 5, 1788. Henry fears the power of the new government over its citizens. [5]

Here is a revolution as radical as that which separated us from Great Britain. It is as radical, if in this transition our rights and privileges are endangered and the sovereignty of the states be relinquished. And cannot we plainly see that this is actually the case? The rights of conscience, trial by jury, liberty of the press— all your immunities and franchises, all pretensions to human rights and privileges—are rendered insecure, if not lost, by this change, so loudly talked of by some and inconsiderately by others. Is this tame relinquishment of rights worthy of free men? Is it worthy of that manly fortitude that ought to characterize republicans? It is said eight states have adopted this plan. I declare that if twelve states and a half had adopted it, I would with manly firmness, and in spite of an erring world, reject it. You are not to inquire how your trade may be increased, nor how you are to become a great and powerful people, but how your liberties can be secured—for liberty ought to be the direct end of your government...

Is it necessary for your liberty that you should abandon those great rights by the adoption of this system? Is the relinquishment of the trial by jury and the liberty of the press necessary for your liberty? Will the abandonment of your most sacred rights tend to the security of your liberty? Liberty, the greatest of all earthly blessings—give us that precious jewel, and you may take everything else!

But I am fearful I have lived long enough to become an old fashioned fellow. Perhaps an invincible attachment to the dearest rights of man may, in these refined enlightened days, be deemed old fashioned. If so, I am contented to be so. I say the time has been when every pulse of my heart beat for American liberty and which, I believe, had a counterpart in the breast of every true American. But suspicions have gone forth—suspicions of my integrity, publicly reported that my professions are not real. Twenty-three years ago was I supposed a traitor to my country. I was then said to be a bane of sedition because I supported the rights of my country. I may be thought suspicious when I say our privileges and rights are in danger. But, sir, a number of the people of this country are weak enough to think these things are too true. I am happy to find that the honorable gentleman on the other side [Henry "Light Horse Harry" Lee] declares they are groundless.

But, sir, suspicion is a virtue, as long as its object is the preservation of the public good, and as long as it stays within proper bounds. Should it fall on me, I am contented. Conscious rectitude is a powerful consolation. I trust there are many who think my professions for the good to be real. Let your suspicion look to both sides. There are many on the other side who possibly may have been persuaded of the necessity of these measures, which I conceive to be dangerous to your liberty. Guard with jealous attention the public liberty. Suspect everyone who approaches that jewel. Unfortunately, nothing will preserve it but downright force...

When the American spirit was in its youth, the language of America was different. Liberty, sir, was then the primary object. We are descended from a people whose government was founded on liberty. Our glorious forefathers of Great Britain made liberty the foundation of everything. That country is become a great, mighty, and splendid nation—not because their government is strong and energetic, but, sir, because liberty is its direct end and foundation. We drew the spirit of liberty from our British ancestors. By that spirit we have triumphed over every difficulty. But now, sir, the American spirit, assisted by the ropes and chains of consolidation, is about to convert this country into a powerful and mighty empire. If you make the citizens of this country agree to become the subjects of one great consolidated empire of America, your government will not have sufficient energy to keep them together. Such a government is incompatible with the genius of republicanism. There will be no checks, no real balances in this government. What can avail your specious, imaginary balances, your rope-dancing, chain-rattling, ridiculous ideal checks and contrivances?

But, sir, we are not feared by foreigners. We do not make nations tremble. Would this, sir, constitute happiness or secure liberty?... Go to the poor man; ask him what he does. He will inform you that he enjoys the fruits of his labor under his own fig tree, with his wife and children around him in peace and security. Go to every other member of society. You will find the same tranquil ease and content. You will find no alarms or disturbances. Why then tell us of dangers to terrify us into an adoption of this new [form of] government? And yet who knows the dangers that this new system may produce? They are out of the sight of the common people. They cannot foresee latent consequences. I dread the operation of it on the middling and lower class of people. It is for them I fear the adoption of this system...

Besides the expenses of maintaining the senate and the other house in as much splendor as they please, there is to be a great and mighty president with very extensive powers—the powers of a king. He is to be supported in extravagant magnificence, so that the whole of our property may be taken by this American government by laying what taxes they please, giving themselves what salaries they please, and suspending our laws at their pleasure. I might be thought too inquisitive, but I believe I should take up very little of your time in enumerating the little power that is left to the government of Virginia, for this power is reduced to little or nothing. Their garrisons, magazines, arsenals, and forts, which will be situated in the strongest places within the states; their ten miles square, with all the fine ornaments of human life added to their powers and taken from the states, will reduce the power of the latter to nothing. The voice of tradition, I trust, will inform posterity of our struggles for freedom. If our descendants be worthy of the name of Americans, they will preserve and hand down to their latest posterity the transactions of the present times. And though I confess my exclamations are not worthy, they will see that I have done my utmost to preserve their liberty...

This constitution is said to have beautiful features, but when I come to examine these features, sir, they appear to me horribly frightful. Among other deformities, it has an awful squinting. It squints towards monarchy. And does not this raise indignation in the breast of every true American? Your president may easily become a king. Your senate is so imperfectly constructed that your dearest rights may be sacrificed by what may be a small minority—and a very small minority may continue forever unchangeably this government, although horridly defective. Where are your checks in this government? Your strongholds will be in the hands of your enemies. It is on the supposition that your American governors shall be honest that all the good qualities of this government are founded. But its defective and imperfect construction puts it in their power to perpetrate the worst of mischiefs should they be bad men. And, sir, would not all the world, from the eastern to the western hemisphere, blame our distracted folly in resting our rights upon the contingency of our rulers being good or bad. Show me that age and country where the rights and liberties of the people were placed on the sole chance of their rulers being good men without a consequent loss of liberty…

This government has not the affection of the people at present. Should it be oppressive, their affection will be totally estranged from it. And, sir, you know that a government without their affections can neither be durable nor happy. I speak as one poor individual—but when I speak, I speak the language of thousands…

(5) Saturday, June 7, 1788. Henry calls for a Bill of Rights similar to the Virginia Declaration of Rights. [6]

That government is no more than a choice among evils is acknowledged by the most intelligent among mankind and has been a standing maxim for ages. If it be demonstrated that the adoption of the new plan is a little or a trifling evil, then, sir, I acknowledge that adoption ought to follow. But, sir, if this be a truth that its adoption may entail misery on the free people of this country, I then insist that rejection ought to follow. Gentlemen strongly urge its adoption will be a mighty benefit to us. But, sir, I am made of such incredulous materials that assertions and declarations do not satisfy me. I must be convinced, sir. I shall retain my infidelity on that subject till I see our liberties secured in a manner perfectly satisfactory to my understanding.

There are certain maxims by which every wise and enlightened people will regulate their conduct. There are certain political maxims which no free people ought ever to abandon—maxims of which the observance is essential to the security of happiness. It is impiously irritating the avenging hand of heaven, when a people who are in the full enjoyment of freedom launch out into the wide ocean of human affairs and desert those maxims which alone can preserve liberty. Such maxims, humble as they are, are those only which can render a nation safe or formidable. Poor little humble republican maxims have attracted the admiration and engaged the attention of the virtuous and wise in all nations and have stood the shock of ages. We do not now admit the validity of maxims which we once delighted in. We have since adopted maxims of a different but more refined nature—new maxims which tend to the prostration of republicanism.

We have one, sir: *That all men are by nature free and independent, and have certain inherent rights, of which, when they enter into society, they cannot by any compact deprive or divest their posterity.* We have a set of maxims of the same spirit, which must be beloved by every friend of liberty, to virtue, to mankind. Our Bill of Rights [Virginia Declaration of Rights] contains those admirable maxims...

(6) Monday, June 9, 1788. Henry's remarks get under Governor Randolph's skin and result in "a very warm debate"—perhaps even a duel is averted. [7]

I beseech gentlemen to consider whether they can say, when trusting power, that a mere patriotic profession will be equally operative and efficacious as the check of self love. In considering the experience of ages, is it not seen that fair, disinterested patriotism and professed attachment to rectitude have never been solely trusted to by any enlightened free people? If you depend on your president's and senators' patriotism, you are gone. Have you a resting place like the British government? Where is the rock of your salvation? The real rock of political salvation is *self-love*, perpetuated from age to age in every breast and manifested in every action. If they can stand the temptations of human nature, you are safe. If you have a good president, senators, and representatives, there is no danger.

But can this be expected from human nature? Without real checks, it will not suffice that some of them are good. A good president, or senator, or representative will have a natural weakness. Virtue will slumber. The wicked will be continually watching. Consequently you will be undone. Where are your checks? You have no hereditary nobility, an order of men to whom human eyes can be cast up for relief. For, says the constitution, there is no title of nobility to be granted—which, by the bye, would not have been so dangerous as the perilous cession of powers contained in that paper. Because, as Montesquieu says, when you give titles of nobility you know what you give, *but when you give power, you know not what you give…*

I am constrained to make a few remarks on the absurdity of adopting this system and relying on the chance of getting it amended afterwards. When it is confessed to be replete with defects, is it not offering to insult your understandings to attempt to reason you out of the propriety of rejecting it till it be amended? Does it not insult your judgments to tell you: Adopt first and then amend? Is your rage for novelty so great that you are first to sign and seal, and then to retract? Is it possible to conceive a greater solecism? I am at a loss what to say. You agree to bind yourselves hand and foot—for the sake of what? Of being unbound. You go into a dungeon—for what? To get out. Is there no danger when you go in that the bolts of federal authority shall shut you in? Human nature will never part with power…

Henry continued speaking for perhaps ten minutes, then concluded with a summary containing this statement:

But I should be led to take that man to be a lunatic who should tell me to run into the adoption of a government, avowedly defective, in hopes of having it amended afterwards…

Henry Lee of Westmoreland County then spoke for approximately thirty minutes in favor of the Constitution. At the conclusion of Lee's speech, Governor Edmund Randolph, who undoubtedly had taken Henry's previous remarks personally and had been boiling ever since, responded to his perceived assailant. Randolph had refused to sign the Constitution in Philadelphia and now, in Richmond, was one of its most ardent advocates. During the previous debates, Patrick Henry had not let him forget this. Randolph defended himself angrily:

Having consumed heretofore so much of your time, I did not intend to trouble you again so soon. But I now call on this committee, by way of right, to permit me to answer some severe charges against the friends of the new constitution. It is a right I am entitled to and shall have. I have spoken twice in this committee. I have shown the principles which actuated the general convention and attempted to prove that after the ratification of the proposed system by so many states, the preservation of the union depended on its adoption by us.

I find myself attacked in the most illiberal manner by the honorable gentleman [Henry]. I disdain his aspersions and his insinuations. His asperity is warranted by no principle of parliamentary decency nor compatible with the least shadow of friendship. And if our friendship must fall, *let it fall like Lucifer, never to rise again*. Let him remember that it is not to answer him, but to answer this respectable audience, that I now get up. He has accused me of inconsistency in this very respectable assembly. Sir, if I do not stand on the bottom of integrity and pure love for Virginia, as much as those who can be more clamorous, I wish to resign my existence.

Consistency consists in actions and not in empty specious words. Ever since the first entrance into that federal business, I have been invariably governed by an invincible attachment to the happiness of the people of America. Federal measures had been before that time repudiated. The augmentation of congressional powers was dreaded. The imbecility of the confederation was proved and acknowledged. When I had the honor of being deputed to the federal convention to revise the existing system, I was impressed with the necessity of a more energetic government, and thoroughly persuaded that the salvation of the people of America depended on an intimate and firm union. The honorable gentleman there can say that when I went thither, no man was a stronger friend to union than myself. I informed you why I refused to sign.

I understand not him who wishes to give a full scope to licentiousness and dissipation—who would advise me to reject the proposed plan and plunge us into anarchy.

At this point, stenographer Robertson ceased taking down the proceedings word for word, and his record assumed the narrative form:

Here his Excellency read the conclusion of his public letter, wherein he says that, notwithstanding his objections to the Constitution, he would adopt it rather than lose the union and proceeded to prove the consistency of his present opinion with his former conduct. Mr. Henry arose and declared that he had no personal intention of offending anyone—that he did his duty, but that he did not mean to wound the feelings of any gentleman, that he was sorry if he offended the honorable gentleman without intending it, and that every gentleman had a right to maintain his opinion. His Excellency then said that he was relieved by what the honorable gentleman said—that were it not for the concession of the gentleman, he would have made some men's hair stand on end by the disclosure of certain facts.

Mr. Henry then requested that if he had anything to say against him, to disclose it. His Excellency then continued: That as there were some gentlemen there who might not be satisfied by the recantation of the honorable gentleman without being informed, he should give them some information on the subject. His ambition had ever been to promote the Union. He was no more attached to it now than he always had been. And he could in some degree prove it by the paper which he held in his hand, which was his public letter. . . He then read a considerable part of his letter... He then read part of [another] letter which he had written to his constituents on the subject, which was expressive of sentiments amicable to a union with the other states. He then threw down the letter on the clerk's table and declared that it might lie there for *the inspection of the curious and malicious...*

Randolph's "curious and malicious" was, of course, a refer-ence to Henry. His good nature not withstanding, Henry felt that Randolph's remark was a rebuke to his honor. That night, accord-ing to Spencer Roane, Henry and his friend, Colonel William Cabell, called on Governor Randolph (see the Prologue, Section Ten). Fortunately, the code duello *had not as yet become an inflex-ible institution. "Henry acted with great firmness and propriety," Judge Roane later heard Colonel Cabell say, but he "let Mr. Randolph down pretty easily, owing to the extreme benignity of his disposition."*

(7) Thursday, June 12, 1788. Henry prophecies: rich vs. poor in running for elective office, federal emoluments vs. those offered by the states, and federal and state courts—running in parallel lines? [8]

Will the Honorable gentleman say that a poor man, as en-lightened as any man in the island [of Great Britain], has an equal chance with a rich man to be elected? He will stand no chance, though he may have the finest understanding as any man in the shire. It will be so here. Where is the chance that a poor man can come forward with the rich?

The honorable gentleman [Edmund Pendleton] will find that instead of supporting democratic principles, it goes absolutely to destroy them. The state governments, says he, will possess greater advantages than the general government and will constantly pre-vail. His opinion and mine are diametrically opposed. Bring forth the federal allurements and compare them with the poor contempt-ible things that the state legislatures can bring forth. On the part of the state legislatures, there are justices of peace and militia of-ficers—and even these justices and officers are bound by oath in favor of the constitution. A constable is the only man who is not obliged to swear paramount allegiance to this beloved congress. On the other hand, there are rich, fat federal emoluments—your rich, snug, fine, fat federal offices. The number of collectors of taxes and excises will outnumber anything from the states. Who can cope with the excise men and the tax men? There are none in this country that can cope with this class of men alone.

But sir, is this the only danger? Would to heaven that it were. If we are to ask which will last the longest—the state or the general government, you must take an army and a navy into account. Lay these things together and add to the enumeration the superior abilities of those who manage the general government. Can then the state governments look it in the face? You dare not look it in the face now, when it is but in *embryo*...

Then the honorable gentleman said that the two judiciaries and legislatures would go in a parallel line and never interfere— that as long as each was confined to its proper objects, that there would be no danger of interference—that like two parallel lines as long as they continue in their parallel direction, they would never meet. With submission to the honorable gentleman's opinion, I assert that there *is* danger of interference because no line is drawn between the powers of the two governments in many instances. And where there is a line, there is no check to prevent the one from encroaching upon the powers of the other. I therefore contend that they must interfere, and that this interference must subvert the state government as being less powerful. Unless your government has checks, it must inevitably terminate in the destruction of your privileges...

(8) Saturday, June 14, 1788. More suspicions of power, and particularly the power given congress of "arming, organizing, and disciplining the militia": [9]

There are suspicions of power on the one hand and absolute and unlimited confidence on the other. I hope to be one of those who have a large portion of suspicion. I leave it to this house if there be not too small a portion on the other side. By giving up too much to that government, you can easily see which is the worst of two extremes. Too much suspicion may be corrected. If you give too little power today, you may give more tomorrow. But the reverse of the proposition will not hold. If you give too much power today, you cannot retake it tomorrow. For tomorrow will never come for *that* purpose...

As my worthy friend [George Mason] said, there is a positive partition of power between the two governments. To congress is given the power of "arming, organizing, and disciplining the militia, and governing such part of them as may be employed in the service of the United States." To the state legislators is given the power of "appointing the officers and training the militia according to the disciplines prescribed by congress." I observed before that if the power be concurrent as to arm them, it is concurrent in other respects. If the states have the right of arming them and etc. concurrently, congress has a concurrent power of appointing the officers and training the militia. If congress has that power, it is absurd. To admit this mutual concurrence of powers will carry you into endless absurdity—that congress has nothing exclusive on the one hand, nor the states on the other! The rational explanation is that congress shall have exclusive power of arming them and etc., and that the state governments shall have exclusive power of appointing the officers and etc.

Let me put it in another light. May *we* not discipline and arm them as well as congress, if the power be concurrent? So that our militia shall have two sets of arms, double sets of regimentals and etc., and thus, at very great cost, we shall be doubly armed. The great object is that every man be armed. But can the people afford to pay for double sets of arms and etc.? Everyone who is able may have a gun. But have we not learned by experience that necessary as it is to have arms, and though our assembly has by a succession of laws for many years endeavored to have the militia completely armed, it is still far from being the case? When this power is given up to congress without limitation or bounds, how will your militia be armed? You trust to chance. For sure I am that that nation which shall trust its liberties in other hands cannot long exist.

If gentlemen are serious when they suppose a concurrent power, where can be the impolicy to amend it? Or, in other words, to say that congress shall not arm or discipline them till the states have refused or neglected to do it? This is my object. I only wish to bring it to what they themselves say is implied. Implication is to be the foundation of our civil liberties, and when you speak of arming the militia by a concurrence of power, you use implication. But implication will not save you when a strong army of veterans comes upon you. You would be laughed at by the whole world for trusting your safety implicitly to implication.

The argument of my honorable friend [George Mason] was that rulers *might* tyrannize. The answer he received was that they *will not*. In saying that they *would not*, he [James Madison] admitted they *might*. In this great, this essential part of the constitution, if you are safe, it is not from the constitution, but from the virtues of the men in government. If gentlemen are willing to trust themselves and posterity to so slender and improbable a chance, they have greater strength of nerves than I have…

(9) Monday, June 16, 1788. Henry insists on "the most express stipulation." [10]

The necessity of a bill of rights appears to me to be greater in this government than ever it was in any government before. I observed already that the sense of the European nations, and particularly Great Britain, is against the construction of rights being retained which are not *expressly* relinquished. I repeat that all nations have adopted this construction—that all rights not expressly and unequivocally reserved to the people are impliedly and incidentally relinquished to rulers as necessarily inseparable from the delegated powers. It is so in Great Britain—for every possible right which is not reserved to the people by some express provision or compact is within the king's prerogative. It is so in that country which is said to be in such full possession of freedom. It is so in Spain, Germany, and other parts of the world.

Let us consider the sentiments which have been entertained by the people of America on this subject. At the revolution, it must be admitted that it was their sense to put down those great rights which ought in all countries to be held inviolable and sacred. Virginia did so, we all remember. She made a compact to reserve, expressly, certain rights. When fortified with full, adequate, and abundant representation, was she satisfied with that representation? No. She most cautiously and guardedly reserved and secured those invaluable, inestimable rights and privileges which no people, inspired with the least glow of the patriotic love of liberty, ever did, or ever can, abandon. She is called upon now to abandon them and dissolve that compact which secured them to her. She is called upon to accede to another compact which most infallibly supercedes and annihilates her present one. Will she do it? This is the question. If you intend to reserve your unalienable rights, you must have the most express stipulation...

A bill of rights may be summed up in a few words. What do they tell us?—that our rights are reserved. Why not say so? Is it because it will consume too much paper? Gentlemen's reasonings against a bill of rights do not satisfy me...

(10) Thursday, June 19, 1788. Henry on the proposed American impeachment: [11]

The minister [of the British Parliament] who will sacrifice the interest of the nation is subject to parliamentary impeachment. This has been ever found to be effectual. But I beg gentlemen to consider the American impeachment. What is it? It is a mere sham—a mere farce. When they do anything derogatory to the honor or interest of their country, they are to try themselves! Is it so in England? The history of that country shows that they have blocks and gibbets. The violators of the public interest have been tried, justly and impartially, and perished by those necessary instruments of justice. Can there be any security where offenders mutually try one another?...

(11) Tuesday, June 24, 1788. Henry declares he abhors slavery, but plays upon the racial fears of the convention. The day concludes with Henry's "thunderstorm speech."

Henry's detestation of slavery, which he had expressed at some length fifteen years earlier in a letter to Quaker leader Robert Pleasants (see Chapter III, 4), was probably sincere. But Henry, who owned slaves himself, was also a consummate trial lawyer who knew how to play upon the fears of his fellow citizens. "They will search that paper and see if they have power of manumission—and have they not, sir?" he warned realistically and prophetically. Perhaps Henry, the self-made man who, as Spencer Roane observed, had lifted himself from "straitened circumstances" and "was too much attached to property," was speaking on this occasion. It was not the Voice of American Liberty's finest hour.

Excerpts from stenographer David Robertson's record: [12]

Among ten thousand implied powers which they [congress] may assume, they may, if we be engaged in war, liberate every one of your slaves, if they please. And this must and will be done by men, a majority of whom have not a common interest with you. They will therefore have no feeling for your interests. It has been repeatedly said here that the great object of a national government was national defense. That power, which is said to be intended for security and safety, may be rendered detestable and oppressive. If you give power to the general government to provide for the general defense, the means must be commensurate to the end. All the means in the possession of the people must be given to the government, which is entrusted with the public defense.

In this state there are 236,000 blacks, and there are many in several other states. But there are few or none in the northern states, and yet if the northern states shall be of opinion that our numbers are numberless, they may call forth every national resource. May congress not say that every black man must fight? Did we not see a little of this last war? We were not so hard pushed as to make emancipation general. But acts of assembly passed that every slave who would go to the army should be free. Another thing will contribute to bring this event about. Slavery is detested. We feel its fatal effects. We deplore it with all the pity of humanity. Let all these considerations at some future period press with full force on the minds of congress—let that urbanity, which I trust will distinguish America, and the necessity of national defense—let all these things operate on their minds. They will search that paper and see if they have power of manumission. And have they not, sir? Have they not power to provide for the general defense and welfare? May they not pronounce all slaves free, and will they not be warranted by that power? There is no ambiguous implication or logical deduction—the paper speaks to the point. They have the power in clear, unequivocal terms and will clearly and certainly exercise it.

As much as I deplore slavery, I see that prudence forbids its abolition. I deny that the general government ought to set them free, because a decided majority of the states have not the ties of sympathy and fellow feeling for those whose interest would be affected by their emancipation. The majority of the congress is to the north, and the slaves are to the south. In this situation, I see a great deal of the property of the people of Virginia in jeopardy and their peace and tranquility gone away. I repeat it again, that it would rejoice my very soul that every one of my fellow beings was emancipated. As we ought with gratitude to admire that decree of heaven which has numbered us among the free, we ought to lament and deplore the necessity of holding our fellow men in bondage. But is it practicable by any human means to liberate them without producing the most dreadful and ruinous consequences? We ought to possess them in the manner we have inherited them from our ancestors, as their manumission is incompatible with the felicity of the country. But we ought to soften, as much as possible, the rigor of their unhappy fate. I know that in a variety of particular instances, the legislature listening to complaints has admitted their emancipation. Let me not dwell on this subject. I will only add that this, as well as every other property of the people of Virginia, is in jeopardy and put in the hands of those who have no similarity of situation with us...

He [James Madison] tells you of important blessings which he imagines will result to us and mankind in general from the adoption of this system. I see the awful immensity of the dangers with which it is pregnant. I see it—I feel it. I see beings of a higher order, anxious concerning our decision. When I see beyond the horizon that binds human eyes, and look at the final consummation of human things, and see those intelligent beings which inhabit the ethereal mansions reviewing the political decisions and revolutions which in the progress of time will happen in America, and the consequent happiness or misery of mankind—I am led to believe that much of the account on one side or the other will depend on what we now decide. Our own happiness alone is not affected by the event. All nations are interested in the determination. We have it in our power to secure the happiness of one half of the human race. Its adoption may involve the misery of the other hemispheres. (Here a violent storm arose, which put the house in such disorder that Mr. Henry was obliged to conclude.)

Spencer Roane's account of the "thunderstorm speech": [13]

The question of adoption was approaching, and from that cause everyone had an awful and anxious feeling. This was, as it were, the parting speech of Mr. Henry, and he was depicting the awful immensity of the question and its consequences as it respected the present and future generations. He stated that the ethereal beings were awaiting with anxiety the decision of a question which involved the happiness or misery of more than half the human race. He had presented such an awful picture, and in such feeling colors, as to interest the feelings of the audience to the highest pitch. When lo! A storm at that moment arose, which shook the building in which the convention were sitting, and broke it up in confusion. So remarkable a coincidence was never before witnessed, and it seemed as if he had indeed the faculty of calling up spirits from the vasty deep.

Archibald Stuart's account of the "thunderstorm speech" in a letter dated August 25, 1816, to William Wirt: [14]

I was with Mr. Henry in the convention when a storm rose in the middle of his speech. I sat too far from him to hear distinctly, but it was said he seemed to rise on the wings of the tempest to seize upon the artillery of heaven and direct it against his adversaries. Much was said of the effort at the time.

Compare Stuart's concise account to Wirt's highly dramatic telling below with footnote: [15]

Towards the close of the session, an incident occurred of a character so extraordinary as to deserve particular notice. The question of adoption or rejection was now approaching. The decision was still uncertain, and every mind and every heart was filled with anxiety. Mr. Henry partook most deeply of this feeling, and while engaged, as it were, in his last effort, availed himself of the strong sensation which he knew to pervade the house and made an appeal to it which, in point of sublimity, has never been surpassed in any age or country of the world.

After describing, in accents which spoke to the soul and to which every other bosom deeply responded, the awful immensity of the question to the present and future generations and the throbbing apprehensions with which he looked to the issue, he passed from the house and from the earth and looking, as he said, 'beyond the horizon which binds mortal eyes, he pointed, with a countenance and action that made the blood run back upon the aching heart, to those celestial beings who were hovering over the scene and waiting with anxiety for a decision which involved the happiness or misery of more than half the human race. To those beings—with the same thrilling look and action—he had just addressed an invocation that made every nerve shudder with supernatural horror. When lo! a storm at that instant arose which shook the whole building, and the spirits whom he had called seemed to have come at his bidding. Nor did his eloquence, or the storm, immediately cease—but, availing himself of the incident with a master's art, he seemed to mix in the fight of his ethereal auxiliaries and, 'rising on the wings of the tempest, to seize upon the artillery of heaven and direct its fiercest thunders against the heads of his adversaries.' The scene became insupportable, and the house rose without the formality of adjournment, the members rushing from their seats with precipitation and confusion. *

* The words above quoted are those of Judge Archibald Stuart; a gentleman who was present, a member of the convention, and one of those who voted against the side of the question supported by Mr. Henry...

(12) Wednesday, June 25, 1788. Henry shows greatness of character in defeat.

Both sides had been counting votes as the convention progressed. By June twenty-fifth, a comfortable margin in favor of ratification seemed apparent. On this final day of debate, Henry once more reminded the delegates: "The great and direct end of government is liberty. Secure our liberty and privileges, and the end of government is answered." Henry then made his final address to the convention: [16]

I beg pardon of this house for having taken up more time than came to my share, and I thank them for the patience and polite attention with which I have been heard. If I shall be in the minority, I shall have those painful sensations which arise from a conviction of being overpowered in a good cause. Yet I will be a peaceable citizen! My head, my hand, and my heart shall be at liberty to retrieve the loss of liberty and remove the defects of that system—in a constitutional way. I wish not to go to violence, but will wait with hopes that the spirit which predominated in the Revolution is not yet gone, nor the cause of those who are attached to the Revolution yet lost. I shall therefore patiently wait in expectation of seeing that government changed so as to be compatible with the safety, liberty, and happiness of the people.

Shortly after Henry's speech, the Constitution of the United States was ratified by the Virginia Convention: Ayes 89, Noes 79.

CHAPTER IX

THE BATTLE FOR AMENDMENTS, 1788-1791

"I firmly believe the American union depends
on the success of amendments."
—Patrick Henry to Richard Henry Lee,
November 15, 1788

(1) James Madison expresses his concern to George Washington over the fate of the newly-ratified constitution.

Article V of the Constitution of the United States provided two ways for initiating the amendment process: "Congress, whenever two-thirds of both houses shall deem it necessary, shall propose amendments to this constitution, or, on the application of the legislatures of two-thirds of the several states, shall call a convention for proposing amendments..." On June 27, 1788, two days after ratification, the Virginia Convention proposed forty amendments (twenty were structural changes to the new document and twenty were offered as "a declaration or bill of rights"). The same day James Madison wrote to George Washington: [1]

The convention came to a final adjournment today. The enclosed is a copy of their act of ratification with the yeas and nays. A variety of amendments has been since recommended—several of them highly objectionable, but which could not be parried...

Mr. Henry declared previous to the final question that although he should submit as a quiet citizen, he should seize the first moment that offered for shaking off the yoke in a *constitutional* way. I suspect the plan will be to engage two-thirds of the legislatures in the task of undoing the work, or to get a congress appointed in the first instance that will commit suicide on their own authority.

(2) October–November 1788: Henry fights for amendments by proposing a national convention.

On October 20, 1788, the Virginia legislature convened in Richmond. Patrick Henry, its most influential member, declared that he would "oppose every measure" for putting the constitution into motion unless the legislature called for a national convention to consider amendments. Henry charged that under the new document "the most precious rights of the people if not cancelled are rendered insecure." [2]

The first of the resolutions offered by Henry for amending the constitution through a new convention: [3]

That for quieting the minds of the good citizens of this commonwealth and securing their dearest rights and liberties, and preventing those disorders which must arise under a government not founded on the confidence of the people, application be made to the Congress of the United States, as soon as they shall assemble under the said constitution, to call a convention for proposing amendments to the same according to the mode therein directed.

Excerpt from a letter dated November 17, 1788, from George Washington to James Madison: [4]

The accounts from Richmond are indeed very unpropitious to federal measures. The whole proceedings of the assembly *it is said* may be summed up in one word—to wit—that the edicts of Mr. Henry are enregistered with less opposition by the majority of that body than those of the grand monarch are in the parliaments of France. He has only to say let this be law, and it is law.

(3) Henry puts a legislative opponent in his place during the debate for amendments.

This story from the debate in the Virginia legislature came to William Wirt from a correspondent whom he did not identify. Spencer Roane, who was a member of that body in 1788 and 1789 refers to it in his memo to Wirt (Prologue, Section Eight), so there seems to be no doubt that the incident actually took place. It illustrates most vividly Henry's consummate acting talent "in the comic line" and his remarkable ability to blandly demolish an adversary, both of which, it is said, he used sparingly. [5]

It was in the course of the debate, which has just been mentioned, that Mr. Henry was driven from his usual decorum into a retaliation that became a theme of great merriment at the time, and has continued ever since one of the most popular anecdotes that relate to him. He had insisted, it seems, with great force that the speedy adoption of the amendments was the only measure that could secure the great and inalienable rights of the free men of this country—that the people were known to be exceedingly anxious for this measure—that it was the only step that could reconcile them to the new constitution and assure that public contentment, security, and confidence, which were the sole objects of the government and without which no government could stand—that whatever might be the individual sentiments of the gentlemen, yet the wishes of the people, the foundation of all authority, being known, they were bound to conform to those wishes—that, for his own part, he considered his opinion as nothing when opposed to those of his constituents; and that he was ready and willing *at all times and on all occasions "to bow with the utmost deference to the majesty of the people."*

A young gentleman of the federal side of the house [Francis Corbin], who had been a member of the late convention and had in that body received, on one occasion, a slight touch of Mr. Henry's lash, resolved now, in an ill-fated moment, to make a set charge upon the veteran and brave him to the combat. He possessed fancy, a graceful address, and an easy, sprightly elocution, and had been sent by his father (an opulent man, and an officer of high rank and trust under the regal government) to finish his education in the colleges of England and acquire the polish of the Court of St. James, *where he had passed the whole period of the American Revolution.*

Returning with advantages which were rare in this country and with the confidence natural to his years presuming a little too far upon those advantages, he seized upon the words "bow to the majesty of the people," which Mr. Henry had used, and rung the changes upon them with considerable felicity. He denied the solicitude of the people for the amendments so strenuously urged on the other side. He insisted that the people thought their "*great* and *unalienable* rights" sufficiently secured by the constitution which they had adopted—that the preamble of the constitution itself, which was now to be considered as the language of the people, declared its objects to be, among others, the security of those very rights. The people then declared the constitution the guarantee of their rights, while the gentleman, in opposition to this public declaration of their sentiments, insists upon his amendments as furnishing that guarantee. Yet the gentleman tells us that "he bows to the majesty of the people." Those words he accompanied with a most graceful bow.

"The gentleman," he proceeded, "had set himself in opposition to the people throughout the course of this transaction. The people approved of the constitution. The suffrage of their constituents in the last convention had proved it. The people wished—most anxiously wished—the adoption of the constitution as the only means of saving the credit and honor of the country and producing the stability of the union. The gentleman, on the contrary, had placed himself at the head of those who opposed its adoption—*yet the gentleman is ever ready and willing to bow to the majesty of the people* (with another profound and graceful bow). Thus he proceeded through a number of animated sentences, winding up each one with the same words sarcastically repeated and the accompaniment of the same graceful obeisance. Among other things, he said it was of little importance whether a country was ruled by a despot with a tiara on his head or by a demagogue in a red cloak, a caul-bare wig, and etc. (describing Mr. Henry's dress so minutely as to draw every eye upon him) although he *should profess on all occasions to bow to the majesty of the people.*

A gentleman who was present and who, struck with the singularity of the attack, had the curiosity to number the vibrations on those words and the accompanying action, states that he counted thirteen of the most graceful bows he had ever beheld. The friends of Mr. Henry considered such an attack on a man of his years and high character as very little short of sacrilege. And on the other side of the house, there was, indeed, a smothered sort of dubious laugh, in which there seemed to be at least as much apprehension as enjoyment. Mr. Henry had heard the whole of it without any apparent mark of attention.

The young gentleman having finished his philippic, very much at least to his own satisfaction, took his seat with the gayest expression of triumph in his countenance:

"Heu! Nescia mens hominum fati; sortisque futurus! [From Vergil's *Aeneid*: "Alas! The mind of men, ignorant of fate and its future destiny!"]

Mr. Henry raised himself up heavily and with affected awkwardness. "Mr. Speaker," said he, "I am a plain man and have been educated altogether in Virginia. My whole life has been spent among planters and other plain men of similar education, who have never had the advantages of that polish which a court alone can give and which the gentleman over the way has so happily acquired. Indeed, sir, the gentleman's employments and mine (in common with the great mass of his countrymen) have been as widely different as our fortunes. For while that gentleman was availing himself of the opportunity, which a splendid fortune afforded him, of acquiring a foreign education, mixing among the great, attending levees and courts, *basking in the beams of royal favor at St. James,* and exchanging courtesies with crown heads (here he imitated Mr. Corbin's bows at court, making one elegant but most obsequious and sycophantic bow), I was engaged in the arduous toils of the Revolution and was probably as far from thinking of acquiring those polite accomplishments, which the gentleman has so successfully cultivated, as that gentleman *then* was from sharing in the toils and dangers in which his *unpolished countrymen* were engaged. I will not therefore presume to vie with the gentleman in those courtly accomplishments, of which he has just given the house so agreeable a specimen. Yet such a bow as I can make shall ever be at the service of the people."

Herewith, although there was no man who could make a more graceful bow than Mr. Henry, he made one so ludicrously awkward and clownish, as took the house by surprise and put them in a roar of laughter. "The gentleman, I hope, will commiserate the disadvantages of education under which I have labored, and will be pleased to remember that I have never been a favorite with that monarch whose gracious smile he has had the happiness to enjoy." He pursued this contrast of situations and engagements for fifteen or twenty minutes, without a smile and without the smallest token of resentment, either in countenance, expression, or manner. "You would almost have sworn," says a correspondent, "that he thought himself making his apology for his own awkwardness before a full drawing room at St. James."

I believe there was not a person that heard him, the sufferer himself excepted, who did not feel every risible nerve affected. His adversary meantime hung down his head and, sinking lower and lower until he was almost concealed behind the interposing forms, submitted to the discipline as quietly as a Russian malefactor who had been beaten with the knout till all sense of feeling was lost.

(4) Excerpts from a letter by Patrick Henry to Richard Henry Lee, one of Virginia's two initial United States Senators, November 15, 1788

Although he was beginning to withdraw from public life, Henry still had the business of amendments to finish. Henry could have easily been elected by the Virginia legislature as one of the state's initial United States senators. Instead, he saw that Richard Henry Lee and William Grayson, two political allies, were named. "The friends of the system are much displeased that Mr. Madison was left out of the choice," noted Henry to Lee with no little satisfaction. [6]

I postponed answering your favor until I could have the plea-sure of congratulating you on your election to the office of Senator for Virginia in the new congress, which I now do. The friends of the system are much displeased that Mr. Madison was left out of the choice. They urged his election most warmly, claiming as a sort of right the admission of one Federal member.

But in vain—for to no purpose must the efforts of Virginia have been expected to procure amendments, if one of her sena-tors had been found adverse to that scheme. The universal cry is for amendments, and the Federals are obliged to join in it—but whether to amuse or conceal other views seems dubious. You have been too long used to political measures not to see the grounds of this doubt and how little dependence can be placed on such occa-sional conformity. And you know too well the value of the matters in contest to trust their safety to those whose late proceedings, if they do not manifest enmity to public liberty, yet show too little solicitude or zeal for its preservation…

I firmly believe the American union depends on the success of amendments. God grant I may never see the day when it shall be the duty of whiggish Americans to seek for shelter under any other government than that of the United States. The old charges of turbulence and ambition have been plentifully bestowed on me. You have not escaped—but as to us who have so long been accus-tomed to despise these attempts, they will have little effect further than to excite pity…

(5) Henry's resolutions passed in the Virginia legislature on November 20, 1788, but not without rancor on the part of his opponents.

Excerpt from a letter by Tobias Lear, George Washington's secretary, to the governor of New Hampshire, January 31, 1789: [7]

In plain English, he ruled a majority of the assembly. . . And after he had settled everything to his satisfaction, he mounted his horse and rode home, leaving the little business of the state to be done by anybody who chose to give themselves the trouble of attending to it.

During the winter of 1789, "Decius," who is thought to have been Federalist John Nicholas of Albemarle County, published a series of attacks on Henry in Richmond's Virginia Independent Chronicle, *accusing him of being motivated by "ambition, avarice, envy, hatred, and revenge," which were "the secret promoters of all the late noise about liberty."*

Spencer Roane remembered that "[Henry] evinced no feeling on the occasion and far less condescended to parry the effects thereof on the public mind (see the Prologue, Section Two)." Apparently Roane was unaware of Henry's bitter outburst to Senator William Grayson in this letter of March 31, 1789: [8]

What Decius says of me and others say of me the gazettes have told you. I have not seen them except a few numbers (about 5). In these he was not lucky enough to hit upon one charge that is warranted by truth. How lucky it is that he knew me no better, for I know of many deficiencies in my own conduct—that I can easily consider myself an unprofitable servant. But alas! How difficult it is for human pride to submit to that appellation from others! It is not candid to characterize a system of government from the men who will ever form the fag end of human society—from the political understrappers who ever follow the footsteps of power and whine and fawn or snarl a bark as they are bid; who ape their betters and are content with their leavings, as the wages of the dirty work assigned them. Such men are found in most governments and no doubt in the American. But whether their superiors will be more tolerant is yet to learn. That dirty scribblers will be disowned by their own party I doubt not—but that they are encouraged also as little doubt.

The attacks on Henry by "Decius" prompted the staunch Federalist James Innes to write him on March 28, 1799: [9]

...I now find that the papers of Decius are also imputed to me... I take this opportunity to declare that I neither am the author, nor do I know who he is, that I am not directly or indirectly concerned in the publication, nor have I ever approved of it. I will only take the liberty to add that I am with sentiments of very high and respect, dear sir.

Excerpt from a letter by Edmund Randolph to James Madison, March 27, 1789. Patrick Henry's grandson and biographer, William Wirt Henry, pointed out, "As [this letter] was never designed to meet Mr. Henry's eyes, [it] is the more valuable as an estimation of the attack." [10]

Although I am convinced that nothing will soften the rancor of some men, I believe that moderate and conciliatory conduct on the part of our federal rulers will detach from their virulence those who have been opposed from principle. A very injudicious and ill-written publication, which you have seen, under the signature of "Decius," may impede perhaps the salutary effect by keeping in a state of irritation those minds which are well affected to the object of his bitterness. His facts are of a trivial cast, and his assertions are not always correct; and he thus becomes vulnerable in almost every part... Those who deserve well of their country... should not be assailed by an enemy in disguise and have their characters deeply wounded before they can prepare for their defense...

(6) Excerpt from a Letter by Patrick Henry to James Monroe, January 24, 1791

Henry concluded his service in the Virginia legislature with the 1790 session. He declined re-election and never again sat in another deliberative body. In March 1790, Henry wrote from his home in Prince Edward County to James Monroe, who had become a United States senator upon the death of William Grayson. [11]

The form of government into which my countrymen determined to place themselves had my enmity. Yet as we are one and all embarked, it is natural to care for the crazy machine—at least so long as we are out of sight of a port to refit. I have therefore my anxieties to hear and know what is doing and to what point the state pilots are steering, and, to keep up the metaphor, whether there is no appearance of storms on our horizon?

Representative James Madison was successful in adding amendments guaranteeing individual liberties to the Constitution while avoiding structural changes.[12] On September 25, 1789, Congress transmitted to the state legislatures twelve proposed amendments, two of which, having to do with congressional representation and pay, were not adopted. The remaining ten amendments, the Bill of Rights, went into effect on December 15, 1791, when the Virginia Assembly (the Senate following the earlier House vote) ratified them while meeting at the Capitol in Richmond. Virginia was the eleventh, and thus the enabling, state.

CHAPTER X

HENRY RETURNS TO THE COURTROOM, 1790s

"I hope you will hear me with patience,
when you consider that blood is concerned."
—The Reverend Conrad Speece,
quoting Henry as attorney for the defense
in a murder trial during the 1790s

Upon his retirement from the Virginia legislature in 1790, Henry devoted his full attention to his financial situation. His family responsibilities included not only his own large brood of children, but the orphaned children of his sister Anne Christian and those of his eldest daughter Martha Fontaine, who had lost their father. "What a weight of worldly concerns rests upon this old man's shoulders," *Samuel Venable of Prince Edward County wrote in his diary of his fifty-six-year-old neighbor in 1792.* "He supports it with strength and fortitude, but nature must sink under the load ere long..."* [1]

"Your tongue will soon pay your debts," another friend predicted, and Henry's law practice flourished. [2] *Despite continuing bouts of ill health, the prematurely aged orator came to life in a courtroom. Indeed, representation by Henry was so highly valued in the 1790s that clients were often willing to hire a second attorney to undertake the legal research for their cases. Henry's talents as a defense lawyer were in particular demand, and persons facing a capital murder charge were especially motivated to find the wherewithal to obtain his services.*

Spencer Roane's comments on a number of Henry's better-known cases appear in Section Eight of this book's Prologue. Several others for which eyewitness accounts exist follow:

(1) A description of Henry in the circuit court of Prince Edward County during the mid-1790s by Rev. Archibald Alexander (1772-1851)

In 1794 Rev. Alexander was called as pastor of two Presbyterian churches, in Charlotte County and in Prince Edward County, where he first heard Patrick Henry. In 1796 he became president of nearby Hampden-Sydney College. [3]

It was with some difficulty I obtained a seat in front of the bar, where I could have a full view of the speaker, as well as hear him distinctly. But I had to submit to a severe penance in gratifying my curiosity; for the whole day was occupied with the examination of witnesses, in which Mr. Henry was aided by two other lawyers.

In person, Mr. Henry was lean rather than fleshy. He was rather above than below the common height, but had a stoop in the shoulders, which prevented him from appearing as tall as he really was. In his moments of animation, he had the habit of straightening his frame and adding to his apparent stature.

He wore a brown wig, which exhibited no great care in dressing. Over his shoulders he wore a brown camlet [wool] cloak. Under this his clothing was black, something the worse for wear. The expression of his countenance was that of solemnity and deep earnestness. His mind appeared to be always absorbed in what, for the time, occupied his attention. His forehead was high and spacious, and the skin of his face more than usually wrinkled for a man of fifty [Henry was about fifty-eight at this time]. His eyes were small and deeply set in his head, but were of a bright blue color and twinkled much in their sockets. In short, Mr. Henry's appearance had nothing very remarkable as he sat at rest. You might readily have taken him for a common planter who cared very little about his personal appearance. In his manners he was uniformly respectful and courteous.

Candles were brought into the courthouse, and the judges put it to the option of the bar whether they would go on with the argument that night or adjourn until the next day. Paul Carrington, Jr., the attorney for the state, a man of large size and uncommon dignity of person and manner, and also an accomplished lawyer, professed his willingness to proceed immediately, while the testimony was fresh in the minds of all.

Now for the first time I heard Mr. Henry make anything of a speech, and though it was short, it satisfied me on one thing which I had particularly desired to have decided, namely whether like a player he merely assumed the appearance of feeling.

He would be willing to proceed with the trial, but, said he, "My heart is so oppressed with the weight of responsibility which rests upon me, having the lives of three fellow beings depending probably upon the exertions which I may be able to make in their behalf (here he turned to the prisoners behind him), that I do not feel able to proceed tonight. I hope the court will indulge me and postpone the trial till the morning."

The impression made by these few words was such as I assure myself no one can ever conceive by seeing them in print. In the countenance, action, and intonation of the speaker, there was expressed such an intensity of feeling that all my doubts were dispelled. Never again did I question whether Henry felt, or only acted a feeling. Indeed, I experienced an instantaneous sympathy with him in the emotions which he expressed, and I have no doubt the same sympathy was felt by every hearer.

(2) Henry's victory in court over a suspected Tory sympathizer on September 19, 1789, at New London, near Lynchburg

The famous "Beef Case," to which Spencer Roane referred in his memo to William Wirt, is often cited as a prime example of Patrick Henry's courtroom skill "in the comic line."

The "Beef Case" according to Judge Archibald Stuart in a letter to William Wirt, August 24, 1816: [4]

I also witnessed extraordinary efforts from Mr. Henry's forensic eloquence in the trial of a cause in the district court of New London. John Hook had brought a suit against a Mr. Venable, who as a commissary had taken two of his steers to feed the army during the administration of General Thomas Nelson. The act had not been strictly legal. Mr. H. appeared for the defendant. On the trial the cause being one of considerable expectation, the courthouse was crowded.

After Mr. Henry became animated in his cause, he appeared to have complete control over the passions of his audience. At one time he excited their indignation vs. Hook. Vengeance was visible in every countenance. Again, when he chose to relax and ridicule him, the whole audience was in a roar of laughter. The cause was all but decided by acclamation. The jury retired for form's sake and instantly returned with a verdict for the defendant.

Wirt took Archibald Stuart's account, added additional details he had heard over almost a dozen years of research (and very likely a few touches of his own), and produced this version for his Sketches of the Life and Character of Patrick Henry: [5]

The case of John Hook, to which my correspondent [Wirt refers here to Spencer Roane] alludes, is worthy of insertion. Hook was a Scotchman, a man of wealth, and suspected of being unfriendly to the American cause. During the distresses of the American army, consequent on the joint invasion of Cornwallis and Phillips in 1781, a Mr. Venable, an army commissary, had taken two of Hook's steers for the use of the troops. The act had not been strictly legal, and on the establishment of peace, Hook, under the advice of Mr. Cowan, a gentleman of some distinction in the law, thought proper to bring an action of trespass against Mr. Venable in the district court of New London.

Mr. Henry appeared for the defendant and is said to have disported himself in this cause to the infinite enjoyment of his hearers, the unfortunate Hook always excepted. After Mr. Henry became animated in the cause, says my correspondent [here Wirt notes "Judge Stuart"], he appeared to have complete control over the passions of his audience. At one time he excited their indignation against Hook; vengeance was visible in every countenance.

Again, when he chose to relax and ridicule him, the whole audience was in a roar of laughter.

He painted the distresses of the American army, exposed almost naked to the rigor of a winter's sky, and marking the ground over which they marched with the blood of their unshod feet. "Where was the man," he said, "who had an American heart in his bosom, who would not have thrown open his fields, his barns, his cellars, the doors of his house, the portals of his breast, to have received with open arms the meanest soldier in that little band of famished patriots? *There* he stands, but whether the heart of an American beats in his bosom, you, gentlemen, are to judge."

He then carried the jury, by the powers of his imagination, to the plains around Yorktown, the surrender of which had followed shortly after the act complained of. He depicted the surrender in the most glowing and noble colors of his eloquence. The audience saw before their eyes the humiliation and dejection of the British as they marched out of their trenches. They saw the triumph which lighted up every patriot face, and heard the shouts of victory and the cry of "Washington!" and "Liberty!" as it rung and echoed through the American ranks and was reverberated from the hills and shores of the neighboring river.

But hark! What notes of discord are these which disturb the general joy and silence the acclamations of victory? They are the notes of *John Hook*, hoarsely bawling through the American camp, "*beef! beef! beef!* "

The whole audience was convulsed. A particular incident will give a better idea of the effect than any general description. The clerk of court, unable to command himself and unwilling to commit any breach of decorum in his place, rushed out of the courthouse and threw himself on the grass in the most violent paroxysm of laughter—where he was rolling, when Hook, with very different feelings, came out for relief into the yard also.

"Jemmy [James] Steptoe," said he to the clerk, "what the devil ails ye, mon?" Mr. Steptoe was only able to say that he could not help it. "Never mind ye," said Hook, "wait 'til Billy Cowan gets up—he'll show them the law." Mr. Cowan, however, was so completely overwhelmed by the torrent which bore upon his client that when he rose to reply to Mr. Henry, he was scarcely able to make an intelligible or audible remark.

The jury retired for form's sake and instantly returned with a verdict for the defendant. Nor did the effect of Mr. Henry's speech stop here. The people were so highly excited by the Tory audacity of such a suit that Hook began to hear around him a cry more terrible than that of *beef*! It was the cry of *tar and feathers*!—from the application of which, it is said, that nothing saved him but a precipitate flight and the speed of his horse.

(3) Henry's ability during the early 1790s to sway an entire courtroom with a single phrase, as told by Rev. Conrad Speece (1776-1836): [6]

Many years ago, I was at the trial in one of our district courts of a man charged with murder. The case was briefly this: The accused, in execution of his office as constable, had gone to arrest a slave who had been guilty of some misconduct and bring him to justice. Expecting opposition in the business, the constable took several men with him, some of them armed. They found the slave on the plantation of his master, within view of his house, and proceeded to seize and bind him. His mistress, seeing the arrest, came down and remonstrated vehemently against it. Finding her efforts unavailing, she went off to a barn where her husband was, who was presently seen running briskly to the house. It was known he always kept a loaded rifle over his door.

The constable now desired his company to remain where they were, taking care to keep the slave in custody, while he himself would go to the house to prevent mischief. He accordingly ran towards the house. When he arrived within a short distance of it, the master appeared coming out of the door with his rifle in his hand. Some witnesses said that as he came to the door, he drew the cock of the piece and was seen in the act of raising it to the position of firing. But upon these points there was not an entire agreement in the evidence. The constable, standing near a small building in the yard, at this instant fired, and the fire had a fatal effect.

No previous malice was proved against him, and his plea upon trial was that he had taken the life of his assailant in necessary self defense. A great mass of testimony was delivered. This was commented upon with considerable ability by the lawyer for the commonwealth and by another lawyer engaged by the friends of the deceased for the prosecution. The prisoner was also defended in elaborate speeches by two respectable advocates. These proceedings brought the day to a close. The general whisper through a crowded house was that the man was guilty and could not be saved.

About dusk, candles were brought out, and Henry arose. His manner was that which the *British Spy* [a popular book by William Wirt, published in 1803] describes with so much felicity—plain, simple, and entirely unassuming. "Gentlemen of the jury," said he, "I dare say we are all very much fatigued with this tedious trial. The prisoner at the bar has been well defended already, but it is my duty to offer you some further observations in behalf of this unfortunate man. I shall aim at brevity. But should I take up more of your time than you expect, I hope you will hear me with patience, when you consider *that blood is concerned*."

I cannot admit the possibility that anyone who never heard Henry speak should be made fully to conceive the force of expression which he gave to those few words, *"blood is concerned."* I had been on my feet through the day, pushed about in the crowd, and was excessively weary. I was strongly of the opinion too, notwithstanding all the previous defensive pleadings, that the prisoner was guilty of murder, and I felt anxious to know how the matter would terminate. Yet when Henry uttered these words, my feelings underwent an instant change. I found that everything within me answered at once, *"Yes,* since *blood* is concerned, in the name of all that is righteous, go on. We will hear you with patience until the rising of tomorrow's sun."

This bowing of the soul must have been universal, for the profoundest silence reigned, as if our breath had been suspended.

The spell of the magician was upon us, and we stood like statues around him. Under the touch of his genius, every particular of the story assumed a new aspect, and his cause became continually more bright and promising. At length he arrived at the fatal act. "You have been told, gentlemen, that the prisoner was bound by every obligation to avoid the supposed necessity of firing by leaping behind a house near which he stood at that moment. Had he been attacked with a club or with stones, the argument would have been unanswerable, and I should feel myself compelled to give up the defense in despair. But surely I need not tell you, gentlemen, how wide is the difference between sticks or stones and double-triggered, *loaded rifles cocked at your breast.*" The effect of this terrific image, exhibited in this great orator's peerless manner, cannot be described. I dare not attempt to delineate the paroxysm of emotion which it excited in every heart. The result of the whole was that the prisoner was acquitted, with the perfect approbation, I believe, of the numerous assembly who attended the trial.

What was it that gave such transcendent force to the eloquence of Henry? His reasoning powers were good, but they have been equaled by those of many other men. His imagination was exceeding quick and commanded all the stores of nature as materials for illustrating his subject. His voice and delivery were inexpressibly happy. But his most irresistible charm was the vivid feeling of his cause with which he spoke. Such feeling infallibly communicates itself to the breast of the hearer.

(4) The British Debts Case, Richmond, November 1791

Henry's advocacy on behalf of Americans who owed pre-war debts to the British seems to have been prompted by what he regarded as moral considerations rather than self-interest (little, if any, of his own money appears to have been involved). John Marshall, future Chief Justice of the United States Supreme Court, appeared with Henry as co-counsel. On November 14, 1791, the Virginia House of Delegates adjourned to hear the opening argu-

ments. Onlookers crowded the courtroom and spilled out onto the portico of the Capitol where the case was tried.

The favorable outcome Henry obtained for his clients during 1791 and 1793 sessions of the District Court of Richmond was appealed and eventually overturned by the United States Supreme Court in 1796, two years after Henry had retired from the practice of law. He had, however, bought time for his clients and, ultimately, that proved to be enough. Much of the British debt was paid by the United States government or never paid.

The British Debts Case is of particular interest for two reasons: As during the Virginia Convention of 1788, stenographer David Robertson was on hand to take down the proceedings—if imperfectly. In addition, Henry, not usually a detail man in his courtroom preparation, this time shut himself up in his law office to study the case's legal precedents. Even Thomas Jefferson had to admit "he had exerted a degree of industry in that case totally foreign to his character, and not only seemed, but had made himself really learned on the subject." [7]

The orator's opening observations concerning the duty of a Christian were a paraphrase of a sermon by the Reverend Samuel Davies, the Presbyterian evangelist and later president of the college which became Princeton University. Henry's oratorical style is said to have been inspired by Davies whom he had heard in Hanover County perhaps forty years earlier. [8]

I stand here, may it please your honors, to support, according to my power, that side of the question which respects the American debtor. I beg leave to beseech the patience of this honorable court, because the subject is very great and important and because I have not only the greatness of the subject to consider, but those numerous observations which have come from the opposing counsel to answer. Thus, therefore, the matter proper for my discussion is unavoidably accumulated.

Sir, there is a circumstance in this case that is more to be deplored than that which I have just mentioned, and that is this: those animosities, which the injustice of the British nation hath produced and which I had well hoped would never again be the subject of discussion, are necessarily brought forth. The conduct of that nation, which bore so hard upon us in the late contest, becomes once more the subject of investigation. I know, sir, how well it becomes a liberal man and a Christian to forget and forgive. As individuals professing a holy religion, it is our bounden duty to forgive injuries done us as individuals. But when to the character of Christian you add the character of patriot, you are in a different situation.

Our mild and holy system of religion inculcates an admirable maxim of forbearance. If your enemy smite one cheek, turn the other to him. But you must stop there. You cannot apply this to your country. As members of a social community, this maxim does not apply to you. When you consider injuries done to your country, your political duty tells you of vengeance. Forgive as a private man, but never forgive public injuries. Observations of this nature are exceedingly unpleasant, but it is my duty to use them.

Henry then went straight to the heart of his argument:

The first point which I shall wish to establish will be that debts in common wars become subject to forfeiture. And if forfeited in common wars, much more so must they be in a revolutionary war, as the late contest was. In considering this subject, it will be necessary to define what a debt is. I mean by it an engagement, or promise, by one man to pay another for a valuable consideration an adequate price. By a contract thus made for a valuable consideration, there arises what in the law phrase is called a lien on the body and goods of his debtor. This interest, which the creditor becomes entitled to, in the goods and body of his debtor is such as may be taken from the creditor if he be found the subject of a hostile country. This position is supported by the following authorities:

Henry then cited "copius extracts" from the works of such authorities on international law as Hugo Grotius (1583-1645) and Emerich de Vattel (1714-1767), but it was probably his more visceral arguments, such as these, that convinced his listeners of the righteousness of his cause:

What would have been the consequences, sir, if we had been conquered? Were we not fighting against that majesty [the might of the British empire] ? Would the justice of our opposition have been considered? The most horrid forfeitures, confiscations, and attainders would have been pronounced against us. Consider their history from the time of William the First [William the Conqueror] until this day. Were not his Normans gratified with the confiscation of the richest estates in England? Read the excessive cruelties, attainders, and confiscations of that reign. England depopulated, it inhabitants stripped of the dearest privileges of humanity, degraded with the most ignominious badges of bondage, and totally deprived of the power of resistance to usurpation and tyranny.

This inability continued to the time of Henry the Eighth. In his reign, the business of confiscation and attainder made considerable havoc. After his reign, some stop was put to that effusion of blood which preceded and happened under it. Recollect the sad and lamentable effects of the York and Lancastrian wars. Remember the rancorous hatred and inveterate detestations of contending factions—the distinction of the white and red roses. To come a little lower, what happened in that island in the rebellions of 1715 and 1745? If we had been conquered, would not our men have shared the fate of the people of Ireland? A great part of that island was confiscated, though the Irish people thought themselves engaged in a laudable cause. What confiscations and punishments were inflicted in Scotland? The plains of Culloden and the neighboring gibbets would show you. I thank heaven that the spirit of liberty, under the protection of the Almighty, saved us from experiencing so hard a destiny.

But had we been subdued, would not every right have been wrested from us? What right would have been saved? Would debts have been saved? Would it not be absurd to save debts, while they should burn, hang, and destroy?…

Hardin Burnley, who later served as Acting Governor of Virginia, was present at the British War Debts Trial and described the famous Henry "war cant," as pictured in the portrait by Thomas Sully, to William Wirt: [9]

Mr. Henry had taken ample notes of the arguments of his adversaries. The people would give him his own time to examine his notes and select the argument or remark that he meant to make the subject of his comments, observing in these pauses the most profound silence. If the answer which he was about to give was a short one, he would give it without removing his spectacles from his nose—but if he was ever seen to give his spectacles a cant to the top of his wig, *it was a declaration of war*, and his adversaries must stand clear.

In this anecdote from the British Debts Case, William Ronald, an attorney for the other side, was the target of Patrick Henry's "war cant." [10]

Mr. Ronald was a native of Scotland, and at the commencement of the Revolutionary War, at least, had been suspected of being not very warm in the American cause. He had urged the objection to the national competency of Virginia at the time of the passage of those laws of confiscation and forfeiture [by its legislature during the Revolution] on which the defendant relied. In the course of his observations, Ronald had unfortunately used the remark that Virginia was, at the time, nothing more than a *revolted* colony.

When Mr. Henry came to notice this remark, he gave his spectacles the *war cant*: "But another observation," said he, "was made that by the law of nations we had not a right to legislate on the subject of British debts—we were not an independent nation. And I thought," he said, raising himself aloft while his frame dilated itself beyond the ordinary size, "that I heard the word *revolt!*" At this word, he turned upon Mr. Ronald his piercing eye and knit his brows at him, with an expression of indignation and contempt which seemed almost to annihilate him. It was like a stroke of lightning.

Mr. Ronald shrunk from the withering look, and, pale and breathless, cast down his eyes, seeming, says my informant, to be in quest of an auger hole, by which he might drop through the floor and escape forever from mortal sight. Mr. Henry perceived his suffering, and his usual good nature returned to him. He raised his eyes gently towards the court and, shaking his head slowly with an expression of regret, added, "I wish I had not heard it. For although innocently meant (and I am sure that it was so, from the character of the gentleman who mentioned it), yet the sound displeases me—it is unpleasant."

Mr. Ronald breathed again and looked up. His generous adversary dismissed the topic, to resume it no more.

CHAPTER XI

HENRY SETTLES INTO RETIREMENT, DECLINES BOTH FEDERAL AND STATE SERVICE, AND MEDITATES ON GOD AND COUNTRY, LATE 1790S

"The American Revolution was the grand operation which seemed to be assigned by the Deity to the men of this age in our country, over and above the common duties of life."
—Patrick Henry to Governor Henry Lee,
June 27, 1795

Patrick Henry was offered a number of positions in the federal government during the two terms of George Washington's presidency and the presidency of John Adams. He could have been a United States Senator, Chief Justice of the Supreme Court, Secretary of State, and an ambassador to France or Spain. In November 1796 he also declined election by the Virginia Legislature to a sixth term as governor. His polite refusals were based on issues of family, finances, and declining health. These were all valid reasons, and despite overtures from both Federalists and Republicans, Henry had no desire to get himself involved in the factionalism of party politics that had grown even more ugly since his retirement from public life.

(1) Excerpt from a letter from Thomas Jefferson at Monticello to his friend and political ally, Archibald Stuart, in Staunton, April 18, 1795

Jefferson knew that Henry did not approve of his support of the French Revolution. Jefferson had also been told that Henry, upon hearing of his French cooking at Monticello, remarked that he did not approve of gentlemen "abjuring their native victuals"— perhaps the only personal remark against Jefferson by Henry on record. Nevertheless, Jefferson discussed with Stuart the possibility of enlisting Henry in the cause of the Republican Party. Their hoped-for meeting with him, however, never took place. [1]

With respect to the gentleman [Henry] we expected to see there [the Bedford County Court], satisfy him, if you please, that there is no remain of disagreeable sentiment towards him on my part. I was once sincerely affectioned [sic] towards him, and it accords with my philosophy to encourage the tranquillizing passions.

(2) Patrick Henry to Governor Henry Lee, from his home, Red Hill, in Southside Virginia, June 27, 1795

Henry reflects on the Revolution, thanks Governor Lee for reassuring him that there are no hard feelings on President Washington's part toward him, and expresses the hope of spending the rest of his days in privacy. [2]

My Dear Sir:

Your very friendly communication of so much of the President's letter [to Lee] as relates to me demands my sincere thanks. Retired as I am from the busy world, it is still grateful to me to know that some portion of regard remains for me amongst my countrymen, especially those of them whose opinions I most value. But the esteem of that personage who is contemplated in this correspondence is highly flattering indeed.

The American Revolution was the grand operation which seemed to be assigned by the Deity to the men of this age in our country, over and above the common duties of life. I ever prized at a high rate the superior privilege of being one in that chosen age to which Providence entrusted its favorite work. With this impression, it was impossible for me to resist the impulse I felt to contribute my mite toward accomplishing that event which in future will give a superior aspect to the men of these times. To the man especially who led our armies will that aspect belong, and it is not in nature for one with my feelings to revere the Revolution without including him who stood foremost in its establishment.

Every insinuation that taught me to believe I had forfeited the good will of that personage to whom the world had agreed to ascribe the appellation of good and great must needs give me pain—particularly as he had opportunities of knowing my character, both in public and private life. The intimation now given me that there was no ground to believe I had incurred his censure, gives very great pleasure.

Since the adoption of the present constitution, I have generally moved in a narrow circle. But in that I have never omitted to inculcate a strict adherence to the principles of it. And I have the satisfaction to think that in no part of the union have the laws been more pointedly obeyed than in that where I have resided and spent my time. Projects, indeed, of a contrary tendency have been hinted to me, but the treatment of the projectors has been such as to prevent all intercourse with them for a long time. Although a democrat myself, I like not the late democratic societies. As little do I like their suppression by law. Silly things may amuse for a while, but in a little time men will perceive their delusions. The way to preserve in men's minds a value for them is to enact laws against them.

My present views are to spend my days in privacy. If, however, it shall please God during my life so to order the course of events as to render my feeble efforts necessary for the safety of the country in any, even the smallest, degree, that little which I can do shall be done. Whenever you may have an opportunity, I shall be much obliged by your presenting my best respects and duty to the President, assuring him of my gratitude for his favorable sentiments towards me.

Be assured, my dear sir, of the esteem and regard with which I am yours.

Patrick Henry

(3) Patrick Henry to the President of the United States from his home at Long Island in Campbell County, October 16, 1795

In a letter dated October 9, 1795, Washington offered Henry an appointment as Secretary of State to succeed Edmund Randolph. Henry respectfully declined, stating personal reasons rather than political differences. [3]

Honored Sir:

Your favor of the ninth of this month is at this moment brought to me by an express from Richmond. The contents of it make a deep impression on my mind. To disobey the call of my country into service when her venerable chief makes the demand of it must be a crime, unless the most substantial reasons justify declining it. I must trust in your goodness and candor to excuse me for not accepting the appointment you are pleased to offer me.

My domestic situation pleads strongly against a removal to Philadelphia, having no less than eight children by my present marriage, and Mrs. Henry's situation now forbidding her approach to the small pox, which neither herself nor any of our family ever had. To this may be added other considerations arising from loss of crops and consequent derangement of my finances. And what is of decisive weight with me, my own health and strength, I believe, are unequal to the duties of the station you are pleased to offer me. This detail, composed so much of particulars uninteresting to the public, I am emboldened to lay before you from the very friendly and unreserved sentiments you are pleased to express towards me.

Permit me to add that having devoted many years of the prime of my life to the public service and thereby injured my circumstances, I have been obliged to resume my profession and go to the bar, at a time of life too advanced to support the fatigues of it. By this means my health has been injured. When these things are considered, may I hope for your favorable judgement on the motives by which I am actuated?

Believe me, sir, I have bid adieu to the distinction of Federal and Anti-federal ever since the commencement of the present government, and in the circle of my friends have often expressed my fears of disunion amongst the states from collision of interests—but especially from the baneful effects of faction. The most I can say is that if my country is destined in my day to encounter the horrors of anarchy, every power of mind or body which I possess will be exerted in support of the government under which I live, and which has been fairly sanctioned by my countrymen. I should be unworthy the character of a republican or an honest man if I withheld from the government my best and most zealous efforts because in its adoption I opposed it in its unamended form. And I do most cordially execrate the conduct of those men who lose sight of the public interest from personal motives. It is with painful regret that I perceive any occurrences of late have given you uneasiness. Indeed, sir, I did hope and pray that it might be your lot to feel as small a portion of that as the most favored condition of humanity can experience. And if it eventually comes to pass that evil instead of good grows out of the public measures you may adopt, I confide that our country will not so far depart from her character as to judge from the events, but give full credit to the motives and decide from those alone.

Forgive, sir, these effusions, and permit me to add to them one more, which is an ardent wish that the best rewards which are due to a well-spent life may be yours. With the most sincere esteem and high regard I ever am, dear sir, your much obliged and very humble servant.

Patrick Henry

In his August 4, 1805, letter to William Wirt, Thomas Jefferson stated his conviction that Henry was incapable of performing the duties of Secretary of State, an office which he had been the first to hold. [4]

General Washington flattered him by an appointment to a mission to Spain, which however he declined, and by proposing to him the office of Secretary of State on the earnest solicitation of General Henry Lee, who pledged himself that Henry should not accept it. General Washington knew that he was entirely unqualified for it, and moreover that his self esteem had never suffered him to act as second to any man on earth. I had this fact from information, but that of the mission to Spain is of my own knowledge, because, after my retiring from the office of Secretary of State, General Washington passed the papers to Mr. Henry through my hands.

In his Life of Washington*, John Marshall contradicted Jefferson's version of Washington's appointment of Henry as Secretary of State.* [5]

This place was offered to Mr. Henry, a gentleman of eminent talents, great influence, and most commanding eloquence. He had led the opposition to the constitution in Virginia, but after its adoption his hostility had in some measure subsided. He was truly the personal friend of the president, and had lately manifested a temper not inimical to the administration. The chief magistrate was anxious to engage him in the public service, but was aware of the embarrassments which must result from placing in so confidential a station a person whose opinions might lead him to thwart every measure of the executive. It was therefore necessary to come to some explanation with Mr. Henry on this subject, and the letter which invited him into the Department of State, opened the way for this explanation by stating the views and character of the administration.

Marshall then quoted this passage from Washington's October 9, 1795, letter to Henry:

"I persuade myself, sir, it has not escaped your observation that a crisis is approaching that must, if it cannot be arrested, soon decide whether order and confusion ensue. I can most religiously aver I have no wish that is incompatible with the dignity, happiness, and true interest of the people of this country.

"My ardent desire is and my aim has been, as far as depended upon the executive department, to comply strictly with all our engagements, foreign and domestic; but to keep the United States free from political connections with every other country, to see them independent of all and under the influence of none. In a word, I want an *American* character, that the powers of Europe may be convinced we act for *ourselves* and not for others. This in my judgment is the only way to be respected abroad and happy at home; and not by becoming the partisans of Great Britain or France, create dissensions, disturb the public tranquility, and destroy, perhaps forever, the cement which binds the union.

"I am satisfied these sentiments cannot be otherwise than congenial to you. Your aid therefore in carrying them into effect would be flattering and pleasing to [me]."

Marshall then concluded his note with this assertion:

This accurate chart of the road he was invited to travel presented in itself no impediments which to Mr. Henry appeared insurmountable. By private considerations alone was he restrained from proceeding in it.

(4) Henry to his daughter, Elizabeth Aylett, from his home at Red Hill in Charlotte and Campbell counties, August 20, 1796

Henry is disenchanted with the current political situation and is shocked by the attacks on President Washington, whom he greatly admires. He takes consolation in his religion and his retirement. [6]

My Dear Betsey,

Mr. William Aylett's arrival here with your letter gave me the pleasure of hearing of your welfare, and to hear of that is highly gratifying to me, as I so seldom see you… [The rest of this paragraph is devoted to family affairs.]

As to the reports you have heard of my changing sides in politics, I can only say they are not true. I am too old to exchange my former opinions, which have grown up into fixed habits of thinking. True it is I have condemned the conduct of our members in congress because, in refusing to raise money for the purposes of the British treaty [secured by John Jay and ratified by congress the previous year], they would have surrendered our country bound, hand and foot, to the power of the British nation. This must have been the consequences, I think, but the reasons for thinking so are too tedious to trouble you with. But what must I think of those men [Madison and others who supported the ratification of the Constitution] whom I myself warned of the danger of giving the power of making laws by means of treaty to the president and senate, when I see these same men denying the existence of that power which they insisted, in our convention [the Virginia Convention of 1788 on the Ratification of the Constitution], ought properly to be exercised by the president and senate and by none other?

The policy of these men, both then and now, appears to me quite void of wisdom and foresight. These sentiments I did mention in conversation in Richmond and perhaps others, which I don't remember. But sure I am my first principle is, that from the British we have everything to dread when opportunities of oppressing us shall offer. It seems that every word was watched which I casually dropped and wrested to answer party views.

Who can have been so meanly employed, I know not— nor do I care. For I no longer consider myself as an actor on the stage of public life. It is time for me to retire, and I shall never more appear in a public character unless some unlooked-for circumstance shall demand from me a transient effort not inconsistent with private life—in which I am determined to continue.

I see with concern our old commander in chief most abusively treated. Nor are his long and great services remembered as any apology for his mistakes in an office to which he was totally unaccustomed. If he, whose character as our leader during the whole war was above all praise, is so roughly handled in his old age, what may be expected by men of the common standard of character? I ever wished he might keep himself clear of the office he bears and its attendant difficulties, but I am sorry to see the gross abuse which is published of him.

Thus, my dear daughter, have I pestered you with a long letter on politics, which is a subject little interesting to you, except as it may involve my reputation. I have long learned the little value which is to be placed on popularity acquired by any other way than virtue. I have also learned that it is often attained by other means. The view which the rising greatness of our country presents to my eye is greatly tarnished by the general prevalence of deism, which with me is but another name for vice and depravity. I am, however, much consoled by reflecting that the religion of Christ has, from its first appearance in the world, been attacked in vain by all the wits, philosophers, and wise ones, aided by every power of man, and its triumph has been complete. What is there in the wit or wisdom of the present deistical writers or professors that can compare them with Hume, Shaftsbury, Bolingbroke [David Hume (1711-1760), Anthony Ashley Cooper, Earl of Shaftsbury (1621-1683), and Henry St. John, Viscount Bolingbroke (1678-1751); all English authors], and others? And yet these have been confuted and their fame decaying, insomuch that the puny efforts of [Thomas] Paine [*Age of Reason*] are thrown in to prop their tottering fabric, whose foundations cannot stand the test of time.

Amongst other strange things said of me, I hear it is said by the deists that I am one of their number, and indeed that some good people think I am no Christian. This thought gives me much more pain than the appellation of Tory—because I think religion of infinitely higher importance than politics, and I find much cause to reproach myself that I have lived so long and have given no decided proofs of my being a Christian. But indeed, my dear child, this is a character I prize far above all this world has or can boast.

And amongst all the handsome things I hear said of you, what gives me the greatest pleasure is to be told of your piety and steady virtue. Be assured there is not one tittle, as to disposition or character, in which my parental affection for you would suffer a wish for your changing, and it flatters my pride to have you spoken of as you are.

Perhaps Mr. [Spencer] Roane and Anne [Henry Roane, Patrick Henry's daughter] may have heard the reports you mention. If it will be any object with them to see what I write, show them this. But my wish is to pass the rest of my days, as much as may be, unobserved by the critics of the world, who show but little sympathy for the deficiencies to which old age is liable. May God bless you, my dear Betsey, and your children. Give my love to Mr. Aylett and believe me ever

Your affectionate father,
P. Henry

CHAPTER XII

VIRGINIA AND THE UNITED STATES IN CRISIS, 1799; WASHINGTON CALLS ON HENRY, AND HENRY ANSWERS

"It is more than probable that certain leaders meditate a change in government. To effect this, I see no way so practicable as dissolving the confederacy."
—Patrick Henry to Archibald Blair,
January 8, 1799

During the last years of the Adams administration, Virginia was politically divided between the Federalists, whose prominent members were George Washington, John Adams, and Alexander Hamilton, and the emerging Democratic Republicans (generally referred to as the Republican Party), headed by Thomas Jefferson and James Madison. The Federalist-inspired Alien and Sedition acts, passed in Congress in the summer of 1798 during the Adams administration, convinced Republicans that the national government was committed to a policy of repression. A result of this conflict was the Republican-inspired Kentucky Resolutions, masterminded by Jefferson, and the Virginia Resolutions, guided by Madison, which proclaimed the states' right to ignore federal laws which infringed on their sovereignty.

(1) Patrick Henry to Archibald Blair, January 8, 1799

Blair, the clerk of Virginia's Executive Council, had written Henry on December 28, 1798, enclosing a copy of the Virginia Resolutions. These caused much alarm, not only to Henry, but also to ex-President George Washington—as did the Republicans' backing of France against what they perceived were the best inter-

ests of the United States. France had been through its revolution's bloody Reign of Terror five years earlier and was, at the beginning of 1799, under the rule of a corrupt five-man Directory.

Virginian John Marshall, the future Chief Justice of the United States Supreme Court, had during the previous year returned from a mission to France. While there, Marshall, together with fellow diplomats Charles Cotesworth Pinckney of South Carolina and Elbridge Gerry of Massachusetts, spurned an attempt by the French government to extort a bribe from the United States. This incident became known as the "X Y Z Affair" and resulted in the slogan, "Millions for Defense, but Not One Cent for Tribute."

A concerned ex-president Washington persuaded John Marshall to run for Congress from the Richmond district as the Federalist candidate against Republican John Clopton. Marshall received Henry's endorsement and won the election by a small margin.

Although Spencer Roane states that Henry suffered a "gradual decline" during the last two years of his life (see the Prologue, Section Eleven), which made him "querulous" on the subject of politics, his letter to Blair shows no decline of his mental faculties. [1]

Dear Sir:

Your favor of the twenty-eighth of last month I have received. Its contents are a fresh proof that there is cause for lamentation over the present state of things in Virginia. It is possible that most of the individuals who compose the contending factions are sincere and act from honest motives. But it is more than probable that certain leaders meditate a change in government. To effect this, I see no way so practicable as dissolving the confederacy. And I am free to own that, in my judgment, most of the measures lately pursued by the opposition party directly and certainly lead to that end. If this is not the system of the party, they have none and act *ex tempore*.

I do acknowledge that I am not capable to form a correct judgment on the present polities of the world. The wide extent to which the present contentions have gone will scarcely permit any observer to see enough in detail to enable him to form anything like a tolerable judgment on the final result as it may respect the nations in general. But, as to France, I have no doubt in saying that to her it will be calamitous. Her conduct has made it the interest of the great family of mankind to wish the downfall of her present government, because its existence is incompatible with that of all others within its reach. And whilst I see the dangers that threaten ours from her intrigues and her arms, I am not so much alarmed as at the apprehension of her destroying the pillars of all government and of social life—I mean virtue, morality, and religion. This is the armor, my friend, and this alone that renders us invincible. These are the tactics we should study. If we lose these, we are conquered indeed.

Today?

In vain may France show and vaunt her diplomatic skill and brave troops. So long as our manners and principles remain sound, there is no danger. But believing as I do that these are in danger, that infidelity in it broadest sense, under the name of philosophy is fast spreading, and that under the patronage of French manners and principles, everything that ought to be dear to man is covertly but successfully assailed, I feel the value of those men amongst us who hold out to the world the idea that our continent is to exhibit an originality of character. And that instead of that imitation and inferiority which the countries of the old world have been in the habit of exacting from the new, we shall maintain that high ground upon which nature has placed us, and that Europe will alike cease to rule us and give us modes of thinking.

But I must stop short, or else this letter will be all preface. The prefatory remarks, however, I thought proper to make, as they point out the kind of character amongst our countrymen most estimable in my eyes.

General Marshall and his colleagues exhibited the American character as respectable. France, in the period of her most triumphant fortune, beheld them as unappalled. Her threats left them as she found them—mild, temperate, firm. Can it be thought that with these sentiments I should utter anything tending to prejudice General Marshall's election? Very far from it indeed. Independently of the high gratification I felt from his public ministry, he ever stood high in my esteem as a private citizen. His temper and disposition were always pleasant, his talents and integrity unquestioned. These things are sufficient to place that gentleman far above any competitor in the district for congress. But when you add the particular information and insight which he has gained and is able to communicate to our public councils, it is really astonishing that even blindness itself should hesitate in the choice. But it is to be observed that the efforts of France are to loosen the confidence of the people everywhere in the public functionaries and to blacken the characters most eminently distinguished for virtue, talents, and public confidence—thus smoothing the way to conquest, or those claims of superiority as abhorrent to my mind as conquest from whatever quarter they may come.

Tell Marshall I love him, because he felt and acted as a republican—as an American. The story of the Scotch merchants and old Tories voting for him is too stale, childish, and foolish, and is a French *finesse*—an appeal to prejudice, not reason and good sense. If they say in the daytime the sun shines, we must say it is the moon; if again, we ought to eat our victuals. No, say we, unless it is ragout or fricassee. And so on to turn fools in the same proportion as they grow wise. But enough of such nonsense.

As to the particular words stated by you and said to come from me, I do not recollect saying them. But certain I am I never said anything derogatory to General Marshall. But on the contrary, I really should give him my vote for Congress, preferably to any citizen in the state at this juncture—one only excepted—and that one is another line.

I am too old and infirm ever again to undertake public concerns. I live much retired, amidst a multiplicity of blessings from that Gracious Ruler of all things, to whom I owe unceasing acknowledgements for his unmerited goodness to me. And if I was permitted to add to this catalog one other blessing, it would be that my countrymen should learn wisdom and virtue, and in this their day know the things that pertain to their peace.

Farewell. I am, dear sir, yours,

Patrick Henry

(2) George Washington to Patrick Henry from Mount Vernon, January 15, 1799

Henry feared a civil war or a revolution similar to the one that had taken place in France. Washington played upon both Henry's fear of anarchy, which he shared, and Henry's horror of French deism. The Father of His Country importuned his admirer to come forward for election to the Virginia House of Delegates as "a rallying point for the timid and an attraction for the wavering." This was no flattery, for even in retirement and despite the rising Republican tide in Virginia, Henry exerted a remarkable amount of political influence. [2]

Dear Sir:

At the threshold of this letter I ought to make an apology for its contents. But if you will give me credit for my motives, I will contend for no more, however erroneous my sentiments appear to you.

It would be a waste of time to attempt to bring to the view of a person of your observation and discernment the endeavors of a certain party among us to disquiet the public mind with unfounded alarms, to arraign every act of the administration, to set the people at variance with their government, and to embarrass all its measures. Equally useless would it be to predict what must be the inevitable consequences of such a policy, if it cannot be arrested.

Unfortunately—and extremely do I regret it—the State of Virginia has taken the lead in this opposition [Madison's Virginia Resolutions]. I have said the *state*, because the conduct of its legislature in the eyes of the world will authorize the expression, and because it is an incontrovertible fact that the principal leaders of the opposition [Jefferson and Madison] dwell in it, and because no doubt is entertained, I believe, that with the help of the chiefs in the other states, all the plans are arranged and systematically pursued by their followers in other parts of the union—though in no state, except Kentucky [Jefferson's Kentucky Resolutions], that I have heard of, has legislative countenance been obtained beyond Virginia.

It has been said that the great mass of the citizens of this state are well affected, notwithstanding, to the general government and the union, and I am willing to believe it—nay do believe it. But how is this to be reconciled with their suffrages at the elections of representatives, both to congress and their state legislature, who are men opposed to the first, and by the tendency of their measures would destroy the latter? Some among us have endeavored to account for this inconsistency, and though convinced themselves of its truth, they are unable to convince others who are unacquainted with the internal polity of the state.

One of the reasons assigned is that the most respectable and best qualified characters among us will not come forward. Easy and happy in their circumstances at home and believing themselves secure in their liberties and property, they will not forsake them, or their occupations, and engage in the turmoil of public business, or expose themselves to the calumnies of their opponents, whose weapons are detraction.

But at such a crisis as this, when everything dear and valuable to us is assailed—when this party hangs upon the wheels of government as a dead weight, opposing every measure that is calculated for defense and self-preservation, abetting the nefarious views of another nation upon our rights, preferring as long as they dare contend openly against the spirit and resentment of the people the interest of France to the welfare of their own country, justifying the first at the expense of the latter—when every act of their own government is tortured by constructions they will not bear into attempts to infringe and trample upon the Constitution with a view to introduce monarchy.

When the most unceasing and purest exertions were being made to maintain a neutrality which had been proclaimed by the executive, approved unequivocally by Congress, by the state legislatures—nay by the people themselves—in various meetings and to preserve the country in peace, are charged as a measure calculated to favor Great Britain at the expense of France, and all those who had any agency in it are accused of being under the influence of the former and her pensioners; when measures are systematically and pertinaciously pursued which must eventually dissolve the union or produce coercion—I say, when these things have become so obvious, ought characters who are best able to rescue their country from the pending evil to remain at home? Rather, ought they not to come forward, and, by their talents and influence, stand in the breach which such conduct has made on the peace and happiness of this country and oppose the widening of it?

Vain will it be to look for peace and happiness or for the security of liberty and prosperity, if civil discord should ensue. And what else can result from the policy of those among us, who, by all the means in their power, are driving matters to extremity, if they cannot be counteracted effectually? The views of men can only be known, or guessed at, by their words or actions. Can those of the *leaders* of opposition be mistaken then, if judged by this rule? That they are *followed* by numbers who are unacquainted with their designs and suspect as little the tendency of their principles, I am fully persuaded. But, if their conduct is viewed with indifference, if there is activity and misrepresentation on one side and supineness on the other, their numbers accumulated by intriguing and discontented foreigners under proscription who were at war with their own government and the greater part of them with *all* governments, their number will increase, and nothing short of omniscience can foretell the consequences.

I come now, my good sir, to the object of my letter, which is to express a hope and an earnest wish that you would come forward at the ensuing elections (if not for Congress, which you may think would take you too long from home) as a candidate for representative in the General Assembly of this commonwealth.

There are, I have no doubt, very many sensible men who oppose themselves to the torrent that carries away others who had rather swim with, than stem it, without an able pilot to conduct them—but these are neither old in legislation nor well known in the community. Your weight of character and influence in the House of Representatives would be a bulwark against such dangerous sentiments as are delivered there at present. It would be a rallying point for the timid and an attraction of the wavering. In a word, I conceive it to be of immense importance at this crisis that you should be there, and I would fain hope that all minor considerations will be made to yield to the measure.

If I have erroneously supposed that your sentiments on these subjects are in union with mine, or if I have assumed a liberty which the occasion does not warrant, I must conclude, as I began, with praying that my motives may be received as an apology. My fears that the tranquility of the union, and of this state in particular, is hastening to an awful crisis have extorted them from me.

With great and very sincere regard and respect, I am, dear sir,

> Your most obedient and very humble servant,
> George Washington

(3) Henry's last speech at Charlotte County Court House, March 1799

Unable to refuse his former commander in chief, Patrick Henry announced his candidacy for the Virginia Legislature. Although unopposed and much weakened by the illness that would take his life three months later, he traveled to the county seat to speak on court day. Henry's biographer, Henry Mayer, has written: "He went in homage to Washington and to the remembered ideals of the Revolution, and he spoke less as a partisan than as an embodiment of political virtue." The following four versions of Henry's speech are arranged in what the editor regards as their order of credibility. [3]

The speech as recalled by the Reverend Archibald Alexander:

The Reverend Alexander, at the time president of nearby Hampden-Sydney College, dismissed classes and traveled with his students to Charlotte Court House to hear the old orator. [4]

I heard the last speech which Mr. Henry ever made… [Here Alexander refutes details of an account of the speech in the *New Edinburgh Encyclopedia*.] There is more truth in the statements contained in Mr. Wirt's memoir. In point of fact, the performance made little impression beyond the transient pleasure afforded to the friends of the administration and the pain inflicted on the Anti-federalists, [Henry's] former political friends. Mr. Henry came to the place with difficulty, and was plainly destitute of his unwonted vigor and commanding power. The speech was nevertheless a noble effort, such as could have proceeded from none but a noble heart.

William Wirt in his biography appended to his account: "This was the substance *of the speech written down at the time by one of his hearers. 'There was,' says the writer [whose name Wirt did not reveal], 'an emphasis in his language to which, like the force of his articulation and the commanding expression of his eye, no representation* can *do justice; yet I am conscious of having given a correct transcript of his opinions, and, in many instances, his very expression.'"* [5]

He told [the people] that the late proceedings of the Virginia Assembly had filled him with apprehension and alarm. They had planted thorns upon his pillow; they had drawn him from that happy retirement which it had pleased a bountiful Providence to bestow, and in which he had hoped to pass, in quiet, the remainder of his days. He declared that the state had quitted the sphere in which she had been placed by the constitution, and in daring to pronounce upon the validity of federal laws had gone out of her jurisdiction in a manner not warranted by any authority and in the highest degree alarming to every considerate man. Such opposition on the part of Virginia to the acts of the general government must beget their enforcement by military power. This would prob-ably produce civil war—civil war and foreign alliances. And that foreign alliances must necessarily end in subjugation to the pow-ers called in. He conjured the people to pause and consider well before they rushed into such a desperate condition, from which there could be no retreat.

He painted to their imaginations Washington at the head of a numerous and well-appointed army, inflicting upon them military execution. "And where (he asked) are our resources to meet such a conflict? Where is the citizen of America who will dare to lift a hand against the father of his country?" A drunken man in the crowd threw up his arm and exclaimed that he dared do it. "No," answered Mr. Henry, rising aloft in all his majesty, *"you dare not do it. In such a parricidal attempt, the steel would drop from your nerveless arm!"* "The look and gesture at this moment," says a correspondent [again unnamed by Wirt], "gave to these words an energy on my mind unequalled by anything that I have ever wit-nessed."

Mr. Henry, proceeding in his address, asked whether the County of Charlotte would have any authority to dispute an obedi-ence to the laws of Virginia, and he pronounced Virginia to be to the union what the County of Charlotte was to *her*. Having denied the right of a state to decide upon the constitutionality of federal laws, he added that perhaps it might be necessary to say some-thing of the merits of the laws in question [the Alien and Sedition Acts]. His private opinion was that they were "*good* and *proper*." But whatever might be their merits, it belonged to the people, who held the reins over the head of Congress, and to them alone, to say whether they were acceptable or otherwise to Virginians. This must be done by way of petition. Congress was as much our representatives as the assembly and had as good a right to our confidence. He had seen with regret the unlimited power over the purse and sword consigned to the general government, but he had been overruled, and it was now necessary to submit to the consti-tutional exercise of that power.

"If," said he, "I am asked what is to be done when a people feel themselves intolerably oppressed, my answer is ready: *Overturn the government*. But do not, I beseech you, carry matters to this length without provocation. Wait at least until some infringement is made upon your rights which cannot be otherwise addressed. For if ever you recur to another change, you may bid adieu forever to representative government. You can never exchange the present government but for a monarchy. If the administration has gone wrong, let us all go wrong together, rather than split into factions, which must destroy that *union* upon which our existence hangs. Let us preserve our strength for the French, the English, the Germans, or whoever else shall dare invade our territory, and not exhaust it in civil commotions and intestine wars."

He concluded by declaring his design to exert himself in the endeavor to allay the heart burnings and jealousies which had been fomented in the state legislature. And he fervently prayed, if he was deemed worthy to effect it, that it might be reserved to some other and abler hand to extend this blessing over the community.

William Wirt Henry's account of 1891 follows William Wirt's fairly closely, except that he quotes the testimony of Dr. John H. Rice (1777-1831) and Dr. John Miller of South Carolina. Dr. Rice was at the time of Patrick Henry's Charlotte Court House speech a tutor at Hampden-Sydney and later became a founder of Richmond's Union Seminary; Dr. Miller was a student at the college. W. W. Henry also cites "a manuscript found among Mr. Wirt's papers in the handwriting of John Randolph [of Roanoke, who appeared that day as a candidate for Congress]." Of the hated Alien and Sedition Laws, according to Randolph's manuscript (which cannot be located today), the orator declared: [6]

. . . that these laws were too deep for him, they might be right and they might be wrong. But whatever might be their merits or demerits, it belonged to the people who held the reins over the head of Congress, and to them alone, to say whether they were acceptable or otherwise to Virginians; and that this must be done by way of petition.

Patrick Henry's great-grandson, Edward Fontaine, wrote: "I have the narratives of several intelligent men who heard [Patrick Henry's] dying effort. But I prefer giving that of Dr. John Miller of South Carolina as he gave it to me in Pontotoc, Mississippi, in 1838." According to Dr. Miller: [7]

The substance of his speech among other topics contained a severe denunciation of the Alien and Sedition Laws, of the designs of the agrarians and red republicans of France, which had caused their enactment. He uttered a solemn warning against the doctrines and principles of the infidel philosophers of that country, who were at war with the Majesty of Heaven and the welfare of the earth; and which were poisoning the minds and infecting the morals of the most talented youths of Virginia. He vindicated nobly the character of Washington from the charge of treason and toryism…

Henry was elected easily, but as Thomas Jefferson correctly noted, he faced the prospect of being vigorously opposed in the Virginia Legislature. On May 14, 1799, Jefferson wrote to his political ally, Archibald Stuart: [8]

The state elections have generally gone well. Mr. Henry will have the mortification of encountering such a mass of talents as he has never met before. For from everything I can learn, we never had an abler nor a sounder legislature. His apostacy[9] must be unaccountable to those who do not know all the recesses of his heart. The cause of republicanism, triumphing in Europe, can never fail to do so here in the long run.

Jefferson was not, however, accurate in his prediction of republicanism triumphing in Europe. During the following year, 1800, Napoleon Bonaparte, whose armies were causing havoc there and in the Middle East, established himself as First Consul of France. On December 2, 1804, in the Cathedral of Notre Dame, he crowned himself Emperor in the presence of Pope Pius VII, who had come to Paris expecting to do it.

CHAPTER XIII

THE DEATH OF PATRICK HENRY
AT RED HILL, JUNE 6, 1799;
HIS ADVICE TO FUTURE GENERATIONS

"Whether [American independence] will prove a blessing or a curse will depend upon the use our people make of the blessings which a gracious God hath bestowed upon us…"
—From a letter found with Patrick Henry's will after his death at Red Hill on June 6, 1799

(1) George Dabney to William Wirt, May 14, 1806 [1]

He died about the year 1800 [1799] being, I think, in his 64th year. He had a lingering disorder, which gave him great time to prepare for death. I am told that one of his neighbors, going to see him sometime before his death, found him reading the Bible. Holding the book in his hand, he observed, "That book is worth all the books that ever were printed, and it has been my misfortune that I have never found time to read it until lately."

(2) A Henry family narrative of his death as set down by Patrick Henry's great-grandson

Edward Fontaine, the author, undoubtedly heard a first-hand account from his father, Patrick Henry Fontaine, Patrick Henry's oldest grandson, who was present at the orator's death. Although the story was undoubtedly embellished over the years, its essential points are in character with all we know about both Patrick Henry and his physician, Dr. George Cabell. Dr. Cabell was a graduate of the University of Pennsylvania Medical School and was consid-

ered an excellent doctor. His treatment of Henry conformed to the accepted standards of the time. [2]

About the first of June 1799, a letter from [Patrick Henry] to my grandmother in Henry County, Virginia, commencing with the alarming words, "Dear Patsy [Martha Henry Fontaine], I am very unwell and have Dr. Cabell with me," announced to his family living in that part of the state that his end was approaching. My grandmother, father [Patrick Henry Fontaine], mother, and aunt had only time, after two days traveling, to reach Red Hill to see him die.

They found him sitting in a large old fashioned armchair, in which he was easier than upon a bed. Dr. Cabell, a distinguished physician and devoted friend, had come from Lynchburg to attend him. He handed him a small vial of liquid mercury to remove the [intestinal] obstruction… all other remedies having failed to relieve him. [Henry] held the dose and looked at it for a moment and said, "I suppose, doctor, this is your last resort." He replied, "I am sorry to say, Governor, that it is. Acute inflammation of the intestine has already taken place, and unless it is removed, mortification will ensue—if it has not already commenced, which I fear."

"What will be the effect of this medicine?" said the old man. "It will give you immediate relief, or—" the kind-hearted physician could not finish the sentence. But the dying man calmly said, "You mean, doctor, that it will give relief or will prove fatal *immediately*?" The doctor answered: "You can only live a very short time without it, and it may possibly relieve you."

Then [Henry] drew a silk cap, which he usually wore instead of his wig, over his eyes and said, "Excuse me for a few minutes, doctor." And still holding the vial in his hand he bowed his head sitting in his chair and prayed audibly a child-like fervent prayer for a preparation for death and for the welfare of his family and country. He then swallowed the mercury without any emotion.

In the meantime, Dr. Cabell, who was a skeptic, had left the house, and overwhelmed with sorrow, had thrown himself upon the ground underneath one of the trees in the yard, where he wept bitterly. But he soon returned to his patient whom he found sitting, looking at the blood congealing under the nails of his fingers and comforting his wife and family weeping around him. Among other things which he said, after expressing his gratitude for the goodness of God to him all his days: "I feel truly thankful to my Heavenly Father, who after blessing me *all my life is permitting me now to die without any pain.*

His voice was clear and distinct, and his last words were addressed to his friend, Dr. Cabell. He fixed his eyes affectionately upon him and said, "Doctor, I have used many arguments to prove to you the truth of the Christian Religion. *I will now give you my last argument by showing you how a Christian can die.*" In a few moments more he ceased to breathe, and without giving the signal of a parting pang to the peaceful body, his mighty spirit passed away from earth and time.

(3) Excerpt from a letter by Henry's widow, Dorothea Dandridge Henry, to her stepdaughter, Elizabeth Henry Aylett, written after his death: [3]

My loss, my dear Betsey, can never be repaired in this life. But oh that I may be enabled to imitate the virtues of your dear and honored father, and that my latter end may be like his. He met death with firmness and in full confidence that through the merits of a bleeding savior that his sins would be pardoned. Oh, my dear Betsey, what a scene have I been witness to. I wish the great Jefferson and all the heroes of the deistical party could have seen my ever dear and honored husband pay his last debt to nature.

(4) Obituary of the *Virginia Gazette*, June 14, 1799: [4]

Mourn, Virginia, mourn! Your Henry is gone! Ye friends to liberty in every clime, drop a tear.

No more will his social feelings spread delight through his happy house. No more will his edifying example dictate to his numerous offspring the sweetness of virtue and the majesty of his patriotism. No more will his sage advice, guided by zeal for the common happiness, impart light and utility to his caressing neighbors.

No more will he illuminate the public councils with sentiments drawn from the cabinet of his own mind, ever directed to his country's good and clothed in eloquence sublime, delightful, and commanding.

Farewell, first-rate patriot, farewell! As long as our rivers flow or mountains stand—so long will your excellence and worth be the theme of homage and endearment. And Virginia, bearing in mind her loss, will say to rising generations, "Imitate my HENRY!"

(5) Reflections on Patrick Henry by his political contemporaries after his death

Excerpt from a letter from John Marshall to George Washington, June 12, 1799: [5]

Virginia has sustained a very serious loss, which all good men will long lament, in the death of Mr. Henry.

Excerpt from a letter of George Washington to John Marshall, June 16, 1799: [6]

In the death of Mr. Henry… not only Virginia but our country at large has sustained a very serious loss. I sincerely lament his death as a friend, and the loss of his eminent talents as a patriot I consider as peculiarly unfortunate…

Although elected to the General Assembly, Henry died before he could take his seat. According to William Wirt, "A federal member of the house moved the following resolution… All the angry passions of the house immediately arose at such a proposition… It was laid upon the table and has been heard of no more." [7]

The General Assembly of Virginia, as a testimonial of their veneration for the character of their late illustrious fellow-citizen, Patrick Henry, whose unrivalled eloquence and superior talents were, in times of peculiar peril and distress, so uniformly, so powerfully, and so successfully devoted to the cause of freedom, and of his country—and in order to invite the present and future generations to an imitation of his virtues, and an emulation of his fame—

Resolved: That the executive be authorized and requested to procure a marble bust of the said Patrick Henry at the public expense, and to cause the same to be placed in one of the niches of the hall of the House of Delegates.

Thomas Jefferson was elected President of the United States in 1800, the year after the death of Patrick Henry (and also of George Washington), and served for two terms. On August 4, 1805, he wrote to William Wirt: [8]

Mr. Henry's apostasy, sunk him to nothing in the estimation of his country. He lost at once all that influence which federalism had hoped, by cajoling him, to transfer with him to itself, and a man, who through a long and active life, had been the idol of his country, beyond anyone that ever lived, descended to the grave with less than its indifference and verified the saying of the philosopher that no man must be called happy till he is dead.

In his 1884 history of the Tyler family, Lyon G. Tyler wrote, "From the faded MS of Judge Tyler [like Jefferson a Republican] to William Wirt, I decipher the following allusion to Henry… The words in brackets mine; manuscript obliterated where they occur." [9]

The close of his life was clouded in the opinion of many of his friends, supposing he was attached to the aristocratic party. But however he might have been [erred in] his opinions in his aged and infirm state, it was impossible he could be an aristocrat. His [conceptions] were too well fixed. His love [of liberty grew] always tenfold [stronger]. I lament that I could not see him [before he died]. He sent me a message expressing his desire to satisfy me how much he had been misrepresented. "Men might differ in ways and means, and not in principles," said he.

(6) Patrick Henry's messages to his family and to posterity

The penultimate paragraph of Patrick Henry's will, dated November 20, 1798: [10]

This is all the inheritance I can give to my dear family. The religion of Christ can give them one which will make them rich indeed.

With Patrick Henry's will was found a sealed letter, in which was written, "Enclosed are the resolutions of the Virginia Assembly, in 1765, concerning the Stamp Act. Let my executors open this paper." On the back of the paper containing the resolutions was this statement: [11]

The within resolutions passed the House of Burgesses in May 1765. They formed the first opposition to the Stamp Act and the scheme of taxing America by the British Parliament. All the colonies, either through fear or from influence of some kind or other, had remained silent.

I had been for the first time elected a burgess a few days before, was young, inexperienced, unacquainted with the forms of the House and the members that composed it. Finding the men of weight averse to opposition and the commencement of the tax at hand, and that no person was likely to step forth, I determined to venture, and alone, unadvised, and unassisted on a blank leaf of an old law book wrote the within. Upon offering them to the House, violent debates ensued. Many threats were uttered, and much abuse cast on me by the party for submission. After a long and warm contest, the resolutions passed by a very small majority, perhaps of one or two only. The alarm spread throughout America with astonishing quickness, and the ministerial party was over-whelmed. The great point of resistance to British taxation was universally established in the colonies. This brought on the war which finally separated the countries and gave independence to ours.

Whether this will prove a blessing or a curse will depend upon the use our people make of the blessings which a gracious God hath bestowed upon us. If they be wise, they will be great and happy. If they are of a contrary nature, they will be miserable. Righteousness alone can exalt them as a nation. Reader! Whoever thou art, remember this, and in thy sphere practice virtue thyself and encourage it in others.

P. Henry

REMEMBRANCES OF PATRICK HENRY BY TWO FORMER POLITICAL ADVERSARIES

One – Thomas Jefferson to Daniel Webster, 1824

"He was as well suited to the times as any man ever was, and it is not now easy to say what we should have done without Patrick Henry… He was a man of very little knowledge of any sort; he read nothing and had no books…"

Jefferson's view of Henry a quarter century after his death

In December 1824, Daniel Webster (1782-1852), the Massachusetts orator and statesman, accompanied by Professor George Ticknor of Harvard and Mrs. Ticknor, visited Jefferson at Monticello a year and a half before his death. They made a record of their host's remarks, for which Professor Ticknor wrote in his introduction:

> *[These notes] were written down on the very evening on which we left Monticello at a little tavern kept by a Mrs. Clarke, where we stopped for the night early in the afternoon because it was the only tolerable inn within our reach. We had therefore a long winter evening before us, and we got rid of it by making these notes, which are here copied with care, and without a change of any sort from the identical manuscript in which they were originally recorded…*

Although the Webster-Ticknor memorandum covers a number of subjects, it begins with Jefferson's comments relating to Patrick Henry. They reveal that his contradictory feelings about the man who was, as he said, " our leader in the measures of the Revolution in Virginia" had, if anything, intensified after his correspondence with William Wirt for Henry's biography. In the editor's opinion, the reasons for Jefferson's bipolar opinion of Henry are best explained—insofar as it is humanly possible—in essays written by Henry biographer Henry Mayer and Jefferson historian Andrew Burstein. [1]

The Henry section of the Webster-Ticknor memorandum begins with a dozen or so sentences concerning the orator's early life similar to those found in Jefferson's August 5, 1805, letter to William Wirt. It continues as follows: [2]

He was as well suited to the times as any man ever was, and it is not now easy to say what we should have done without Patrick Henry. He was far before all in maintaining the spirit of the Revolution. His influence was most extensive with the members from the upper counties, and his boldness and their votes overawed and controlled the more cool or the more timid aristocratic gentlemen of the lower part of the state. His eloquence was peculiar, if indeed it should be called eloquence, for it was impressive and sublime beyond what can be imagined. Although it was difficult when he had spoken in opposition to my opinion, had produced a great effect, and I myself been highly delighted and moved, I have asked myself when he ceased, "What the d—l has he said?" and could never answer the inquiry. His person was of full size, and his manner and voice free and manly, his utterance neither very fast nor very slow. His speeches generally short, from a quarter to half an hour. His pronunciation was vulgar and vicious, but it was forgotten while he was speaking.

He was a man of very little knowledge of any sort; he read nothing and had no books. Returning one November from Albemarle court, he borrowed of me *Hume's Essays* in two volumes, saying he should have leisure in the winter for reading. In the spring he returned them and declared he had not been able to go further than twenty or thirty pages in the first volume. He wrote almost nothing—he could not write. The [Stamp Act] resolutions which have been ascribed to him, have by many been supposed to have been written by Mr. Johnston, who acted as his second on that occasion. But if they were written by Henry himself, they are not such as to prove any power of composition. Neither in politics nor in his profession was he a man of business; he was a man for debate only. His biographer says that he read Plutarch every year. I doubt whether he ever read a volume of it in his life.

His temper was excellent, and he generally observed decorum in debate. On one or two occasions I have seen him angry and his anger was terrible; those who witnessed it were not disposed to rouse it again. [Jefferson seems to have been the only person to have gone on record as seeing an angry Henry.] In his opinions he was yielding and practicable and not disposed to differ from his friends. In private conversation, he was agreeable and facetious, and, while in genteel society, appeared to understand all the decencies and proprieties of it—but in his heart he preferred low society and sought it as often as possible. He would hunt in the pine woods of Fluvannah with overseers and people of that description, living in a camp for a fortnight at a time without a change of raiment.

I have often been astonished at his command of proper language. How he attained the knowledge of it, I never could find out as he read so little and conversed little with educated men. After all, it must be allowed that he was our leader in the measures of the Revolution in Virginia. In that respect more was due to him than any other person. If we had not had him, we should probably have got on pretty well, as you did, by a number of men of nearly equal talents, but he left us all far behind. His biographer sent the sheets of his work to me as they were printed, and at the end asked for my opinion. I told him it would be a question hereafter, whether his work should be placed on the shelf of history or of panegyric. It is a poor book, written in bad taste, and gives so imperfect an idea of Patrick Henry that it seems intended to show off the writer more than the subject of the work.

Nevertheless, two years later, in 1826, Henry's biographer, William Wirt, was offered the office of President of Mr. Jefferson's University of Virginia. The position was created by the university's board, despite Jefferson's dissenting opinion, as an inducement to Wirt to accept the professorship of law offered with it. Wirt declined both positions. [3]

Two - Edmund Randolph, circa 1810

"For grand impressions in the defense of liberty, the western world has not yet been able to exhibit a rival."

Praise for Patrick Henry in Randolph's *History of Virginia*

Edmund Randolph (1753-1813), a member of one of Virginia's wealthiest and most aristocratic families, was, at twenty-three, the youngest delegate to the Virginia Convention of 1776. He was a member, with Patrick Henry, George Mason, and James Madison, of the committee to draft a declaration of rights and a constitution for the self-declared independent commonwealth, became Virginia's first attorney general, and served in the Continental Congress.

Randolph succeeded Henry as governor of Virginia in 1786 and was in his second one-year term when they clashed at the 1788 Virginia Convention on the Ratification of the United States Constitution. It was then the "very warm debate" occurred, which, it was said, almost led to a duel between the young governor and the aging orator (see Chapter VIII, Section 6). Randolph later served as Attorney General and Secretary of State in the Washington administration.

Edmund Randolph, the only man known to have come close to a physical confrontation with Patrick Henry, had perhaps two decades after the Virginia Convention to reflect on the accomplishments of his one-time political opponent before beginning to write about him in his History of Virginia. *During that interval, whatever resentments Randolph may have had against Henry seem to have changed into admiration, as the passage quoted below from the history bears out (note particularly "His style of oratory was vehement, without transporting him beyond the power of self command or wounding his opponents by deliberate offense."). As the history's twentieth-century editor, Arthur H. Shaffer, observed in his introduction:*

> *Considering Henry's reputation as a firebrand, it seems odd that Randolph should cast him as the prototype of a ruling group celebrated for its decorum, moderation, and learning. But Randolph had grasped an important point; despite Henry's flamboyant behavior and seemingly radical tone, he was an establishment man who played by the rules of the game of Virginia politics... Even his vehement and often sarcastic tone was softened "by a demeanor inoffensive, conciliating, and abounding in good humor." In short, Henry differed from his fellows only in his individual capabilities and personality, not in basic assumptions about the rules of the game and the social order.* [1]

To Patrick Henry the first place is due as being the first who broke the influence of that aristocracy. Little and feeble as it was and incapable of daring to assert any privilege, clashing with the right of the people at large, it was no small exertion in him to surprise them with the fact that a new path was opened to the temple of honor, besides that which led through the favor of the king. He was respectable in his parentage, but the patrimony of his ancestors and of himself was too scanty to feed ostentation or luxury. From education he derived those manners which belonged to the real Virginian planter and which were his ornament, in no less disdaining an abridgement of personal independence than in observing every decorum interwoven with the comfort of society.

Within his years the unbought means of popularity increased. Identified with the people, they clothed him with the confidence of a favorite son. Until his resolutions on the Stamp Act, he had been unknown, except to those with whom he had associated in the hardy sports of the field and the avowed neglect of literature. Still he did not escape notice, as occasionally retiring within himself in silent reflection and sometimes descanting with peculiar emphasis on the martyrs in the cause of liberty. This enthusiasm was nourished by his partiality for the dissenters from the established church. He often listened to them while they were waging their steady and finally effectual war against the burdens of that church, and from a repetition of his sympathy with the history of their sufferings, he unlocked the human heart and transferred into civil discussions many of the bold licenses which prevailed in the religions. If he was not a constant hearer and admirer of that stupendous master of the human passions, [the evangelist] George Whitefield, he was a follower, a devotee of some of his most powerful disciples at least.

All these advantages he employed by a demeanor inoffensive, conciliating, and abounding in good humor. For a short time he practiced the law in an humble sphere, too humble for the real height of his powers. He then took a seat at the bar of the General Court, the supreme tribunal of Virginia, among a constellation of eminent lawyers and scholars and was in great request even on questions for which he had not been prepared by much previous erudition. Upon the theater of legislation he entered, regardless of that criticism which was profusely bestowed on his language, pronunciation, and gesture. Nor was he absolutely exempt from an irregularity in his language, a certain homespun pronunciation, and a degree of awkwardness in the cold commencement of his gesture. But the corresponding looks and emotions of those whom he addressed speedily announced that language may be sometimes peculiar and even quaint, while it is at the same time expressive and appropriate; that a pronunciation which might disgust in a drawing room may yet find access to the hearts of a popular assembly; and that a gesture at first too much the effect of indolence may expand itself in the progress of delivery into forms which would be above the rule and compass but strictly within the prompting of nature…

He transfused into the breast of others the earnestness depicted in his own features, which ever forbade a doubt of sincerity. In others rhetorical artifice and unmeaning expletives have been often employed as scouts to seize the wandering attention of the audience. In him the absence of trick constituted the triumph of nature. His was the only monotony which I ever heard reconcilable with true eloquence. Its chief note was melodious, but the sameness was diversified by a mixture of sensations which a dramatic versatility of action and of countenance produced. His pauses, which for their length might sometimes be feared to dispel the attention, riveted it the more by raising the expectation of renewed brilliancy. In pure reasoning, he encountered many successful competitors. In the wisdom of looks, many superiors. But although he might be inconclusive, he was never frivolous, and arguments which at first seemed strange were afterwards discovered to be select in their kind, because adapted to some peculiarity in his audience.

His style of oratory was vehement, without transporting him beyond the power of self command or wounding his opponents by deliberate offense. After a debate had ceased, he was surrounded by them on the first occasion with pleasantry on some of its incidents. His figures of speech, when borrowed, were often borrowed from the scriptures. The prototypes of others the sublime scenes and objects of nature, and an occurrence at the same instant he never failed to employ with all the energy of which it was capable. His lightning consisted in quick successive flashes, which rested only to alarm the more. His ability as a writer cannot be insisted on, nor was he fond of a length of details. But for grand impressions in the defense of liberty, the western world has not yet been able to exhibit a rival…

APPENDIX A

EDMUND WINSTON'S MEMORANDUM TO WILLIAM WIRT, CA. 1805

Edmund Winston (1745-1818), nine years younger than Patrick Henry, was the son of Henry's maternal uncle, William ("Langloo") Winston. Edmund Winston was not only Patrick Henry's first cousin but a longtime friend, with many close professional, as well as personal, associations. He was an ardent revolutionary patriot, a state legislator, a prosecuting attorney, and Judge of the General Court. Although, like Henry, he was brought up in Hanover County, by 1768 Judge Winston had migrated to the Piedmont frontier. During the Revolution he was established at his estate "Chestnut Hill," two miles south of Lynch's Ferry, which in 1786 was chartered as Lynchburg.

The Winston-Henry family connections eventually became almost too many to count. Edmund Winston's son, George, married Dorothea Spotswood Henry, Patrick Henry's oldest child by his second marriage to Dorothea Dandridge. Judge Winston and Patrick Henry were appointed two of the three executors of the will of Sarah Winston Henry, Patrick Henry's mother. Edmund Winston and his son George were two of three executors of Patrick Henry's will. In this instance, Judge Winston performed his duties so well he married the patriot's widow, Dorothea, in 1801, two years after Henry's death.

Patrick Henry's will (see Appendix D) stated: "But in case my said wife shall marry again, in that case I revoke and make void every gift, legacy, authority, or power herein mentioned; and order, will, and direct she, my wife, shall have no more of my estate than she can recover by law. Nor shall she be guardian to any of my children or executrix of my will." Despite the obvious disregard of this provision, there is no record of any attempt to penalize Dorothea for her remarriage. Edmund Winston died in 1818 at Point of Honor, the Lynchburg home of Dr. George Cabell, Patrick

Henry's physician. His obituary in the Richmond Enquirer *noted that he had served with distinction as Judge of the Circuit Court for many years, and added, "for his public services and private virtues he received the esteem of numerous acquaintances, and his death will be universally regretted."*

Dorothea Dandridge Henry Winston died on February 19, 1831, at the home of a daughter, "Seven Islands," on the Staunton River near Brookneal. She is buried in the family cemetery at Red Hill beside her first husband. Her tombstone bears the inscription: "Dorothea Dandridge, wife of Patrick Henry." [1]

[One – Henry's early life until he received his law license]

Patrick Henry, the second son of John Henry, was born the twenty-ninth of May 1736, in Hanover County at the place ["Studley"] which is now the seat of Judge Peter Lyons. His father was a Scotch gentleman of very considerable literary attainments and had been for some years Surveyor of Hanover County and Colonel of the Militia. After his marriage, he lived on the estate with his wife without engaging in any other business. Mr. Henry's mother was the daughter of Isaac Winston, a reputable planter in the county. She had been married before to a Mr. Syme, who died leaving her a widow with one son. Colonel Henry died in 1770 [actually 1773. The next line in the manuscript is blurred.].

Mr. Henry was never sent to a school. However, he acquired under the direction of his father an imperfect knowledge of the Latin language, and he lived in the family till his marriage, except about a year that he was employed as an assistant in a retail store.

In May 1754, at the age of eighteen, he married the daughter of Mr. John Shelton, a planter living in the neighborhood, and soon after removed to a small farm and other properties given him by his father and father-in-law. Here he was obliged to labor with his own hands to obtain a scanty support for his family.

In the year 1758, he engaged in merchandise, which he continued but a short time, and this adventure nearly ruined him. In the winter of 1760, he obtained a license to practice law, after six weeks reading such books as he could borrow, *without other* assistance. He may be considered to have been at this time a virtuous young man, unconscious of the power of his own mind—in very narrow circumstances, making a last effort to supply the wants of his family.

[Two – Henry from the Parson's Cause to the onset of the Revolution; his early law practice]

He was not distinguished at the bar for nearly four years. It will be recollected the stipends to the ministers of the Church of England were levied on the people in tobacco. The crop of 1758 was so scanty that the price of this article rose to 50 percent [hundred] weight, about thrice the usual rate. The legislature passed an act directing the pay to be made in money at the rate of 16/8 percent [hundred]. The royal assent was not obtained to this act. A minister instituted a suit to recover the difference between this rate and the actual value [the Parson's Cause]. The suit came on to be tried in Hanover County Court in the fall of 1763, and Mr. Henry was the counsel for the defendants.

The question was whether the act had the force of a law before it was assented to by the King. Mr. Henry in his argument insisted on the mutual obligation between the King and his people—that delaying his assent to this act was an instance of misrule and neglect of the interests of the colony, which made it necessary they should provide for their own safety by adhering to the direction of the act. The jury found for the defendants. I believe in this suit he gave the first indication of superior talents. I was not present, but a few days after, Colonel Henry [John Henry, Patrick's father] mentioned it to me in nearly the following words: "Patrick spoke in this cause for near an hour, without hesitation or embarrassment, and in a manner that surprised me, and showed himself well informed on a subject of which I did not think he had any knowledge." Soon afterwards a professor at William and Mary College published some strictures on this proceeding, in which he mentioned Mr. Henry as an obscure attorney.

In 1764 he attended the Committee of Privileges, as counsel in a contested election to the House of Burgesses. Some time after, a member of the House, speaking to me of this occurrence, observed he had for a day or two observed an ill-dressed young man sauntering in the lobby. He seemed to be a stranger to everybody, and he had not the curiosity to inquire his name. But attending when the case of the contested election came on before the committee, he was surprised to find this same person was counsel for one of the parties, and still more so when he delivered an argument superior to anything he had ever heard.

In winter of 1765, Mr. Henry was elected a member [of the House of Burgesses] for Louisa County, to which he had just before removed, and attended the session in the following May. I have been told he took no part in the business of the House till he presented several resolutions expressing in clear terms objections to the Stamp Act. Those resolutions and the speech with which he ushered them into the House are well remembered. I understood from him he communicated the resolutions to only two members before they were offered to the House. These were (I think) John Fleming, member for Cumberland, and George Johnston, for Fairfax.

The members that I recollect as the most distinguished at that period were Mr. [John] Robinson, speaker; Peyton Randolph, attorney general; Landon Carter; Benjamin Harrison; Richard Bland; Edmund Pendleton; Richard Henry Lee. Except the two last named, these were men of very ordinary talents, but derived great influence from their stations, their wealth, and connections.

In 1766, the Treasurer of the Colony died, and Mr. Henry supported the proposition to separate the speaker's chair from the treasury—the offices being till that time united in the same person. He also joined in promoting an inquiry into the conduct of the late treasurer, who was supposed to have misapplied the public money to a great amount.

In 1769 he went to the bar of the General Court. The profits of his practice must have been very moderate, for about this time he thought his property was [illegible] worth not more than 1,400 pounds, adding [illegible]. He entered here into a competition [in the practice of law] with Mr. Pendleton, the Attorney General John Randolph, Mr. Wythe, Mr. Nicholas, Mr. Mercer, and Mr. Jefferson, all of them men of eminence in their profession. It will perhaps be admitted that in reasoning on general principles, he did not lose in a comparison with any man, and I never heard that he betrayed a want of legal knowledge. It will naturally be asked, how is that possible? To which I can only answer that without much labor, he acquired that information which, in the case of other men, is the result of painful research.

[Three - Henry from the onset of the Revolution (1775) through his final service to the State of Virginia (1790)]

He continued a member from Louisa till he was in the year 1770 [actually, 1769] elected from Hanover, and shortly after removed to that county. He represented this county till the year 1775, and was a member of the First and Second Continental Congresses. [Illegible] the latter part of 1775, he was appointed [illegible, possibly "commander of the"] First Virginia Regiment. Retaining this position for a few months, he [illegible] for Hanover County [illegible] to the Declaration of [illegible]. By his conduct in relation to the Stamp Act and in the following year, Mr. Henry had exposed himself to the dislike of men of great influence in this county. He was reproached on account of his poverty, and the fact could not be questioned. It was said to be a great presumption in a young, ignorant, and obscure man to interfere in the deliberations of the legislature on subjects of which he was not competent to judge. For all this, he was consoled by the most unequivocal expressions of the public approbation. Long before the war with England, his character was out of the reach of any attack.

So soon as he believed a war with England inevitable, he labored in congress and in the convention of Virginia to get the country armed and put into as good a condition for defense as circumstances admitted. And perhaps he never exerted his talents more successfully in respect to the public interest [illegible] to his own reputation as a patriot and [illegible] this occasion.

Immediately after the formation of the new government, he was elected governor, [illegible, possibly "and served until"] his *resignation* in the May session of 1779. During his administration, he acted in great harmony with the legislature, this country (Virginia) enjoyed internal tranquility, and did not become the seat of war till after his retirement from office. On his retirement, he moved to Henry County, 200 miles west of Richmond. The next spring, he was annually elected a delegate for the county and continued to serve till he was chosen governor in the fall of 1784. He resigned this in fall 1786 and retired to Prince Edward County. The following spring he was elected a delegate for the county and was annually elected till he declined to serve in 1791.

[Four – Henry's opposition to the U. S. Constitution; his later practice of law; Henry declines Federal appointments]

Mr. Henry was chosen a member to serve in the convention to be held in 1787 to consider and amend the Constitution. He did not however attend the meeting. He had never been in easy circumstance, [illegible] after his removal to Prince Edward County [illegible] happened to express to a neighbor [illegible] some debts, that he was not [illegible]. The reply was to this effect [illegible] your tongue will soon pay your debts [illegible] you will promise to go, I will give you a retainer.

This blunt advice determined him to return to the practice of the law, which he did in the beginning of 1788, and for six years he attended the Prince Edward and New London District Courts. He was occasionally employed to argue causes of consequence, depending [pending] in distant courts. It is, I believe, singular that his clients were obliged to employ other counsel, since he would only argue their cases.

He was chosen from Prince Edward County a member of the Convention [on the Ratification of the United States Constitution] which met in Richmond in June 1788. He was altogether opposed to the plan of government offered for their consideration. He was obliged to support that side of the question almost singly. This he did most ably in a discussion that lasted more than two weeks.

After his retirement from the legislature in 1790, President Washington offered him the embassy to Spain. He was elected Governor of Virginia, a member to serve in the Senate of the United States, and President Adams offered him the embassy to France. All these appointments he declined.

[Five – Henry's library; his eloquence as a speaker]

I have been told in Mr. Henry's family that he employed a considerable part of his time in reading. His library, however (except his law books) seems not to have been very well chosen, and it is, I believe, impossible to point out by what course of study he attained that intellectual excellence he certainly possessed. As a public speaker, his manner was temperate, yet impressive and animated. He presented his subject in a light new and unexpected. His recollection enabled him to avoid repetition, and he had a happy facility of varying his expression, so that the ear was not offended by the frequent recurrence of the same words.

Perhaps the cast of his eloquence will be more easily distinguished by describing the effect of it. In 1788 the opposition to the new frame of government before the convention devolved on him, almost alone. This occasioned him to speak sometimes near three hours. While he was speaking, there was a perfect stillness throughout the house and in the galleries. There was no inattention or appearance of weariness. When any other member spoke, the members and the audience would in half an hour be going out or moving from their seats. In 1792, he argued the case of the debtors to British subjects before the Federal Court. During two days which he occupied on this subject, the Speaker of the Delegates was obliged to adjourn the House, who attended the argument. Before and after, the court had only the usual attendance.

[Six – Family matters; Henry, "a sincere Christian"]

He was uniformly an affectionate husband and parent and a kind master to his servants. He removed four times to places where he was personally a stranger, and always on acquaintance became a favorite neighbor. He was throughout his life negligent of his dress, yet he had the manners of a gentleman. In conversation he was cheerful and not improperly reserved.

I believe he was a sincere Christian after a form of his own, for he was never attached to any religious society [Colonel Meredith's memorandum appears to be more accurate on this subject]. He advocated a bill for incorporating the Episcopal clergy in 1784. He was for a general assessment. He traveled (about 179[4?] on a circuit (Nelson and White, judges) carrying Soame Jennings [Soame Jenyns, *View of the Internal Evidence of the Christian Religion*, London, 1776] [2] of which he gave the judges a copy, desiring them at the same time not to "take him for a traveling monk"—on this [illegible] he condemned the warmth of Colonel James Monroe's expressing [presenting?] the *colors* to the French Directory. One of the judges observed he was growing [illegible] as he was growing old and [illegible].

He lost his first wife in 1775. By her he had six children, of whom only two survived him. In 1777, he married Dorothea, the daughter of Nathaniel West Dandridge of the County of Hanover, who survived him and is now living. By her he had six sons and three daughters, who survived him.

He left no compositions [formal literary productions].

After 1794, when he gave up the practice of law, Mr. Henry passed his remaining days in the bosom of his family. After a *gradual decline* for about two years, he died on the sixth of June 1799, at the age of sixty-three.

APPENDIX B

SAMUEL MEREDITH'S MEMORANDUM TO WILLIAM WIRT, 1805

Samuel Meredith (1732-1808) was four years older than Patrick Henry and lived close to him as a boy growing up in Hanover County. Colonel Meredith married Henry's sister, Jane, the one of eight sisters closest in age to Patrick.

After the death of Patrick and Jane's father, John Henry, in 1773, their mother, Sarah Winston Syme Henry, became a resident in the Meredith household in Hanover County. In 1780, Colonel Meredith acquired a large estate known as Winton in Amherst County, approximately twenty miles north of Lynchburg (it continues today as a country club). Sarah Henry moved there with the Merediths and lived with them until her death in November 1784. Patrick Henry's son, Edward (known as "Neddy") was also living at Winton when he died at age twenty-three in 1794. He is buried in the family cemetery there with his grandmother, his aunt, and Colonel Meredith.

Samuel Meredith was about seventy-three years old when his memoir of Patrick Henry to William Wirt was taken down by Judge William H. Cabell; the narrative therefore is written entirely in the third person. It appears to be most useful in its description of Henry's early life and matters pertaining to his family, although some of the dates are incorrect. The long section toward the end, which Colonel Meredith titled "Hanover Volunteers," dealing with their march on Williamsburg in 1775, does not appear to be accurate in a number of important respects—chiefly, Meredith gives himself far too important a role in the incident. Historians have found other accounts more reliable. [1]

Colonel Meredith's Statement

[One – Henry's early youth]

Patrick Henry was born in Hanover, May 18, 1736 [according to the "old style" calendar—May 29 according to the "new style"]. His father was a Scotchman from Aberdeen of a very liberal and extensive education. He was sent to a common English school until about the age of ten years, where he learned to read and write and acquired some little knowledge of arithmetic. He never went to any other school, public or private, but remained with his father, who was his only tutor. With him he acquired a knowledge of the Latin language and a smattering of the Greek. He became well acquainted with the mathematics of which he was very fond. At the age of fifteen he was well versed in both ancient and modern history. His uncle [Rev. Patrick Henry Sr.] had nothing to do with his education.

Until he arrived to eminence at the bar, there was nothing very remarkable in the person, mind, or manners of Mr. Henry. His disposition was very mild, benevolent, and humane. He was quiet and inclined to be thoughtful, but fond of society. From his earliest days he was an attentive observer of everything of consequence that passed before him. Nothing escaped his attention. He was fond of reading, but indulged much in innocent amusements. He was remarkably fond of his gun. He interested himself much in the happiness of others, particularly of his sisters, of whom he had eight, and whose advocate he always was when any favor or indulgence was to be procured from their mother.

In his youth he seemed regardless of the appearance of his outside dress, but was unusually attentive in having clean linen and stockings. He was not remarkable for an uncouth or genteel appearance (the preceding remarks are particularly applicable to Mr. Henry's youth), and in fact there was nothing in early life for which he was remarkable, except his invariable habit of close and attentive observation. He had a nice ear for music, and when he was about the age of twelve, he had his collarbone broken, and during the confinement learned to play very well on the flute. He was also an excellent performer on the violin, but the whole story of his keeping the bar of a tavern is utterly false. Colonel Meredith was about four years older than P. Henry, and lived within four miles of him from his birth until he (P. H.) left Hanover, and declares that there is no man to whom such an occupation would have been more abhorrent. [See note 4 in the Prologue, Section Three, which seems to contradict this.]

He was in early youth, as in advanced life, plain and easy in his manners, exempt from that bashfulness often so distressing to young persons who have not seen much company.

It is not true that he left his father. On the contrary, he was one of the most dutiful sons that ever lived. Colonel Meredith often heard this observation made by his father.

Although an excellent performer on the violin, he never played but in select companies and for the amusement of particular friends.

[Two – Henry's religious background and influences]

One thing is remarkable in Mr. Henry—and this information comes from his sister, Mrs. Meredith, a very pious woman—that he was never known in his life to utter the name of God, except on a necessary or proper occasion. He was through life a warm friend of the Christian religion. He was an Episcopalian, but very friendly to all other sects, particularly the Presbyterian. His father was an Episcopalian, but his mother a Presbyterian. [Henry is said to have been greatly influenced as a young man in both his religious beliefs and style of oratory by the "New Light" Presbyterian minister Samuel Davies, whom he heard preach in Hanover County.] He was so pleased with Soame Jenyns' *Internal View of the Christian Religion* that, meeting with a copy of it when he was governor, or shortly after, he had several hundred copies printed and distributed at his own expense.[2] Doddridge's *Rise and Progress of Religion* was his favorite author on the subject of religion.[3]

[Three – Family matters; Henry's study and practice of the law]

About the age of fifteen [Henry] became clerk for some merchant in Hanover. He continued in that employment for one year, when his father purchased a parcel of goods for him and his brother William, and they commenced business on their own account. They were jointly interested, but Patrick was the principal manager. They, however, did not continue business longer than one year when it was found necessary to abandon it, as they had injured themselves by granting too extensive credit.

P. H. was then engaged in winding up the business of the concern until he was married, the fall after he was eighteen, to a daughter of Mr. John Shelton, who lived in the forks of Hanover. She was a woman of some fortune and much respectability, by whom he had six children. She died about the year 1770 or 1771 [correct date, 1775]. In April 1776 [correct date, 1777] he was married to a daughter of Mr. Nathaniel Dandridge, now the wife of Judge Edmund Winston, by whom he had nine children—living at, or some short time before, his death.

P. H. lived in Hanover until about the year 1764 or 1765, when he removed to Louisa, which county he represented when he made the famous stand against the Stamp Act. He returned to Hanover in 1767 or 1768 where he purchased Scotchtown, a noted place, the former seat of Colonel Chiswell, where he remained until he was elected governor. On his resignation as governor, he removed to Leatherwood, in Henry County, where he had purchased a large body of land. He remained there several years, then gave the most of his land there to his children by his first wife, retaining the balance. [During his two additional terms as governor (1784-1786), he lived in or near Richmond.] He then removed to Prince Edward, where he continued for six or seven years and then moved to Long Island in Campbell County, where he continued three or four years, and then moved to Booker's Ferry on the Staunton River, where he lived until his death, except that he occasionally moved from Booker's Ferry, or Red Hill (the name of his seat) to Long Island during the sickly months.

His furniture was all of the plainest sort, consisting of necessaries only—nothing for show or ornament. He regarded as nothing the trouble of moving, and would change his dwelling with as little concern as a common man would change a coat of which he was tired. He was uncommonly hospitable. His attentions were not confined to the rich, the great, or wise, but he was familiar with every man of good character.

On his first marriage, he received from his father-in-law a tract of land and fourteen or fifteen Negroes, and also a tract of land and four or five Negroes from his father. He then commenced law, about eighteen months before the trial in Hanover Court of the famous cause commonly called the Parson's Cause. [Actually Henry received his license about three and one-half years before the Parson's Cause.]

He did not read law under the direction of any person. It was not even made known to any of his friends until he consulted his friend John Lewis as to his fitness to commence the practice, who encouraged him to apply for a license, in which application he was successful.

He began the practice in Hanover and Louisa, but got little or no business and made no figure until the above-mentioned trial in Hanover. It should have been observed that he was not more than six or eight months [others say six *weeks*] engaged in the study of the law, during which time he secluded himself from the world, availing himself of the use of a few law books owned by his father.

On the day of the trial in Hanover, [Patrick Henry] appeared as a volunteer on the side of the people in opposition to the clergy, of whom at least twenty attended. Among them was the uncle of P. H. [Patrick Henry Sr., one of the "parsons" on whose behalf the suit was brought] who rode to the courthouse in his carriage. As soon as he alighted, he was met by P. H., who accosted him most respectfully and requested him not to appear in the courthouse on that day.

"Why?" said the gentleman. "Because I am engaged in opposition to the clergy, and your appearance there might strike me with such awe as to prevent me from doing justice to my cause."

"Rather than that effect should be produced, Patrick," said his uncle, "I will not only absent myself from the courthouse but return home." And accordingly, he got into his carriage and drove off. Patrick Henry [Jr.] delighted and astonished the audience and the court. His father was then sitting as the judge of the court and shed tears [of pride at the demonstration of his son's forensic abilities] most profusely. The issue of the trial is well known. The people were so delighted that they carried him about the yard on their shoulders. Here began his fame and his popularity. From this time his rise was rapid. He went to the bar of the General Court around '67 or '68 [1769], as well as Colonel Meredith recollects. Colonel Meredith was present at the trial in Hanover and heard the conversation that passed between Patrick Henry and his uncle.

Colonel John Henry, the father of Patrick Henry, had one other son named William, and seven [actually eight] daughters. William received an estate from his father in Fluvanna County, near the mouth of the Hardware River, where he died, leaving only one child, which died a short time after.

About the year 1764 or 1765, Colonel John Henry's fortune, having been much reduced from a want of good management and knowledge of plantation affairs, he engaged in the business of keeping a school and took charge of ten or twelve boys, whom he taught for about twelve months, when he was assisted by a Scotchman whose name was Walker. He then took about twenty scholars, and continued for four or five years to teach that number, when he died.

[Four – See the note in the final paragraph of the introduction concerning the reliability of this section.]

Hanover Volunteers

Patrick Henry knew nothing of the first meeting or first movements of the Hanover Volunteers. Colonel Meredith was the captain of this company and their meeting (for the purpose of going to Williamsburg) was occasioned by a letter written to him as the captain of this company by Robert Carter Nicholas, Chairman of the Common Hall of the City of Williamsburg. Colonel Meredith has been unable to find this letter. He is positive, however, of its contents. It informed him of the then-governor [Lord Dunmore] having seized and taken away the arms, ammunition, etc., at Williamsburg, that the people of that city apprehended very violent measures from Dunmore and requested that he, Captain Meredith, with his company would go down for their protection.

Samuel Meredith immediately dispatched expresses [express riders] to different parts of the county, and in less than two days they assembled to the number of one hundred and sixty odd at New Castle (you are not to understand this as the first formation of the company, for they had been constituted some time before). As S. M. was on his way to New Castle, he fell in with the present Judge Peter Lyons, Mr. [blank] Griffin, Richard Adams, and some others who had taken a station with a view of meeting him (S. M.) as he supposes. They all, and particularly Mr. Lyons, seemed very uneasy at the movements of the Hanover Volunteers, fearing that they contemplated some rash or violent measure.

Mr. Lyons solicited to know of S. M. the precise object of the Hanover Volunteers, but S. M. declined making any communication. On S. M. refusing to make known the object of the Hanover Volunteers, he went on to New Castle, the place of rendezvous, and Mr. Lyons and his party went to Colonel Syme's [John Syme, Patrick Henry's older half- brother], who then lived where Nathaniel Syme now lives near or adjoining New Castle. They prevailed on Colonel Syme to dispatch a messenger with a letter from Syme to Patrick Henry, who was then actually on his way between Hanover Court House and Littlepage Bridge to the first [actually, Second Continental] Congress, requesting him to return and use his influence with his brother-in-law, S. M., and the Hanover Volunteers to find out their real objects.

P. H. returned on the same day to Colonel Syme's who was with the Volunteers in the fields in the lower end of the town and sent for S. M. He asked him to walk in the garden, showed him the letter he had received from Colonel Syme, and asked him if he had confidence enough in him to acquaint him with the views of the Volunteers. S. M. without hesitation told him the contents of the letter from Nicholas and that the Volunteers intended to go to Williamsburg for the purpose of protecting the inhabitants of that city against any acts of violence that might be offered by Dunmore—that they intended to compel a restitution of, or a compensation for, the arms, ammunition, etc., taken away by Dunmore—that for this purpose they intended to seize on as much of the money of the Crown in the hands of the Receiver General— or even if that effort should fail, to seize even the person of the Governor and detain him without offering any violence until he should restore the arms, etc., or pay their fair value. (It is to be re-membered that the letter from Mr. Nicholas to S. M. was silent as to restitution or compensation for the arms, etc., but only prayed protection from the violence of Dunmore.) The idea of recovering the arms, etc., or their value by seizing the money of the Crown or the person of the Governor originated with the Volunteers, after their meeting at New Castle and before the conversation with P. Henry. As soon as these objects were made known to P. H., he expressed the most hearty approbation of them. S. M. then asked him if he had any objection to making known to the officers of the Volunteers that the plans received his approbation. He replied that he had none. S. M. then carried up the officers and several respectable gentlemen of the company to whom P. H. made the same communications he had made to Colonel Meredith. They then pressed him to make known his approbation to the company in the form of an address to which he consented, on condition that it should be done so privately as that none but the company should hear it.

When he [Henry] retired for the purpose of preparing to go and address the company, it was proposed by S. Meredith that every effort should be made to induce P. H. to take the command of the company—that they stood in need of his wisdom to direct them, and his eloquence and his reputation to protect them in case their schemes should fail or be disapproved. This proposition met with universal approbation. It was accordingly agreed that as soon as P. H. should finish his address, Colonel Meredith should resign in his favor, that they should drown all his objections by their cries of approbation and that he should be forcibly invested with the *hunting shirt* and the uniform of the times—S. M. to remain second in command.

The plan was carried into effect, for as soon as he had finished his address (and an elegant one it was), Colonel Meredith resigned the command. Captain Edmund Winston and others clothed Patrick Henry in the hunting shirt. He was an entire stranger to the plan until the moment of its execution and resisted their importunities as long as he could, urging the necessity of his presence in Congress. But at length, finding all resistance vain, he yielded to their entreaties and declared that he would not refuse to execute plans which had been sanctioned by his advice.

Afterwards on the same day it was determined to send a party to King and Queen County to take the person of Colonel Corbin, the Receiver General, in order to ensure payment from the money of the Crown for the military stores taken by Dunmore. But strict orders were given to do no injury to his person. This party was to meet the main body at Armistead's Tavern in New Kent [County]. They went to Colonel Corbin's, but he was from home. On the same day that Patrick Henry was elected to the command, the company marched on Park's Spring, from thence, the next day, to New Kent Court House, where they were met by Mr. Norton, a son-in-law of Robert C. Nicholas, sent up by him to know the extent of the objects of the volunteers, which by this time had been variously conjectured and related, for the people in Williamsburg particularly had become alarmed at the great force which was collecting from various parts. The example of the Hanover Volunteers, headed by a man of Patrick Henry's reputation and a member of Congress had excited a similar spirit in the adjoining counties.

Norton was prevented by P. H. from returning, and all persons traveling towards Williamsburg were arrested in their progress. The next day they proceeded to Doncastle's. That night another messenger arrived from Mr. Nicholas, as the Chairman of the Common Council of the City of Williamsburg, with the information that Dunmore had gone on board the man of war, that the people of Williamsburg were relieved of their apprehensions, and praying the Volunteers might proceed no further. The next day the men were enrolled and consisted of 1,500. Patrick Henry, in answer to Mr. Nicholas, sent him a letter by Holt Richardson (with whom Norton was permitted to return), detailing to him the objects of the Volunteers and requesting a valuation of the military stores, etc. Richardson returned with the valuation, amounting to about 360 pounds sterling, and in his company, or very shortly after him, came Mr. Carter Braxton, who was the son-in-law of Colonel Corbin and had been made acquainted with the objects of the Volunteers, and sent him to make satisfaction for the military stores according to their valuation, and tendered bills drawn by Corbin on Hanberry of London, which were refused by Patrick Henry, although Braxton offered to indorse them. Braxton was much mortified, and expressed his surprise that he should be refused as endorser for so small a sum as 360 pounds sterling. P. H. acted in such a manner as to convince Mr. Braxton that he refused him as endorser because he was suspicious, not of his ability, but of his political attachments. He certainly treated him with great coolness and reserve, for he was writing at the time Mr. Braxton first entered the room, and Samuel Meredith, who was present during the whole interview, is not certain that Mr. H. rose from his chair. P. H. told Mr. Braxton that Dunmore had already gone on board the man of war and was ready to protect and carry off any person or persons friendly to his views, that Corbin, his father-in-law, was agent of the Crown, and he, Carter Braxton, was the agent of Corbin giving him thus clearly to understand that he was with Dunmore. Thus the main object of the Volunteers compensation for the arms, etc., would be defeated.

Colonel Meredith is positive that the cool treatment Braxton received from P. H. arose altogether from the suspicions entertained of Braxton by P. H., and that his suspicions had been excited by no other cause than the near connection existing between Braxton and Colonel Corbin, who was agent of the Crown. Therefore he (Corbin) was suspected by Mr. H. Mr. Braxton had not then given the evidence which his subsequent conduct afforded of the attachment to the cause of the Revolution. P. H. in a private conversation with Samuel Meredith after Braxton retired did not hesitate to declare to him the reason of his conduct towards Braxton and the nature and cause of his suspicions. He informed Mr. Braxton before he retired that he would take as endorser any responsible character of known attachment to the Revolutionary cause. On Carter Braxton mentioning Colonel [Thomas] Nelson [Sr.], P. H. said he would receive him very willingly. Some time after, Colonel Nelson arrived at Doncastle's. Mr. B. was with him, but whether Mr. Braxton had gone to Williamsburg for him, or met him on the way, or whether Mr. [Colonel?] Nelson found Mr. Braxton at Doncastle's is not certain in the recollection of Samuel Meredith. As soon as Patrick Henry heard of the arrival of Colonel Nelson, he ran out of the house, bareheaded, and received him with the utmost warmth of friendship. The bills were endorsed by Colonel Nelson, received by P. H., and the troops, except the Hanover Volunteers, dismissed.

Colonel Meredith is convinced by the subsequent conduct of Carter Braxton that Mr. Henry's suspicions of him were not well founded. But as P. H. did entertain them, there is nothing in his conduct towards Carter Braxton that ought to surprise any friend of the Revolution. There is nothing in it that ought to injure Patrick Henry. It arose from no personal ill will toward Carter Braxton but from an ardent desire to carry into effect the object of the Volunteers to avoid what might defeat it.

The halt at Duncastle's was produced by the letter by R. C. Nicholas to Mr. Henry above stated and not by the aversion of Mr. Henry to military operations. The Hanover Volunteers returned with Mr. Henry to Hanover. He then proceeded to Congress where he negotiated the bills received in Duncastle's, laid out the amount in arms, etc., which he forwarded to Virginia to the Committee of Safety.

There is a space here in the manuscript. The following paragraphs may have been added as an afterthought.

[Five – Henry's resignation from the military; his "management of children"]

P. H. in a communication to Colonel Meredith stated his motive for resigning his commission as colonel. He conceived himself neglected by younger officers having been put above him and preferred to him, particularly in the affair of the Great Bridge, where he wished to have command [see Chapter V (2)], but Colonel [William] Woodford received that appointment. He disliked being kept in and about Williamsburg and not appointed to some more important post or expedition. He was thus induced to think he was neglected by those who had the power of appointment [a "Committee of Safety" presided over by Henry's nemesis, Edmund Pendleton]. He therefore resigned.

In the management of children Mr. Henry seemed to think the most important thing is in the first place to give them good constitutions. They were six or seven years old before they were permitted to wear shoes, and thirteen or fourteen before they were confined to books or received any kind of literary instruction. In the meantime they were as wild as young colts and permitted to run quite at large. He seemed to think that nature ought to be permitted to give and show its own impulse and that then it is our duty to pursue it. His children were on the most familiar footing with him, and he treated them as companions and friends.— End

MEMORANDUMS TO WILLIAM WIRT OF GEORGE DABNEY, CHARLES DABNEY, WILLIAM O. WINSTON, AND NATHANIEL POPE, JR.

In the preface to his Sketches of the Life and Character of Patrick Henry, *William Wirt wrote:*

There were [at the time Wirt began his biography] living in the county of Hanover, three gentlemen of the first respectability, who had been the companions of Mr. Henry's childhood and youth [They were also Henry's cousins]; these were, Colonel Charles Dabney, Captain George Dabney, and Colonel William O. Winston; the first two of whom are still living. Not having the pleasure of a personal acquaintance with these gentlemen, the author interested the late Mr. Nathaniel Pope in his object and, by his instrumentality, procured all the useful information which was in their possession.

Nathaniel Pope was most energetic in obtaining information for Wirt from 1805 up until 1809, when Pope "fell a victim to that savage practice, which, under the false name of honour, continued to prevail too long." Much of the material Pope collected for Wirt repeats what Wirt learned from the far more detailed and generally more accurate memoranda sent him by Spencer Roane, Edmund Winston and Samuel Meredith. The memoir of George Dabney [1740-1824], however, contains several items of interest not found in any of the others.[1]

George Dabney's Memorandum to William Wirt

[One – Henry from his youth to the Revolution]

The late Patrick Henry was born in Hanover about the year 1737 [1736]. His father, John Henry, was a Scotchman. The business of his coming to America I do not know. He married the widow of John Syme, mother of the present Colonel John Syme. He was a man of a liberal education, and to support a large family he kept a grammar school at his own house, in which his son Patrick took the rudiments of his education. He quitted school at about sixteen years of age and entered into a business of merchandise with his brother William, which was dissolved the first year.

He married the daughter of John Shelton, a near neighbor, and settled on a piece of land of his father-in-law's. For about two years he had a very difficult and a [illegible] life. He was a careless, wild, youth, but free from the vices attending such a life.

He then sold off part of his property and again entered into merchandise, but not succeeding in that [illegible], he determined to study law. Applying to the late Judge Pendleton, he procured the loan of some law books [Spencer Roane disagrees with this statement. See the Prologue, Section Four]. He did not read law more than 6 or 8 months before he applied for a license. I heard one of the gentlemen who licensed him say that he was so ignorant of law at the time that he should not have passed him if he had not discovered his great genius.

He commenced the practice of law at about twenty-two and removed to Louisa [County] where he was soon after elected a representative to the Assembly. He was not long after chosen to represent Hanover though a non-resident and without his soliciting it. Indeed he did not appear at the elections. He continued a member of the Assembly until he was appointed to command the First Virginia Regiment at the commencement of the Revolution.

He continued the practice of law in the county courts of Hanover, Louisa, and Goochland during this period. His competitors at the bar of any celebrity were Lewis, Lyons, and Semple. He maintained his integrity, [rest of the sentence illegible]. His morals were exemplary and he had a great respect for the Christian religion, though he never joined any particular sect. He was remarkably temperate in his eating and drinking from his youth through life. In his friendships he was sincere, of a cheerful disposition, and an agreeable companion. He was a kind, affectionate husband and parent, and a very humane master.

He first distinguished himself at the bar in defiance of the parish of St. Paul in a suit brought by [his] uncle, a minister of that parish for his salary [the clergyman was actually the Reverend James Maury]. Claiming his [illegible] in tobacco and expecting to receive it in money at [illegible] as settled by act of assembly. He first, I think, distinguished himself in the assembly in a warm debate on continuing the union of the chair and treasury on the death of Robinson, who had been the speaker and treasurer. It was attempted to unite them again, but Henry by his eloquence prevented it. His celebrated resolves against the Stamp Act are generally known. These he carried though opposed by all the men of influence in the assembly and charged with treason from the chair.

[Two - Henry during the Gunpowder Expedition]

From the *commencement of the Revolution* it was his opinion that an eternal separation would take place between Britain and the United States. Indeed it appears that as a politician he saw further into consequences than all others at that day. I will mention one remarkable instance. When Dunmore seized upon the arms and the ammunition in the magazine [at Williamsburg], Henry proposed raising a company of volunteers to recover them. This was generally condemned by most of our leading men as imprudent and impolitic. But Henry's views extended further than recovering [the arms and ammunition?].

On his way to meet a committee which was to confer on the occasion, he observed to Colonel Richard Morris and myself that it was a fortunate circumstance, which would arouse the people from north to south: "You may in vain maintain the duties to them upon tea and etc. These things they will say do not affect them. But tell them of the robbery of the magazine and that the next step will be to disarm them, and they will be ready to fly to arms to defend their independence."[2]

[Three - Henry from his residence in Scotchtown until his death at Red Hill]

Soon after he was elected for Hanover, he removed into that county to a seat called Scotchtown, which he had purchased. He remained there until [obliterated]. Having lost his wife, he sold his seat, and having married the daughter of Nathaniel Dandridge [in 1777 while living in the Governor's Palace in Williamsburg, at the conclusion of his third term as governor] he removed to Prince Edward [County]. He did not long remain there, but while he did, returned to the practice of the law again [Dabney here omits Henry's Henry County years, 1779-1784, and two additional terms as governor, 1784-1786, and picks him up at their conclusion]. His apology for doing so was that he had purchased some valuable lands on the Roanoke River [his Long Island plantation] and must raise the money to pay for them. He soon after moved there and quitted the bar. He then died about the year 1800 [1799], being, I think, in his sixty-fourth year. He had a lingering disorder which gave him great time to prepare for death. I am told that one of his neighbors, going to see him sometime before his death found him reading the Bible. Holding the book in his hand, he observed, "That book is worth all the books that ever were printed, and it has been my misfortune that I have never found time to read it until lately."

I was upon a footing of intimacy with him from his youth and a great part of the time [illegible section] in giving Mr. Wirt this information, [illegible section] in handing down to posterity [illegible] of this great man.

George Dabney, May 14, 1805

APPENDIX D

PATRICK HENRY'S WILL

Patrick Henry had six children by his first wife, Sarah Shelton, three daughters and three sons. The three daughters, Martha Fontaine, Anne Roane, and Elizabeth (Betsey) Aylett, were presumably furnished suitable dowries upon their marriage, although Anne's husband, Spencer Roane, sued Henry's estate for funds allegedly promised but not paid (see the Prologue, Section Two).

In the seventh paragraph of his will dated November 20, 1798, Henry stated, "I have heretofore provided for the children of my first marriage, but I will to my daughters, Roane and Aylett, two hundred pounds each of them as soon as my estate can conveniently pay it by cropping." In the codicil to his will, dated February 12, 1799, Henry left five hundred dollars to daughter Martha Fontaine, and one thousand dollars each to Anne Roane and Elizabeth Aylett.

All three of Patrick Henry's sons by Sarah Shelton predeceased him: John in 1791, Edward in 1794, and William in 1798. Edward and William died without children. In the sixth paragraph of his will Patrick Henry makes a bequest to his grandson, Edmund Henry, the only son of John.

Six sons and three daughters by Patrick Henry's second marriage to Dorothea Dandridge survived him, and he provided inheritances for them all. It should be noted that there was a second son named John (1796-1868), who was the father of William Wirt Henry (1831-1900), author of Patrick Henry: Life, Correspondence and Speeches *(see "Sources," following this book's appendices). There was also a second son named Edward (1794-1871) who appears in the will as "Edward Winston."*

Patrick Henry's threatened sanctions in the tenth paragraph of his will against his widow Dorothea should she marry again never materialized (see the third paragraph of the introduction to Appendix A, Edmund Winston's Memorandum to William Wirt).[1]

In the name of God, amen. I, Patrick Henry of Charlotte County, at my leisure and in my health, do make this my last will and testament in manner following, and do write it throughout with my own hand. I, knowing my ever dear wife Dorothea to be worthy of the most full and entire confidence, I do will and devise to her the guardianship of my children and do direct and order that she shall not in any manner be accountable to any person for her management therein.

I do give to my said wife Dorothea all my lands at and adjoining my dwelling place called Red Hill, purchased from Fuqua, Booker, Watkins, and others, out of the tract called Watkins' order, to hold during her life, together with twenty of my slaves [out of sixty-six], her choice of them, and at her death the said lands are to be equally divided in value in fee simple between two of my sons by her. And she is to name and point out the two sons that are to take the said lands in fee simple at her discretion.

I will and direct all my lands in my Long Island estate in Campbell County to be divided into two parts by Randolph's old road, till you come along it to the place where the new road going from the overseer's house to Davis's mill crosses it at two white oaks and the stump of a third; from thence by a straight line a few hundred yards to Potts's spring at the old quarter place; from thence as the water runs to the river, which is near to the upper part where Mr. Philip Payne lives, is to be added the Long Island and other islands to the lower part the overseer's residence and also one hundred and fifty acres of the back land out of the upper part. These two estates to be in fee simple to two of my other sons by my said wife, whom she is also to name and point out.

I will and direct that there be raised towards paying my debts one thousand pounds by sale in fee simple out of my following land, viz: Leatherwood, Prince Edward Lands, Kentucky Lands, Seven Island Lands, and those lately purchased of Marshall, Mason, Nowell, Wimbush, Massey, and Prewitt, or such parts thereof as my executors may direct. And the residue thereof I will and direct to be allotted equally in value into two parts for a provision for other two of my sons in fee simple by my said wife, which sons she shall in like manner name and point out. But if the payment of my debts is or can be accomplished without selling any of my slaves or personal estate, then I desire none of these lands to be sold, but they are to be allotted as the provision aforesaid for two of my sons. Thus I have endeavored to provide for my six sons by my dear Dorothea. Their names are Patrick, Fayette, Alexander Spotswood, Nathaniel, Edward Winston, and John.

I will my slaves to be equally divided amongst my children by my present wife, except my daughter [Dorothea] Winston, who has received hers, or nearly so. But the twenty slaves given to my said wife for her life, I desire she may give as she pleases amongst her children by me. I will that my wife have power to execute deeds for any lands I have agreed to sell in the most ample manner. I give to my grandson, Edmund Henry, when he arrives to the age of twenty-one years and not before, in fee simple, the thousand acres of land where his father died, joining Perego's line, Cole's line, and the line of the land intended for my son Edward, deceased, together with the Negroes and other property on the said one thousand acres of land. But in case the said Edmund shall die under the age of twenty-one years, and without issue alive, I will the said land, slaves, and other property to my six sons above mentioned, equally in fee simple.

I have heretofore provided for the children of my first marriage, but I will to my daughters, Roane and Aylett, two hundred pounds each of them as soon as my estate can conveniently pay it by cropping.

In case either of my six sons, viz.: Patrick, Fayette, Alexander Spotswood, Nathaniel, Edward Winston, or John, shall die under the age of twenty-one, unmarried and without issue then living, I will that the estate of such decedent be divided among the survivors of them in such manner as my said wife shall direct.

All the rest and residue of my estate, whether lands, slaves, personal estate, debts and rights of every kind, I give to my ever

dear and beloved wife Dorothea, the better to enable her to edu-
cate and bring up my children by her. And in particular I desire she
may at her discretion collect, accommodate, manage, and dispose
of the debt due to me from the late Judge Wilson [Judge John
Wilson of Norfolk] in such manner as she thinks best without being accountable to any person. But so as that the produce, whether
in lands, slaves, or other effects, be by her given amongst her children by me, as I do hereby direct all the said residue to be given
by her after her decease. If the said debt from the said Wilson can
not be recovered, then I give the lands I covenanted to sell to him,
the said Wilson, lying in Virginia and North Carolina, to my said
wife in fee simple to make the most of and apply for the benefit of
her children by me as aforesaid.

But in case my said wife shall marry again, in that case I revoke and make void every gift, legacy, authority, or power herein
mentioned, and order, will, and direct, she, my said wife, shall
have no more of my estate than she can recover by law. Nor shall
she be guardian to any of my children or executrix of this, my
will.

I will that my daughters, Dorothea S. Winston, M. Catherine
Henry, and Sarah Butler Henry, be made equal in their Negroes. In
case the debt from Judge Wilson's estate be recovered, I do desire
and will that five hundred dollars each be paid to my dear daughters, Anne Roane, Elizabeth Aylett, and Martha Fontaine.

This is all the inheritance I can give to my dear family. The
religion of Christ can give them one which will make them rich
indeed.

I appoint my dear wife Dorothea executrix, my friends
Edmund Winston, Philip Payne, and George D. Winston, execu-
tors of this, my last will, revoking all others. In witness whereof
I have hereunto set my hand and seal this 20th of November 1798.

P. Henry, L. S. [*locus sigili*, place of the seal]

Codicil to my will, written by myself throughout, and by me
annexed and added to the said will and made part thereof in man-

ner following, that is to say: Whereas, since the making of my said will, I have covenanted to sell my lands on Leatherwood to George Hairston, including the 1000 acres intended for my grandson, Edmund Henry, and have agreed to purchase from General Henry Lee two shares of the Saura Town lands, amounting to about 6,314 acres certain, and the debt due me from Wilson's estate is agreed to go in payment for the said purchase, whereby there will exist no necessity to sell any of my estate for payment of my debts.

I do therefore give the said Saura Town lands in fee simple equally to be divided in value to two of my sons by my dear wife Dorothea, and desire her to name the sons who are to take that estate, and it is to be in lieu and place of the Leatherwood, Prince Edward, Kentucky, and Seven Islands, and other lands allotted for two of my sons in my said will, so that the Red Hill estate, Long Island estate, and the Saura Town estate will furnish seats for my six sons by my wife.

In case any part of my lands be evicted or lost for want of title, I will that a contribution of my other sons make good such loss in lands of equal value.

I give to my daughter Fontaine five hundred dollars, to each of my daughters, Anne Roane and Elizabeth Aylett, one thousand dollars, to my daughter Dorothea S. Winston, one thousand dollars, as soon as my estate can conveniently raise these sums. To my daughters, Martha Catharine and Sarah Butler, I give one thousand pounds each, and these legacies to all and each of my daughters are to be in lieu and place of everything before intended for them. And if it is not in the power of my executors to pay my said daughters their legacies in money from my estate, then and in that case, all my said daughters are to take property, real or personal, at fair valuation for their legacies respectively.

And to this end, I give my lands in Kentucky, Prince Edward, at the Seven Islands, all my lands lately purchased near Falling River and its waters containing about 1700 or 1800 acres, and all others not mentioned herein, to my executors for the aforesaid purpose of paying legacies and for allowing my grandson Edmund Henry eight hundred pounds in lieu of the Leatherwood lands, in case he shall attain the age of twenty-one years or marries, but not otherwise. His land, if he has it at all, is to be in fee simple, as also all the lands that may be allotted in lieu of money are to go in fee simple.

I also will that my said dear wife shall at her discretion dispose of three hundred pounds worth of the said last mentioned lands to any of her children by me, and finally of whatsoever residue there may happen to be after satisfying the foregoing demands, and that she have in fee simple all the residue of my estate, real or personal, not disposed of for the intent and purpose of giving the same amongst her children by me.

If she chooses to set free one or two of my slaves, she is to have full power to do so. [Campbell County Order Book 8, p. 169, July 1805: "Ordered that Nancy, Betty, and Phillis, Negroes belonging to the estate of Patrick Henry, deceased, be set free."] In case Judge Wilson's debt is lost by General Lee not taking it in payment, whereby the contract for Saura Town lands becomes void, this codicil is to become of no effect, and is to be void and null. And my executors are to compensate the two of my sons to whom my Leatherwood lands were to go by the lands sold to Judge Wilson. And they are in that case to have all the lands directed to be joined with the Leatherwood and so much money as will make their lots equal in value with the lots of my other sons by my present wife.

In witness whereof I have hereunto set my hand and seal this 12th day of February 1799.

P. Henry, L. S.

Indorsements: The within is my will written throughout in my own hand this 20th day of November 1798.

The codicil also written by myself, February 12th, 1799.

At a court held for Charlotte County the 1st day of July 1799, this last will and testament of Patrick Henry, Esquire, deceased, with the codicil hereto annexed, was presented in court by Edmund Winston, Gentleman, one of the executors herein named, and there being no witness to the said will or codicil, Paul Carrington, Sr., and Paul Carrington, Jr., Gentlemen, being sworn, each deposed that they are well acquainted with the testator's handwriting. Whereupon the said will and codicil are ordered to be recorded. On the motion of Dorothea Henry, the executrix, and the said Edmund Winston and George D. Winston, two of the executors therein named, who made oath according to law, certificate is granted them for obtaining a probate of the said will in due form, they giving security. Whereupon they with Joel Watkins, Paul Carrington, Sr., and Philip Payne, their securities, entered into and acknowledged their bond according to law for that purpose, reserving liberty to Philip Payne, the other executor named in the will, to join in the probate thereof when he shall think fit.

Teste, Thomas Read, Clerk

A true copy, Thomas Read, Clerk

PATRICK HENRY'S BOOKS

*Writers on Henry's life—even sympathetic ones—have won-
dered how the orator could have obtained so much knowledge
on a variety of subjects without a formal education. This bewil-
derment often extended to Henry's alleged lack of an extensive
personal library. Edmund Randolph, who ended his life as a Henry
admirer, nevertheless wrote in his* History of Virginia *of Henry's
"avowed neglect of literature." In their memorandums to William
Wirt, Spencer Roane remarked that the orator's library was not "a
complete or regular one," while Edmund Winston observed that it
seemed "not to have been very well chosen."* [1]

*Thomas Jefferson, among his many other animadversions on
Henry to Wirt, laid particular emphasis on Henry's lack of formal
education. "He was a man of very little knowledge of any sort. He
read nothing and had no books," the eighty-one-year-old Sage
of Monticello told the Massachusetts statesman Daniel Webster
in 1824—then, a few minutes later, confessed with apparent unconscious humor, "I have often been astonished at his command
of proper language. How he attained the knowledge of it, I could
never find out, as he read so little and conversed little with educated men."* [2]

*An inventory of Patrick Henry's property taken a month after
his death in June 1799 included a listing of his books. It shows
a library of about 200 volumes on a variety of subjects (plus a
"parcel" of books in Latin and Greek)—small, without a doubt,
compared to Jefferson's gargantuan collection, but quite respectable for the time. The inventory, written down, as noted by Henry
biographer Robert D. Meade, by someone who "obviously suffered from some of the educational deficiencies of the period," has
been in print for a century, but has only recently been examined
by a scholar capable of accurately discerning the books' titles and
editions.* [3]

Concerning the scope of Henry's library, Kevin J. Hayes, who has completed an extensively annotated study of Henry's books has written: [4]

A number of different subject areas can be discerned. Law, of course, formed the most substantial part of [Henry's] collection, but he also had a number of books devoted to history, geography, and travels. His collection of belles letters included novels, poetry, and essays. And he possessed a number of devotional books, too... Quite modest by standards set among eighteenth-century Virginia's most well-known and well-to-do bookmen, Patrick Henry's library is nonetheless significant enough to refute a notion prevalent among his biographers, that his intellectual powers were a matter of natural ability, not serious study.

SOME PATRICK HENRY APOCRYPHA

It is the duty of the historian to be skeptical. Following are several Henry incidents that very likely did not take place or quotations that Henry almost certainly neither spoke nor wrote:

(1) Henry Defends the Spotsylvania County Baptist Preachers Charged with Preaching without a License, circa 1770—an account from circa 1850

There is no doubt that Henry defended Baptist preachers, and apparently often at his own expense. However, William Wirt Henry believed that the following story had been "made up in after years on doubtful tradition." In it, the orator vehemently addresses the court: [1]

"Did I hear it distinctly, or was it a mistake of my own? Did I hear an expression, as of a crime, that these men whom your worships are about to try for misdemeanor are charged with—with what?... Preaching the gospel of the Son of God?... What laws have they violated?"

All present are overwhelmed with emotion and the magistrate discharges the prisoners. This version seems to have first appeared in William Henry Foote's Sketches of Virginia: Historical and Biographical, *First Series (Richmond, 1850).*

(2) The "Liberty or Death" Speech, 1775; an Account by Edward Fontaine from circa 1872

In his memoir, the Reverend Fontaine (1814-1884), a great-grandson of Patrick Henry, stated that in 1834 he visited the Honorable John Roane of King William County, Virginia, whom he described as " the last surviving elector of the first President of the United States." However, Virginia historian Lyon G. Tyler's Encyclopedia of Virginia Biography *(1915) gives Roane's birth date as 1766, which (if this is the same man) would have made him not more than nine years old had he heard the "Liberty or Death" speech. True or not, this version gives the reader an idea of how the speech had been embellished during the indeterminate number of years—perhaps nearly a century—between the time Henry gave it and Fontaine wrote his report of Roane's recollection.* ²

[Roane] had represented his district in Congress forty years and was more than ninety years old, but his mind was very little impaired by age, and his memory was perfect in retaining past events. He told me many anecdotes about Patrick Henry, and interested me greatly by describing the scene which he witnessed in the House of Burgesses when he made the speech with which every college youth is familiar… During the conversation, animated by his distinct recollection of the sublime scene, the venerable man seemed to forget his age, and in order to enable me to understand his meaning, he arose and acted the conclusion of the speech and imitated, I have no doubt with considerable accuracy, his voice and manner.

His words and gestures were these: "You remember, sir, the conclusion of the speech so often declaimed in various ways by school boys: "Is *peace so sweet,* or *life so dear* as to be purchased at the price of *chains* and *slavery*? Forbid it almighty God! I know not what course others may take, but as for me, give me liberty or give me death!"

He gave each of these words a meaning which is not conveyed by the reading or delivery of them in the ordinary way. When he said, "Is peace so sweet or life so dear as to be purchased at the price of chains and slavery," he stood in the attitude of a condemned galley slave loaded with fetters, awaiting his doom. His form was bowed, his wrists were crossed, *his manacles were almost visible* as he stood like an embodiment of helplessness and agony. After a solemn pause, he raised his eyes and chained hands towards heaven and prayed in words and tones which thrilled every heart, "Forbid it, Almighty God!"

He then turned towards the timid loyalists of the House, who were quaking with terror at the idea of the consequences of participating in proceedings which would be visited with the penalties of treason by the British crown, and he slowly bent his form yet nearer to the earth and said, "I know not what *course others may take,*" and he accomplished the words with his hands still crossed, while seeming to be weighed down with additional chains. The man appeared transformed into an oppressed, heart-broken, and hopeless felon. After remaining in this posture of humiliation long enough to impress the imagination with the condition of the colony under the *iron heel* of *military despotism*, he arose proudly and exclaimed, "but as for me"—and the words hissed through his clenched teeth, while his body was thrown back and every muscle and tendon was strained against the fetters which bound him, and, with his countenance distorted by agony and rage, he looked for a moment like Laocoon in a death struggle with coiling serpents! [Laocoon was a priest of Troy, who unsuccessfully warned the Trojans against bringing into the city the giant horse offered by the Greeks. The god Poseidon, who favored the Greeks, then sent two enormous snakes after Laocoon and his two sons, crushing them to death.]

Then the loud, clear, triumphant notes, *"Give me liberty!!"* electrified the assembly. It was not a prayer, but a *stern demand* which would submit to no refusal or delay! The sound of his voice, as he spoke these memorable words, was like that of a Spartan paean on the field of Plataea [where in 479 BC forces of the Greek city-states under the command of the Spartan general Pausanias decisively defeated the invading Persians]; and, as each syllable of the word *"liberty"* echoed through the building, his fetters were shivered; his arms were hurled apart; and the links of his chains were scattered to the winds! When he spoke the word *"liberty"* with an emphasis never given it before, his hands were open and his arms elevated and extended; his countenance was radiant. He stood erect and defiant, while the sound of his voice and the sublimity of his attitude made him appear a magnificent incarnation of freedom and expressed all that can be acquired or enjoyed by nations and individuals invincible and free.

After a momentary pause, only long enough to permit the echo of the word "liberty" to cease, he let his left hand fall powerless to his side, and clenched his right hand firmly, as if holding a dagger with the point aimed at his breast. He stood like a Roman senator defying Caesar, while the unconquerable spirit of Cato of Utica flashed from every feature, and he closed the grand appeal with the solemn words, "or give me death!" which sounded with the awful cadence of a hero's dirge, fearless of death, and victorious in death; and he suited the action to the word by a blow upon the left breast with the right hand, which seemed to drive the dagger to the patriot's heart!

(3) The Gunpowder Expedition, 1775;
William Wirt's Version, circa 1817

Wirt was sent several memoirs of the so-called "Gunpowder Expedition," but only one, George Dabney's (see Appendix C) contained a direct quotation from Henry. After his account in indirect discourse of Henry's inspirational speech to the Hanover Militia, which appears below, Wirt explained, "These were heads of his harangue. I presume not to give the coloring." But none of it resembles the contents of any of the surviving memoranda he received. [3]

When assembled, he addressed [the Hanover Militia] with all the powers of his eloquence; laid open the plan on which the British Ministry had fallen to reduce the colonies to subjection by robbing them of all the means of defending their rights; spread before their eyes, in colors of vivid description, the fields of Lexington and Concord, still floating with the blood of their countrymen gloriously shed in the general cause; showed them that the recent plunder of the magazine in Williamsburg was nothing more than a part of the general system of subjugation; that the moment was now come in which they were called upon to decide whether they chose to live free and hand down the noble inheritance to their children or to become hewers of wood and drawers of water to those lordlings, who were themselves the tools of a corrupt and tyrannical ministry.

He painted the country in a state of subjugation and drew such pictures of wretched debasement and abject vassalage as filled their souls with horror and indignation. On the other hand, he carried them, by the powers of his eloquence, to an eminence like Mount Pisgah; showed them the land of promise, which was to be won by their valor under the support and guidance of heaven; and sketched a vision of America enjoying the smiles of liberty and peace, the rich productions of her agriculture waving on every field, her commerce whitening every sea in tints so bright, so strong, so glowing, as set the souls of his hearers on fire.

He had no doubt, he said, that God, who in former ages had hardened Pharoah's heart that He might show forth his power and glory in the redemption of His chosen people, had, for similar purposes, permitted the flagrant outrages which had occurred in Williamsburg and throughout the continent. It was for them now to determine whether they were worthy of this divine interference, whether they would accept the high boon now held out to them by heaven. If they would—though it might lead them through a sea of blood—they were to remember that the same God, whose power divided the Red Sea for the deliverance of Israel, still reigned in all his glory, unchanged and unchangeable. [God] was still the enemy of the oppressor and the friend of the oppressed.

For his own part, he was anxious that his native county should distinguish itself in this grand career of liberty and glory and snatch the noble prize which was now offered to their grasp—that no time was to be lost—that it would be easy for them, by a rapid and vigorous movement, to compel the restoration of the powder which had been carried off, or to make a reprisal on the king's revenues in the hands of the receiver-general, which would fairly balance the account—that the Hanover Volunteers would thus have an opportunity of striking the first blow in this colony, in the great cause of American liberty, and would cover themselves with never-fading laurels.

(4) Patrick Henry's Letter to His Daughter Anne on the Eve of Her Marriage to Spencer Roane, September 17, 1786

William Wirt Henry seems to have been the first Patrick Henry biographer to ascribe this letter to his grandfather, noting, "Upon the marriage of this daughter her father wrote her the following letter, which may well challenge comparison with any similar production in the language." To the modern reader, however, the tone of this exposition of marital responsibilities may appear almost unremittingly one-sided, relieved only slightly by the last paragraph in this excerpt.

The letter begins: [4]

My Dear Daughter:

You have just entered into that state which is replete with happiness or misery. The issue depends upon that prudent, amiable, uniform conduct, which wisdom and virtue so strongly recommend on the one hand, or that imprudence which a want of reflection or passion may prompt on the other.

You are allied to a man of honor, of talents, and of an open, generous disposition. You have, therefore, in your power all the essential ingredients of happiness. It cannot be marred, if you now reflect upon that system of conduct which you ought invariably to pursue—if you now see clearly the path from which you will resolve never to deviate. Our conduct is often the result of whim or caprice—often such as will give us many a pang, unless we see beforehand what is always the most praiseworthy and the most essential to happiness...

Mutual politeness between the most intimate friends is essential to that harmony which should never be once broken or interrupted. How important, then, is it between man and wife? The more warm the attachment, the less will either party bear to be slighted or treated with the smallest degree of rudeness or inattention. This politeness, then, if it be not in itself a virtue, is at least the means of giving to real goodness a new luster. It is the means of preventing discontent and even quarrels. It is the oil of intercourse. It removes asperities and gives to everything a smooth, an even, and a pleasant movement...

It now appears that the letter was written by (Episcopal) Bishop James Madison (1742-1812), second cousin to the U. S. president, to his daughter. [5]

(5) Patrick Henry's reason for not attending the Constitutional Convention in Philadelphia, 1787

As stated in the introduction to Chapter VIII, "I smelt a rat," has been attributed to Henry as his reason for not being present. The quote first appeared in Hugh Blair Grigsby's The History of the Virginia Convention of 1788, *published in 1890. Grigsby (1806-1881) lived early enough in the nineteenth century to have known some of the members of the convention as old men. His account of its proceedings is often entertaining, but the three Virginia volumes of the late twentieth-century* Documentary History of the Ratification of the Constitution *(1988) are more reliable.* [6]

(6) The Randolph Murder Trial, Cumberland County, 1792

There is no doubt that the trial took place and was the most sensational of its day in Virginia. However, its records have been lost or destroyed. All the Randolphs involved were young members of one of Virginia's most prominent families. Sisters Nancy and Judith Randolph were distant cousins of Richard Randolph. Nancy Randolph and Richard Randolph, who was Judith's husband, were accused of conceiving a child, aborting it, then hiding the evidence. Richard was arrested and held in the Cumberland County jail.

Richard Randolph engaged John Marshall, the future Chief Justice of the U. S. Supreme Court, and Alexander Campbell of

Richmond for his defense. In addition, he sent a messenger to Patrick Henry at his Long Island plantation, offering the famous advocate a very large fee to argue the case. Henry is said to have refused on the grounds of ill health. Several days later, the messenger reappeared at Long Island with a second offer from Randolph at double the amount.

"Dolly," Henry is supposed to have asked his wife, "Mr. Randolph seems very anxious that I should appear for him, and 500 guineas is a large sum. Don't you think I could make the trip in a carriage?"

The question of Richard and Nancy Randolph's guilt or innocence came down to whether Nancy had actually been pregnant. Ultimately the answer depended on the testimony of Mrs. Carter Page who stated that she confirmed Nancy's condition by peeping through a crack in the door of Nancy's bedroom when Nancy was undressing.

"Which eye did you peep with?" Henry asked the witness, then turning to the court, he declared in a loud voice, "Great God deliver us from eavesdroppers!"

The room exploded in laughter, and Richard Randolph was acquitted. Richard's younger brother, John, later known as John Randolph of Roanoke, is subsequently said to have described Patrick Henry as "the greatest orator that ever lived." He was, Randolph declared, "a Shakespeare and Garrick combined [David Garrick, the great Shakespearean actor of the eighteenth century] and spake as never man spake." [7]

(7) Henry Clay's Patrick Henry Story in the U. S. Senate

When Henry Clay of Kentucky related this apocryphal tale in an 1811 congressional speech, the Voice of American Liberty had been dead only a dozen years, and the memory of his forensic exploits was still green. Like the subject of his anecdote, Mr. Clay was a native of Hanover County, Virginia, and a successful orator and lawyer. Although both he and his listeners knew the story of Patrick Henry's switching sides in mid-argument and still winning his case was a myth, doubtless there remained a kernel of suspicion that it really could have happened.[8]

This was the predicament in which the celebrated orator of Virginia, Patrick Henry, is said to have been placed. Engaged in a most extensive and lucrative practice of law, he mistook in one instance the side of the cause on which he was retained and addressed the court in a very splendid and convincing speech on behalf of his antagonist. His distracted client came up to him whilst he was progressing and, interrupting him, bitterly exclaimed, "You have undone me! You have ruined me!"

"Never mind, give yourself no concern," said the adroit advocate; and turning to the court and jury, continued his argument by observing, "May it please your honors, and you, gentlemen of the jury. I have been stating to you what I presume my adversary may urge on his side. I will now show you how fallacious his reasoning and groundless his pretensions are."

The skillful orator proceeded, satisfactorily refuted every argument which he had advanced, and gained his cause.

Some Contemporary Patrick Henry Apocrypha

(8) What Patrick Henry Did *Not* Say on the Founding of the Country by Christians

Although most of the Founding Fathers were members of the established churches of their respective colonies, few of them could be considered orthodox (or Trinitarian) Christians.[9] *Patrick Henry's writings and reported statements on religion, particularly those towards the end of his life, give every indication that he was a Trinitarian Christian who not only abhorred Thomas Jefferson's support of the French Revolution but his deism as well.*

In recent years there have been attempts by some Christian conservatives to ascribe unsubstantiated statements to the Founders, including Patrick Henry. During the 1990s, the editor frequently encountered the following quote, attributed to Henry, that can be traced to no legitimate source:

It cannot be emphasized too strongly or too often that this nation was founded, not by religionists, but by Christians; not on religions, but on the gospel of Jesus Christ!

(9) Finally: Patrick Henry as Voltaire

In 2005 a colorful new poster was offered for sale on the internet. Beneath a picture of Henry the orator in action was written:

"I may not agree with what you say,
but I will defend to the death your right to say it."
—Patrick Henry

William Wirt's *Sketches of the Life and Character of Patrick Henry* (1817)

"It was all speaking, speaking, speaking. 'Tis true he could talk—Gods how he could talk! But there is no acting the whole… All that is told me is, that on such and such an occasion, he made a distinguished speech. He was a blank military commander, a blank governor, and a blank politician, in all those useful points which depend on composition and detail. In short, it is verily as hopeless a subject as man could well desire." [1]

So wrote William Wirt, Patrick Henry's first biographer, a decade after starting work on a project he believed he could finish relatively quickly. Wirt (1772-1836) was much younger than Henry (1736-1799) and had never met his subject. Beginning in 1805, he struggled for a dozen years with what he discovered to be an appalling lack of documentation concerning the career of the charismatic orator who, after George Washington, had been the most popular man in Revolutionary Virginia. Wirt's frustration with his Henry biography grew during the course of an increasingly successful career that culminated in his becoming a best-selling writer, a much-in-demand speaker, a respected lawyer, and the longest-serving Attorney General of the United States in history. [2]

Wirt's complaint, quoted above, had a solid basis in fact. Unlike most of the Founding Fathers, he discovered, Henry seems to have given little thought as to how posterity would remember him—at least he made no systematic effort to save copies of his correspondence and records.

Wirt consulted official sources, the relatively small number of Henry's personal letters he could find, and the few transcripts of the orator's speeches that existed. In addition, beginning in 1805, Wirt made an effort to contact Henry's contemporaries—relatives, friends, and colleagues in the Revolution—asking them for written memoirs of his hero. On occasion the replies only added to the biographer's aggravation, for he discovered that even those who had known Henry well could not always agree on details concerning his life, which can be explained by the respondents' family and personal interests as well as the inaccuracies of memory. After all, it had been forty-two years since the Parsons' Cause had propelled Henry to fame in Virginia, and he had become a legend in his own lifetime.

When Wirt's *Sketches of the Life and Character of Patrick Henry* at last appeared in 1817, it was a resounding popular success (there were twenty-five editions during the nineteenth century, and the book is in print today). Both the work and its author, however, were also subject to criticism. From the standpoint of scholarship the criticism was often justified, but the invective that sometimes accompanied it was prompted by old political and personal wounds which, even with the commencement of President Monroe's "Era of Good Feelings," had not yet healed.

Wirt ignored most of the unfavorable comments Thomas Jefferson had made on Henry's character during their eleven-year correspondence leading up to the publication of his book, holding steadfast to his original intention of portraying his subject as a noble example of republican virtue to be emulated by the "Young Men of Virginia" to whom the volume was dedicated.[3]

Wirt's *Sketches of the Life and Character of Patrick Henry* is admittedly flawed. But if Wirt had not undertaken the task of writing the first Henry biography, who would have—and when? In a few more years, death or senility would have claimed most of the patriot's contemporaries, and their recollections of him would have been lost. As was the custom of his time, Henry's speeches were not written out. And considering Henry's propensity for seldom saving his correspondence and rarely setting his innermost thoughts down on paper, Wirt did a remarkable job of coming up with the sources that he did and making some sense of them.

Edmund Randolph's *History of Virginia* (circa 1810)

Randolph announced the plan for his history in the December 26, 1809, issue of the Richmond *Enquirer* and finished it sometime before his death in 1813. In the preface to his *Sketches*, William Wirt acknowledged that he had been given access to a copy of the history by Edmund Randolph's son, Peyton. The whereabouts of Randolph's original manuscript and at least two copies cannot be precisely accounted for until the 1870s, when one of the copies, which became the text for the Virginia Historical Society's scholarly edition a century later, came to light.[4] In his introduction editor Arthur H. Shaffer observes:

> Of the fourteen men selected as the best representatives of Virginia's revolutionary leadership, Patrick Henry understandably emerges as the most dramatic but oddly enough as the most representative as well. It was Henry, according to Randolph, who at the outset of the conflict with Great Britain took command of the newly emerging leadership in the House of Burgesses: "They wanted a leader," and "at this critical moment, Patrick Henry appeared as a member from the county of Louisa." [5]

David Robertson's Record of the Virginia Convention on the Ratification of the U. S. Constitution (1788)

Publication of the convention's debates based on the shorthand notes of David Robertson took place as early as 1788. Between 1827 and 1830, Jonathan Elliot published, in four volumes, *The Debates, Resolutions, and other Proceedings in Convention, on the Adoption of the Federal Constitution...* The debates for the Virginia Convention comprised the second volume. Elliot's *Debates* remained the standard source until the publication of *The Documentary History of the Ratification of the Constitution, Virginia* in 1988.[6]

Thomas Jefferson's Letters to William Wirt (1805-1816)

The correspondence was first published in 1910 in the *Pennsylvania Magazine of History and Biography*; again during the following year by John Gribbel of Philadelphia, and yet once more in 1912 by Stan V. Henkels in the same city. The editor's book *Patrick Henry and Thomas Jefferson* contains a reproduction of the 1912 Gribbel edition. Note that not all of Jefferson's animadversions on Henry are covered in this book but are more comprehensively addressed in *PH & TJ*.

Edward Fontaine's Manuscript (1872)

Edward Fontaine's *Patrick Henry: Corrections of biographical mistakes and popular errors in regard to his character. Anecdotes and new facts illustrating his religious and political opinions; & the style & power of his eloquence. A brief account of his last illness & death* is an interesting, if not always accurate, document. Edward Fontaine (1814-1884) was the son of Patrick Henry's oldest grandson, who in turn was the son of Patrick Henry's oldest child, Martha Henry Fontaine. At age seventeen Edward began keeping a diary in which he wrote down all the family lore concerning his famous great-grandfather. An ordained Episcopal minister and a Confederate army officer, Fontaine, himself, was a colorful character.

According to Mark Couvillon, the late twentieth-century transcriber of the Fontaine manuscript, it "is a prime example of the strong Southern patriotism felt after the Civil War. Longing for Virginia's glory days in the midst of Northern reconstruction, [Fontaine] upholds the ideology that the South was the true defender of the revolutionary principles expounded by Patrick Henry and others." The editor, therefore, finds much of the manuscript suspect for reasons of time and filiopietism. Copies of the Couvillon transcription are available through the Patrick Henry Memorial Foundation, Brookneal, VA.

Moses Coit Tyler's *Patrick Henry* (1887)

Tyler (1835-1900) was a respected professor of history at Cornell University. His Henry biography, which appeared as part of a late-nineteenth-century "American Statesman" series is worthy of consideration. Tyler acknowledges with gratitude the assistance of William Wirt Henry, Patrick Henry's grandson (see below). His book was also the first Henry biography to make use of the Fontaine Manuscript, the original of which is in the Cornell University Library.

William Wirt Henry's *Patrick Henry: Life, Correspondence, and Speeches* (1891)

William Wirt Henry (1831-1900) was the son of Patrick Henry's youngest son, John (1796-1868) and was of course named for his grandfather's biographer. Like his father, W. W. Henry was born at Red Hill Plantation in Charlotte and Campbell counties, Patrick Henry's last home and burial place (today Red Hill is the home of the Patrick Henry Memorial Foundation).

In 1855 W. W. Henry was admitted to the bar in Charlotte County and practiced law there until he moved to Richmond in 1873, where he attained considerable prominence in the legal community. He was, for a number of years, the Commonwealth Attorney and served as president of the city and state bar associations, as well as vice president of the American Bar Association. W. W. Henry was a popular speaker and writer on historical topics and was an officer in several state and national historical organizations.

In 1867, it is said, a Richmond newspaper published excerpts from one of the Jefferson letters to William Wirt concerning Patrick Henry. Its contents so incensed W. W. Henry that he embarked upon his own biography, *Patrick Henry: Life, Correspondence, and Speeches*. Its three volumes are thorough and well written, and the author does an excellent job as an advocate for his grandfather. Although Henry describes his sources at some length in his preface, present-day scholars might, however, wish for more specific annotations in the text, especially for the letters. Still, the *Life, Correspondence, and Speeches* has been a treasure trove for later Henry biographers, and as far as the writer knows, the authorship of none of the letters has been disproved, with the exception of the August 1786 letter, alleged to have been written by Patrick Henry to his daughter Anne, described in Appendix F.

George Morgan's *The True Patrick Henry* (1907)

Morgan (1854-1936), a native of Delaware, was a prominent Philadelphia journalist, who also wrote several books on early American history. For his *The True Patrick Henry* Morgan took the trouble to travel to Virginia where Elizabeth Henry Lyons (Patrick Henry's great-granddaughter and daughter of William Wirt Henry) placed "at his service the Henry material collected at Red Hill during the nineteenth century." *The True Patrick Henry*'s appendices, which include transcriptions of almost all of the Roane and Meredith memorandums to William Wirt, Patrick Henry's will, and the inventories of Patrick Henry's estate, have been extremely valuable to subsequent historians like the editor, who have found the original manuscripts difficult to decipher after a century of deterioration since Morgan's time.

Robert Douthat Meade's *Patrick Henry: Patriot in the Making* and *Practical Revolutionary*, and Winston Memorandum

Meade (1903-1974) received criticism from many in the academic community for his *Patrick Henry: Patriot in the Making* (1957) and *Patrick Henry: Practical Revolutionary* (1969). Much of the criticism had a Jeffersonian cast. However, it was also argued that enough source material did not exist to justify Meade's two-volume, 960-page biography.

Whether *Patriot in the Making* and *Practical Revolutionary* tell the reader more than he or she wants to know about Patrick Henry is a judgment for the reader, but this editor can testify that when he was executive vice-president of the Patrick Henry Memorial Foundation, it was Meade he always consulted first in his research. Meade was a thorough scholar and fine writer, as proven by his biography and the introduction, editing, and annotation of his article, "Judge Edmund Winston's Memoir of Patrick Henry" (1961).[7]

NOTES

Abbreviations

Dabney MS	George Dabney memorandum, Henry Papers, Library of Congress.
Doc Hist	*Documentary History of the Ratification of the Constitution—Virginia* (3 vols.).
LC	Library of Congress.
Mayer	Henry Mayer. *A Son of Thunder: Patrick Henry and the American Republic.*
Meade	Robert Meade. *Patrick Henry* (2 vols.).
Meredith MS	Samuel Meredith memorandum, Henry Papers, Library of Congress, and in Morgan.
Morgan	George Morgan. *The True Patrick Henry.*
PGW	*The Papers of George Washington.*
PTJ	*The Papers of Thomas Jefferson.*
PH&TJ	James M. Elson, ed. *Patrick Henry and Thomas Jefferson.*
Randolph	Edmund Randolph. *History of Virginia.*
Roane MS	Spencer Roane memorandum, Henry Papers, Library of Congress, and in Morgan.
Tyler MS	John Tyler memorandum, Henry Papers, Library of Congress.
VMHB	*Virginia Magazine of History and Biography.*
WMQ	*William and Mary Quarterly.*
W. W. Henry	William Wirt Henry. *Patrick Henry: Life, Correspondence, and Speeches* (3 vols.).
Winston MS	Edmund Winston memorandum, Henry Papers, Library of Congress, and Meade, *VMHB* 69 (1961):28-41
Wirt	William Wirt. *Sketches of the Life and Character of Patrick Henry.*

ENDNOTES

PROLOGUE

[1] Roane MS.

[2] F. Thornton Miller, "John Marshall Versus Spencer Roane: A Reevaluation of *Martin v. Hunter's Lessee*," *VMHB* 96 (1988):313.

[3] Meade 2: 306-307, on the Spencer Roane-Anne Henry marriage: "After Henry's death, Roane would make Dolly Henry [his widow] the defendant in a lawsuit over Henry's will, which was hardly to the credit of one of the outstanding American judges."

[4] In a letter dated September 26, 1805, Nathaniel Pope wrote to William Wirt: "Colonel William O. Winston informed me yesterday that to his certain knowledge Mr. Henry did act as a bar keeper for his father-in-law Mr. Shelton at Hanover Court House, that he frequently went to see him while acting in that capacity, that during the time he was clad in an ozna shirt, jump jacket, and drawers of ozna or checks and very often barefooted—that he was very active and attentive to his guests and very frequently amused them with his violin on which he performed very well."

[5] Probably Charles Rollin, *Method of Teaching and Studying the Belles Lettres: Or an Introduction to Languages, Poetry, Rhetoric, History, Moral Philosophy... translated from the French* (London, 1742).

[6] Roane apparently refers to two of the four life portraits of Henry, known as "the Fleming miniature" and "the Meredith miniature." See Virginius Cornick Hall Jr., "Notes on Patrick Henry Portraiture," *VMHB* 71 (1963): 168-184.

Chapter I: Henry's Early Life to the Parsons' Cause Case, 1763

[1] Meredith MS.

[2] Patrick Henry had six children by Sarah Shelton, four of whom predeceased him; he had eleven children by Dorothea Dandridge, two of whom predeceased him.

[3] *PH&TJ*, 25-36.

[4] Jefferson was reluctant to admit that Wythe, his own teacher in the law, had passed Henry. Meade 1:96: "Jefferson's account is more suggestive than literally accurate. From the records of Goochland court we learn that on 'the XV day of the Month Annoque Domini MDCCLX' Patrick Henry produced a license to practice in the county and inferior courts signed by George Wythe and John Randolph and, having taken the prescribed oaths and test, was admitted to the local bar."

[5] Wirt, 34-35. None of the account is found in what remains today of the Tyler MS.

[6] Winston MS.

[7] *PH&TJ*, 26-27, 33-34.

[8] Henry did keep account books, some of which still exist. At the beginning of his career in the law he handled a variety of cases, although he was not always successful in collecting his fees (see Meade 1, Chapter 7, especially 112-113). Upon his return to the bar after his fifth term as governor, Henry did, on occasion, charge large fees in criminal cases (see Meade 2, Chapter 24).

[9] Randolph, 182-183.

[10] From a letter by the Reverend James Maury to the Reverend John Camm, December 12, 1763, in Ann Maury, *Memoirs of a Huguenot Family* (New York, 1853), 428-424.

[11] From a memorandum (1805) by Nathaniel Pope to William Wirt quoting Captain Thomas Trevillian, a spectator at the trial.

[12] Meredith MS.

Chapter II: Henry in the Virginia House of Burgesses; the Stamp Act Speech, 1765

[1] *PH&TJ*, 28.

[2] *PH&TJ*, 37.

[3] Edmund S. Morgan and Helen M. Morgan, *The Stamp Act Crisis* (Chapel Hill: University of North Carolina Press, 1953), 89.

[4] *PH&TJ*, 29-30.

[5] *PH&TJ*, 44.

[6] Wirt, 83. This portion of John Tyler's mutilated MS no longer exists.

[7] Wirt, 83-84. The quote from Jefferson appears in his August 14, 1814, letter to Wirt in another extended passage on the Stamp Act; see *PH&TJ*, 38-41.

[8] Randolph, 167-170; for the Stamp Act Speech quote see 169.

[9] Carrington MS, Patrick Henry Papers, LC.

[10] "Journal of French Traveler in the Colonies, 1765." *American Historical Review*, 26 (1920-1921): 745. The account is no doubt accurate according to the writer's understanding, but see Henry's middle- and late twentieth-century biographers, Mayer (Chapter 5) and especially Meade (1:175-181). It is doubtful that the French (or possible Irish) traveler understood the kind of polite "apology" typical of deferential eighteenth-century parliamentary debate, although he certainly took note of the effect of Henry's speech in the communities he subsequently visited. In any event, Henry's oratory impressed itself on the minds of the members of the House as he intended.

[11] Morgan and Morgan, *The Stamp Act Crisis* (Chapel Hill, 1953), 99.

[12] John Pendleton Kennedy, *Journals of the House of Burgesses, 1761-1765* (Richmond, 1907), 360.

[13] Morgan and Morgan, *The Stamp Act Crisis*, 97: "[T]he evidence that the fifth resolution was the one rescinded rests solely on the copy found among Henry's papers. The copy is not in Henry's hand and is undated, and Henry's endorsement on the back (which states that these were the resolutions passed) was

made many years after the episode. It is certainly not free enough of suspicion to be conclusive."

[14] The second paragraph may still be read in the mutilated Tyler MS in LC.

Chapter III: Towards the First Continental Congress, 1774

[1]   W. W. Henry, 1:112-116.

[2]   Robert B. Semple, *History of the Rise and Progress of the Baptists in Virginia* (Originally published in 1810; rev. ed., Richmond, 1894), 41.

[3]   W. W. Henry, 1:125-127. The Tucker manuscript was destroyed ca. 1900.

[4]   The complete text appears in Meade 1:299-300, who cites a copy at the Library Company of Philadelphia. Morgan, 246, and W. W. Henry 1:152-153 have slightly abbreviated versions.

[5]   Robert A. Rutland, ed., *The Papers of George Mason* (Chapel Hill: The University of North Carolina Press, 1990), 1:190.

[6]   Charles Francis Adams, ed., *The Works of John Adams* (Boston, 1850), 2: 366-367.

[7]   Paul H. Smith et al., eds., *Letter of Members of the Continental Congress: 1774-1789* (Washington, D. C., 1976), 1:62.

[8]   *VMHB* 15 (1907-1908):356.

[9]   Lester J. Cappon, ed., *The Adams-Jefferson Letters* (Chapel Hill: The University of North Carolina Press, 1957), 2:392-393.

[10] Charles Francis Adams, ed., *The Works of John Adams* (Boston, 1850), 10: 277-278.

[11] *PH&TJ*, 30.

Chapter IV: The "Liberty or Death" Speech and the Clash with Dunmore, 1775

[1]   The resolutions, extensively annotated, are found in William J. van Schreeven, compiler, and Robert L. Scribner, ed., *Revolutionary Virginia: The Road to Independence* (Charlottesville: University Press of Virginia, 1975), 2: 366-370. See note 8, p. 369 for the tally of the voting.

[2]   Wirt, 137-142.

[3]   Postscript of a letter from William Wirt to St. George Tucker, August 16, 1815: "I have taken almost entirely Mr. Henry's speech in the convention of '75 from you, as well as your description of its effects on you verbatim." *WMQ*, ser. 1, 22 (1913-1914):252.

[4]   Mark Greenough of Richmond's Living History Associates, Ltd., which managed the re-enactment of the "Liberty or Death" Speech at St. John's Church from 1992-2003, informs the editor: "Wirt's version was first previewed in *Port Folio* magazine in 1816 as an advertisement for the pending biography. Tucker's footnoted remarks in the biography appear directly within the account of the speech as published in the article. Some (including me) feel that the introduction preceding 'Mr. President...' is virtually all Wirt, while most of the

subsequent text is from Tucker. Wirt probably drew from Judge Tyler ('give me liberty or give me death') and Edmund Randolph ('peace, peace, but there is no peace') for certain key phrases."

[5] An excellent analysis of the speech is Charles L. Cohen, "The 'Liberty or Death' Speech: A Note on Religion and Revolutionary Rhetoric," *WMQ*, 3rd ser., 38 (1981):702-717.

[6] See William S. Prince, "St. George Tucker: Bard on the Bench," *VMHB* 84 (1976):266-282.

[7] David A. McCants, "The Authenticity of William Wirt's Version of Patrick Henry's 'Liberty or Death' Speech," *VMHB* 87 (1979): 387-402, cites (p. 395) an article by St. George Tucker's grandson, "Patrick Henry and St. George Tucker" in the *University of Pennsylvania Law Review*, LXVII (1919):70-73, confirming the loss of the Tucker manuscript.

[8] Moses Coit Tyler, *Patrick Henry* (Boston, 1887), 143-144.

[9] Wirt, 140.

[10] Randolph, 212-213.

[11] Copy on microfilm, Virginia State Library.

[12] Randolph, 219-220.

[13] Dabney MS, LC; Wirt, 155.

[14] William J. van Schreeven, compiler, and Robert L. Scribner, ed., *Revolutionary Virginia: The Road to Independence (Charlottesville: University Press of Virginia, 1975)* 3:100-101.

Chapter V: Henry Leads Virginia into the Revolution, 1776

[1] *PH&TJ*, 33.

[2] The full text is in W. W. Henry l:348-350.

[3] Randolph, 227.

[4] *PGW: Revolutionary War Series* (1988), 3:374.

[5] Randolph, 250-251.

[6] Randolph, 252-254.

[7] Randolph, 255-256.

[8] W. W. Henry 1:446-448.

[9] Jack P. Greene, ed., *The Diary of Colonel Landon Carter of Sabine Hall* (Charlottesville: University Press of Virginia, 1965) 2:1057.

[10] H. L. McIlwaine, gen. ed., *Official Letters of the Governors of the State of Virginia* (Richmond: The Virginia State Library, 1926) 1:30.

Chapter VI: Henry as Revolutionary War Governor, 1776-1779

[1] *PGW: Revolutionary War Series* (1994), 6:470.

[2] Ibid. (2002), 12: 564-565.

[3] Ibid. (2002), 12: 636-637.

[4] H. L. McIlwaine, gen. ed., *Official Letters of the Governors of the State of Virginia* (Richmond: The Virginia State Library, 1926) 1: 223.

[5] *PGW: Revolutionary War Series* (2004), 14:328-329.

[6] *PTJ* (1951), 3: 293-294.

[7] Henning, William Waller, ed. *The Statues at Large; Being a Collection of All the Laws of Virginia from the First Session of the Legislature in 1619.* (Richmond, 1822) 10:568.

[8] Randolph, 295-296.

[9] *PTJ* (1952), 6:143.

Chapter VII: Peace: Henry in the Legislature; Governor for a Second Time (1784-1786), and a Family Matter

[1] Robert A. Rutland, ed., *The Papers of George Mason* (Chapel Hill: University of North Carolina Press, 1990), 2:769-773.

[2] Wirt, 254-255. Only a small portion of this section of the mutilated Tyler MS exists today.

[3] Wirt, 250-253. Only a small portion of this section of the mutilated Tyler MS exists today.

[4] Archibald Stuart in a letter dated August 25, 1816, to William Wirt. Original in Henry Papers, LC; appears in Wirt 271-273, also *WMQ*, ser. 2, 6 (1926):340-341.

[5] *PTJ* (1952), 6:204-205.

[6] *PTJ* (1953), 7:558.

[7] Preamble in Wirt, 262, The full text of the bill appears in Thomas E. Buckley, S. J., *Church and State in Revolutionary Virginia, 1776-1787* (Charlottesville: University Press of Virginia, 1977), 188-189. See Chapter 3, "The Legislation of Virtue, 1783-1784, as well as Meade, 2:279-281, for descriptions of the political maneuvers involved.

[8] The text of the second bill is given in full in Wirt, 258-259.

[9] Charles T. Cullen, ed., *The Papers of John Marshall* (Chapel Hill: University of North Carolina Press, 1972), 1:131.

[10] W. W. Henry 2:286-287.

Chapter VIII: Patrick Henry at the Virginia Convention on the Ratification of the Constitution of the United States, Richmond, June 1788

[1] *Doc Hist,* VIII: 79.

[2] Ibid., 88.

[3] Winston MS

[4] *Doc Hist,* IX: 929-931

[5] Ibid., 951-952, 959-964, 967.

[6] Ibid., 1035-1036.

[7] Ibid., 1062, 1070, 1072, 1081-1083.

[8] *Doc Hist,* X: 1217-1219.

[9] Ibid., 1275-1277.

[10] Ibid., 1328-1329, 1331.

[11] Ibid., 1393-1394.
[12] Ibid., 1476-1477, 1506.
[13] Ibid., 1512. Also appears in the Prologue of this book, Section Eight.
[14] Stuart MS, Patrick Henry Papers, LC.
[15] Wirt, 312-313; also *Doc Hist,* X:1511-1512.
[16] *Doc Hist,* X:1536 ("The great and direct end... "); 1537.

Chapter IX: The Battle for Amendments, 1788-1791

[1] *Doc Hist*, X:1550-1558 for the forty proposed amendments; *PGW: Presidential Series* (1987), 1:113-115, for letter of JM to GW.
[2] *Doc Hist,* X:1761-1762.
[3] Ibid., 1764.
[4] *PGW: Presidential Series* (1987) 1:112-115.
[5] Wirt, 320-324; W. W. Henry, 2:418-422.
[6] W. W. Henry, 2:428-430.
[7] Ibid., 2:433.
[8] See Meade, 2:386-390, on Decius; *VMHB*, 14 (1906-1907): 203-204, for text of Henry's letter.
[9] W. W. Henry, 3:436.
[10] Moncure Daniel Conway, *Edmund Randolph* (New York, 1889), 121; W. W. Henry, 2:437.
[11] W. W. Henry, 2:459-462.
[12] Richard Labunski, *James Madison and the Struggle for the Bill of Rights* (New York: Oxford University Press, 2006) is an excellent account of the subject. The pressures and inconveniences Patrick Henry put Madison through to get a Bill of Rights into the Constitution are described in detail, but never, in the opinion of this writer, really acknowledged. And so we refer again to Henry Mayer's quote which appears in the preface to this book: "I will leave to you the beguiling question of apportioning credit for the Bill of Rights between the man who drafted the first ten amendments and the man who made him do it."

Chapter X: Henry Returns to the Courtroom, 1790s

[1] Samuel Venable Diary, Virginia Historical Society.
[2] Winston MS, Section Four.
[3] Archibald Alexander, "Reminiscences of Patrick Henry," *Virginia Historical Register*, 3 (1850):205-213. Also in *The Southern Literary Messenger*, June 1850.
[4] *WMQ*, ser. 2, 6 (1926):341; MS in Henry Papers, LC.
[5] Wirt, 389-391.
[6] Conrad Speece, *The Mountaineer* (Staunton, Virginia, 1823), 22-26; W. W. Henry, 2:486-489.
[7] Wirt (330-331) states that he had access to Robertson's notes, although he admitted that neither he nor Robertson had effectively transcribed their elegance.

"[Henry] had made himself really learned on the subject," wrote Jefferson in regard to the British Debts Case (August 4, 1805), *PH&TJ*, 34-35.

[8] Wirt, 338-340, 364-365; W. W. Henry, 3: 606-607, 629-630. Compare Henry's opening remarks to those of Davies in *Sermons by the Rev. Samuel Davies, A. M., President of the College of New Jersey* (Pittsburg: Solo Dei Gloria Publishers, 1993, reprint of the 1854 edition), 1:115.

[9] Wirt, 381.

[10] Wirt, 384-385; W. W. Henry, 3:647-648. Wirt undoubtedly put together this story from the transcript of the trial and an "informant," perhaps Hardin Burnley, who was present.

Chapter XI: Henry Settles into Retirement, Declines Both Federal and Additional State Service, and Meditates on God and Country, Late 1790s

[1] *PTJ* (2000), 28:331-332. "Native victuals" in Henry S. Randall, *The Life of Thomas Jefferson* (New York, 1858) 3:508.

[2] W. W. Henry 2:550-552.

[3] W. W. Henry 2:558-559.

4 *PH&TJ*, 35.

5 John Marshall, *The Life of Washington* (Philadelphia, 1807) 5: note xviii. The entire text of Washington's letter appears in W. W. Henry, 2:556-557.

6 W. W. Henry, 2:568-571.

Chapter XII: Virginia and the United States in Crisis, 1799; Washington Calls on Henry, and Henry Answers

[1] W. W. Henry, 2:591-594.

[2] *PGW, Retirement Series* (1999), 3:317-320.

[3] Mayer, 471. In an October 17,1996, letter to the editor Mr. Mayer wrote, "I regard the 'last' Charlotte Court House speech of 1799 with great skepticism and did not use it in my book."

[4] Archibald Alexander, "Reminiscences of Patrick Henry" first appeared in *The Princeton Magazine*, then in the *Virginia Historical Register* and *Southern Literary Messenger* during 1850, and finally in James W. Alexander, *Life of Archibald Alexander* in 1854.

[5] Wirt, 408-411.

[6] W. W. Henry, 2:606-614.

[7] "The Fontaine Manuscript," 1872.

[8] *PTJ,* (2004), 31:110.

[9] Some historians have argued that Henry became a Federalist during his last years, but it also might be argued that through their Virginia and Kentucky Resolves Madison and Jefferson became Anti-Federalists. For a spirited defense of Patrick Henry in this matter, see W. W. Henry, 2:614-622.

Chapter XIII: The Death of Patrick Henry at Red Hill, June 6, 1799; His Advice to Future Generations

[1] Dabney MS, LC.

[2] Fontaine MS edited by Couvillon, 30-31. The W. W. Henry version (2: 625-626), which the author indicates is taken from the Moses Coit Tyler biography, is a paraphrase of Fontaine. Dr. Cabell's lengthy obituary in *The Virginian* (Lynchburg), December 2, 1823, leads the editor to conclude that he was, as the story of Henry's death indicates, a "skeptic" or deist. Around 1815 Dr. Cabell built Point of Honor, "an extremely refined essay in the Federal style," preserved in Lynchburg today as a house museum.

[3] Letter donated by a descendant of Patrick Henry to the Patrick Henry Memorial Foundation, 1998.

[4] W. W. Henry, 2:627.

[5] Charles T. Cullen, ed., *The Papers of John Marshall* (Chapel Hill: University of North Carolina Press, 1984), 4:118.

[6] *PGW: Retirement Series 4,* (Charlottesville, 1999), 123.

[7] Wirt, 413.

[8] *PH&TJ*, 35-36. Concerning Henry's alleged "apostacy," see note 9, Chapter XII, above.

[9] Lyon G. Tyler, *Letters and Times of the Tylers* (Richmond, 1884), 1:183.

[10] The will and a codicil, dated February 12, 1799, are reproduced in full in this book as Appendix D.

[11] W. W. Henry, 1:81-82.

Epilogue: Remembrances of Patrick Henry by Two Former Political Adversaries

I – Thomas Jefferson to Daniel Webster (1824)

[1] Henry Mayer's essay "Patrick Henry and Thomas Jefferson" originally appeared in the October 1993 *Newsletter of the Red Hill Patrick Henry National Memorial* and was reprinted in 1997 in the editor's *PH&TJ.* Andrew Burstein's essay, "Forest Demosthenes" appears in Chapter Six of *The Inner Jefferson: Portrait of a Grieving Optimist* (1995).

[2] First published in *The Papers of Daniel Webster* (1857); also Ford, ed., *The Writings of Thomas Jefferson* (New York, 1899), 10:327-331, and *PH&TJ, 59-62*

[3] Dumas Malone. *Jefferson and His Time: The Sage of Monticello* (Boston, 1981), 484.

II – Edmund Randolph (circa 1810)

[1] Randolph, xxvi, 178-181.

Appendix A: Edmund Winston's Memorandum to William Wirt

[1] Of the memorandums sent to William Wirt for his biography of Henry, the Winston memo, in the opinion of the editor, ranks second only to Spencer

Roane's in its scope and accuracy. Winston was about sixty years old when he wrote it (original in PH Papers, LC). In 1969 Henry biographer Robert Douthat Meade published "Judge Edmund Winston's Memoir of Patrick Henry" in *The Virginia Magazine of History and Biography*, 69 (1961):28-41, a heavily annotated transcription of the Winston manuscript with a scholarly eight-page introduction. The notations in brackets in the present version represent either corrections of or additions to the information given by Judge Winston or the inability of Dr. Meade and this editor to fill in missing or illegible portions of the manuscript.

[2] A copy of Jenyns' *View of the Internal Evidence of the Christian Religion*, which was published in Richmond in 1785 and apparently commissioned by Henry, appears on the inventory of Henry's books taken after his death. Samuel Meredith seems to confirm the story of Henry's giving away copies; see Appendix B, Section Two.

Appendix B: Samuel Meredith's Memorandum to William Wirt

[1] The Meredith MS in the Library of Congress was first printed as Appendix A in George Morgan's *The True Patrick Henry* (1907) with the exception of the paragraphs describing the appearance of Henry's uncle, the Reverend Patrick Henry Sr., at the Parsons' Cause, portions of the "Hanover Volunteers" section, and a part of the concluding section. Morgan comments (p. 205) that the "Hanover Volunteers" "has upon it the stain of dubiety as well as the pleasing dinginess of well over a hundred years."

[2] See note 2, Appendix A, above.

[3] Philip Doddridge, *The Rise and Progress of Religion in the Soul*, 1745. Doddridge (1702-1751) was a member of the English "dissenting clergy." Doddridge's book is not listed in the inventory of Patrick Henry's library.

Appendix C: Memorandums to William Wirt of George Dabney, Charles Dabney, William O. Winston, and Nathaniel Pope

[1] Dabney MS in Library of Congress.

[2] Quoted by Wirt, 155.

Appendix D: Patrick Henry's Will

[1] The will appears as Appendix C in Morgan, *The True Patrick Henry* (1907). The original is in the Charlotte County Clerk's office.

Appendix E: Patrick Henry's Books

[1] Randolph in Epilogue Two; Roane in Prologue, Section Four; Edmund Winston's Memorandum, Appendix A, Section Five.

[2] Jefferson to Daniel Webster in Epilogue One.

[3] The first publication of the inventory was in Morgan (1907), 464-468. It later appeared in Meade 2:455-459.

[4] Kevin J. Hayes, *The Library of Patrick Henry*, MS, 204 pages. Dr. Hayes is Associate Professor of English at the University of Central Oklahoma. His books include *Captain John Smith: A Reference Guide* (1991), *Checklist of Melville Reviews* (1991), *Critical Response to Herman Melville's Moby Dick* (1994), *Henry James: The Contemporary Reviews* (1996), and *A Colonial Woman's Bookshelf* (1996).

Appendix F: Some Patrick Henry Apocrypha

[1] W. W. Henry, 1: 119.

[2] Fontaine Manuscript (Couvillon, ed.), 28-30.

[3] Wirt, 156-157.

[4] W. W. Henry, 2:305-309; also quoted in Meade, 2:308-311.

[5] Thomas J. Buckley, S. J., ed. "The Duties of a Wife—Bishop James Madison to His Daughter, 1811." *VMHB*, 91 (1983): 98-104.

[6] Hugh Blair Grigsby, *The History of the Virginia Convention of 1788*, 1:32, note 36. The second volume contains biographies of the convention's participants.

[7] Meade, 2:417-421. For the most lengthy, scholarly, and interesting treatment of the Randolph murder trial see Cynthia A. Kierner, *Scandal at Bizarre: Rumor and Reputation in Jefferson's America* (New York: Palgrave Macmillan, 2004), Chapter 2. David Garrick (1717-1779) was considered the greatest Shakespearean actor of the eighteenth century.

[8] Robert V. Remini, *Henry Clay: Statesman for the Union* (New York: W. W. Norton, 1991), 69.

[9] David L. Holmes. *The Faith of the Founding Fathers* (New York: Oxford, 2006) is an excellent study of the subject.

Sources

[1] John P. Kennedy, *Memoirs of the Life of William Wirt* (Philadelphia, 1856) 1: 345.

[2] An excellent telling of Wirt's life until 1817, his annus mirabilis when he published his successful Henry biography and became U. S. Attorney General, may be found in Joseph C. Robert, "William Wirt, Virginian, *VMHB*, 80 (1972): 388-441; see 431-437 for an entertaining account of the creation of the Henry *Sketches*. See also the delightful "The Benevolently Disposed Mr. Wirt Sends Kisses," Chapter Two of Andrew Burstein's *America's Jubilee* (New York: Vintage Books, 2001), an appraisal of Wirt's life and works from the perspective of the fiftieth anniversary of the United States.

[3] William Robert Taylor, "William Wirt and the Legend of the Old South," *W&MQ*, third ser., xiv (1957):477-493, is a perceptive analysis of Wirt's motives for writing the sketches.

[4] See "The Manuscript, " xxvii-xliv, by John Melville Jennings in Randolph.

[5] Randolph, xxv.

[6] See "Notes on Sources" in *Doc Hist,* viii: xl-xlvii.
[7] *VMHB* 69 (1961): 29-41.

BIBLIOGRAPHY

Manuscripts

Papers of Patrick Henry in the Library of Congress include memorandums and letters from:
Spencer Roane
Samuel Meredith
Edmund Winston
John Tyler
George Dabney, Charles Dabney, William O. Winston, and Nathaniel Pope
Paul Carrington
Archibald Stuart

Thomas Jefferson's Correspondence with William Wirt, 1805-1816, University of Virginia Library (MSS 5622).

Account of a Visit to Monticello by Daniel Webster and George Ticknor, 1824, as taken down by Anna Eliot Ticknor. University of Virginia Library (MSS 5205).

"The Fontaine Manuscript": Edward Fontaine. *Patrick Henry: corrections of biographical mistakes and popular errors in regard to his character. Anecdotes and new facts illustrating his religious and political opinions; & the style & power of his eloquence. A brief account of his last illness and death*, 1872, is in the Cornell University Library.

Patrick Henry's will is at the clerk's office, Charlotte County, Virginia.

Books and Articles

Abbott, W. W., Dorothy Twohig, et al., eds. *The Papers of George Washington: Revolutionary War Series, Presidential Series,* and *Retirement Series.* Charlottesville: University Press of Virginia, 1983—.

Alexander, Archibald. "Reminiscences of Patrick Henry." *Virginia Historical Register* 3 (1850):205-213, and *The Southern Literary Messenger,* 16 (1850):366-368. The same material is found in James W. Alexander, *The Life of Archibald Alexander, D. D.* New York, 1853.

Beeman, Richard R. *Patrick Henry.* New York: McGraw Hill Book Company, 1974. An excellent study, which realizes the author's hope that the reader will gain "a better comprehension of the pressures and principles, the opportunities and anxieties, that guided Patrick Henry's conduct during the Revolutionary era."

Buckley, Thomas E., S. J. *Church and State in Revolutionary Virginia, 1776-1787.* Charlottesville: University Press of Virginia, 1977.

Burstein, Andrew. *The Inner Jefferson: Portrait of a Grieving Optimist.* Charlottesville: University Press of Virginia, 1995. See the "Forest Demosthenes" section, 197-203.

_____ *America's Jubilee.* New York: Vintage Books, 2001. See Chapter Two, "The Benevolently Disposed Mr. Wirt Sends Kisses."

Cohen, Charles L. "The 'Liberty or Death' Speech: A Note on Religion and Revolutionary Rhetoric." *William and Mary Quarterly,* 3rd series, 38 (1981):702-717.

Couvillon, Mark, *Patrick Henry's Virginia: A Guide to the Homes and Sites in the Life of an American Patriot.* Brookneal, Virginia: The Patrick Henry Memorial Foundation, 2001.

Daily, Patrick. *Patrick Henry, The Last Years: 1789-1799.* Brookneal, Virginia: Patrick Henry Memorial Foundation, 1986.

Doddridge, P[hilip]. *The Rise and Progress of Religion in the Soul.* London, 1745. A contemporary reprint of the 1822 edition is available through Kessinger Publications. According to Samuel Meredith, this was Henry's "favorite author" on the subject of religion.

Elson, James M., ed. *Patrick Henry and Thomas Jefferson.* Brookneal, Virginia: Patrick Henry Memorial Foundation, 1997. Contains "Thomas Jefferson's Correspondence with William Wirt" (1805-1816) and "Account of a Visit to Monticello by Daniel Webster" (see "Manuscripts," above), as well as "A Concise Guide to and a Rebuttal of Some of the More Serious Animadversions on Patrick Henry Made by Thomas Jefferson in Correspondence with William Wirt." Brookneal: Patrick Henry Memorial Foundation, 1997.

Fontaine, Edward. *Patrick Henry: corrections of biographical mistakes and popular errors in regard to his character. Anecdotes and new facts illustrating his religious and political opinions; & the style & power of his eloquence. A brief account of his last illness and death* (1872). Transcription and annotation of manuscript (see "Manuscripts" above) by Mark Couvillon. Brookneal, Virginia: Patrick Henry Memorial Foundation, 1996.

Hall Jr., Virginius Cornick. "Notes on Patrick Henry Portraiture." *Virginia Magazine of History and Biography*, 71 (1963):168-184.

Henry, William Wirt. *Patrick Henry: Life Correspondence and Speeches.* 3 vols. New York, 1891; reprint, Harrisonburg, Virginia: Sprinkle Publications, 1993.

Holmes, David L. *The Faiths of the Founding Fathers.* New York: Oxford University Press, 2006.

Jefferson, Thomas. Julian Boyd et al., editors. *The Papers of Thomas Jefferson.* Princeton: Princeton University Press, 1950—.

Jenyns, Soame. *View of the Internal Evidence of the Christian Religion.* Contemporary reprint of the 2nd edition (London, 1776) by Kessinger Publications. This is the book which, according to Samuel Meredith and Edmund Winston, Henry had printed and distributed at his own expense.

"Journal of a French Traveler in the Colonies, 1765." *American Historical Review*, 26 (1921):726-747.

Kaminski, John P., Gaspare J. Saladino, Richard Leffler, et al., eds. *The Documentary History of the Ratification of the Constitution: Volumes VIII, IX, X, Ratification of the Constitution by the States—Virginia*. Madison: State Historical Society of Wisconsin, 1988.

Kennedy, John P. *Memoirs of the Life of William Wirt, Attorney General of the United States*, 2 vols. Philadelphia, 1849.

Kennedy, John Pendleton, ed. *Journals of the House of Burgesses of Virginia,1761-1765*. Richmond, 1907.

Kierner, Cynthia A. *Scandal at Bizarre: Rumor and Reputation in Jefferson's America*. New York: Palgrave Macmillan, 2004.

Labunski, Richard. *James Madison and the Struggle for the Bill of Rights*. New York: Oxford University Press, 2006.

McCants, David A. *Patrick Henry, the Orator*. New York: Greenwood Press, 1990.

_____ . "The Authenticity of William Wirt's Version of Patrick Henry's 'Liberty or Death' Speech." *Virginia Magazine of History and Biography*, 87 (1979):387-402.

McIlwaine, H. L., general editor. *Official Letters of the Governors of the State of Virginia: The Letters of Patrick Henry* (vol.1). Richmond: The Virginia State Library, 1926.

Matthews, Lloyd J. "Patrick Henry's 'Liberty or Death' Speech and Cassius' Speech in Shakespeare's Julius Caesar." *Virginia Magazine of History and Biography*, 86 (1978): 299-305.

Maury, Ann, editor and translator. *Memoirs of a Huguenot Family: Translated and Compiled from the Original Autobiography of the Rev. James Fontaine, and Other Family Manuscripts...* New York, 1853.

Mayer, Henry. *A Son of Thunder: Patrick Henry and the American Republic*. New York: Franklin Watts, 1986 (original hardcover edition). Subsequent paperback editions published by the University Press of Virginia (Charlottesville) in 1991, and

Grove Press (New York), no date. This is the Henry biography to read, if you are reading only one.

Meade, Robert Douthat. *Patrick Henry: Patriot in the Making*, 1957 (vol. 1); *Patrick Henry: Practical* Revolutionary, 1969 (vol. 2). Philadelphia: J. B. Lippincott Company.

_____, editor. "Judge Edmund Winston's Memoir of Patrick Henry." *Virginia Magazine of History and Biography*, 69 (1961): 29-41.

Morgan, Edmund S. and Helen M. Morgan. *The Stamp Act Crisis: Prologue to Revolution.* Chapel Hill: The University of North Carolina Press for The Institute of Early American History and Culture at Williamsburg, Virginia, 1953.

Morgan, George. *The True Patrick Henry*. Philadelphia: J. B. Lippincott Company, 1907. (Published in 1929 as *Patrick Henry*.) Contains transcriptions of the Spencer Roane and Samuel Meredith memoranda, Henry's will, and the inventtory of his property and books.

Prince, William S. "St. George Tucker: Bard on the Bench." *Virginia Magazine of History and* Biography, 84 (1976): 266-282.

Randolph, Edmund. *History of Virginia*. Edited by Arthur H. Shaffer. Charlottesville: The University Press of Virginia for the Virginia Historical Society, 1970.

Robert, Joseph C. "William Wirt, Virginian." *Virginia Magazine of History and Biography*, 80 (1972): 388-441.

Semple, Robert B. *A History of the Rise and Progress of the Baptists in Virginia.* 1810. Revised edition published Richmond, 1894.

Speece, Conrad. *The Mountaineer*. Staunton, Virginia, 1823.

Taylor, William Robert. "William Wirt and the Legend of the Old South." *William and Mary Quarterly*, third series, 14 (1957): 477-493.

Tyler, Moses Coit. *Patrick Henry*. 1887. Reprint, Ithaca: Cornell University Press, 1962.

van Schreeven, William J., compiler, and Robert L. Scribner, editor. *Revolutionary Virginia: The Road to Independence*, 3 vols. Charlottesville: The University Press of Virginia, 1975.

Wirt, William. *Sketches of The Life and Character of Patrick Henry*. ninth edition, Philadelphia, 1836. Reprint, Freeport, New York: Books for Libraries Press, 1970. The *Sketches* was originally published 1817. The page numbers of the Ninth Edition and the 1970 reprint are identical.

INDEX

Patrick Henry's Speeches to Include Court Cases

Patrick Henry in His Own Words

Patrick Henry's Opinions of Others,

as reported by Spencer Roane in the Prologue
(page numbers follow names)

What Others Said About Patrick Henry

How Others Described Patrick Henry

(Listed by chapter, section and paragraph)

Abbreviations: Pro=Prologue (Roane); Ep=Epilogue, [One] Jefferson, [Two] Randolph; App=Appendix, (A) Winston, (B) Meredith, (C), G. Dabney; Sec=Section; par=paragraph number within a section.

Adaptability-Sociability: Pro [Two] par 5, 6; Pro [Three], par 1, 2, 3; Pro [Nine] par 1, 3, 4; Ep [One] par 3; Ep [Two] par 1.

Appearance: Pro [Twelve] par 3, 4; III (3) par 1, 2; X (1), par 1-3.